LEARNING TEXT

FAMILY LAW

The author would like to thank Ado for his understanding
during times of crisis and especially Georgie and her
mother for their help and clotted cream.

LEARNING TEXT

FAMILY LAW

M. E. Rodgers
Solicitor and Senior Lecturer, Nottingham Law School

BLACKSTONE PRESS LIMITED

First published in Great Britain 1998 by Blackstone Press Limited,
Aldine Place, London W12 8AA.   Telephone 0181–740 2277

© Nottingham Law School, Nottingham Trent University, 1998

ISBN: 1 85431 741 5

British Library Cataloguing in Publication Data
A CIP catalogue record for this book is available from the British Library.

Typeset by Style Photosetting Limited, Mayfield, East Sussex
Printed by Livesey Limited, Shrewsbury, Shropshire

FOREWORD

The books in the LLB series have been written for students studying law at undergraduate level. There are two books for each subject. The first is the *Learning Text* which is designed to teach you about the particular subject in question. However, it does much more than that. By means of Activities, Self Assessment, and End of Chapter Questions, the *Learning Text* allows you to test your knowledge and understanding as you work. Each chapter starts with 'Objectives' which indicate what you should be able to do by the end of it. You should use these Objectives in your learning — check them frequently and ask yourself whether you have attained them.

The second book is a volume of *Cases and Materials*. This is cross-referenced from the *Learning Text*. It contains the primary sources of law such as statutes and cases plus subsidiary sources such as extracts from journals, law reform papers and textbooks. This is your portable library. Although each volume can stand alone, they are designed to be complementary.

The two-volume combination aims to support your learning by challenging you to demonstrate your mastery of the principles and application of the law. They are appropriate whatever your mode of study — full-time or part-time.

CONTENTS

Foreword   v

Abbreviations   xi

Table of Cases   xiii

Table of Statutes   xvii

Table of Statutory Instruments   xxii

1   The Family — What?   1

1.1 Objectives — 1.2 Introduction — 1.3 Definitions of the family — 1.4 Social versus legal — 1.5 Prevalent family groupings — 1.6 A change in direction - where is the law enforced? — 1.7 Note on additional reading — 1.8 Summary

2   Marriage — The Starting Point   11

2.1 Objectives — 2.2 Introduction — 2.3 Development of the law — 2.4 The formalities of marriage — 2.5 Registration — 2.6 Consent — 2.7 Consequences of non-compliance with the formalities — 2.8 Summary — 2.9 End of chapter assessment question

3   Nullity and Judicial Separation   22

3.1 Objectives — 3.2 Introduction — 3.3 Void versus voidable — 3.4 Void marriages — 3.5 Voidable marriages — 3.6 Bars to the annulment — 3.7 Who can apply for the marriage to be annulled? — 3.8 Consequences of nullity — 3.9 Judicial separation — 3.10 Summary — 3.11 End of chapter assessment questions

4   The Law on Divorce — The Matrimonial Causes Act 1973   37

4.1 Objectives — 4.2 Introduction — 4.3 A historical perspective — 4.4 The basic presumptions of the modern divorce — 4.5 The grounds for divorce — 4.6 Relationship between the ground for divorce and the facts — 4.7 Which facts are most commonly used? 4.8 Bars to divorce and stopping the clock — 4.9 The divorce process — 4.10 Other problems — 4.11 Summary — 4.12 End of chapter assessment questions

5   The Family Law Act 1996 and Divorce   49

5.1 Objectives — 5.2 Introduction — 5.3 Why the change? — 5.4 The divorce process — 5.5 Mediation — 5.6 Summary — 5.7 End of chapter assessment question

6 Property and Finance on Divorce 66

6.1 Objectives — 6.2 Introduction — 6.3 The concept of maintenance — 6.4 Financial orders: s. 23 — 6.5 Property orders: s. 24 — 6.6 How will the court reach its decision? — 6.7 When will the orders be made? — 6.8 Preventing or delaying the divorce — 6.9 Variation and appealing of orders — 6.10 Summary — 6.11 End of chapter assessment questions

7 Property and Finance Without Divorce 92

7.1 Objectives — 7.2 Introduction — 7.3 Maintenance without divorce — 7.4 Occupation rights and the matrimonial home — 7.5 Rights of ownership — 7.6 Resulting trusts — 7.7 Evaluating shares in equity — 7.8 Proprietary estoppel — 7.9 Summary — 7.10 End of chapter assessment question

8 Domestic Violence 118

8.1 Objectives — 8.2 Introduction — 8.3 Definitions and the historical background — 8.4 Options, other than domestic violence legislation — 8.5 Civil remedies generally — 8.6 The Family Law Act 1996 — 8.7 Stalking — 8.8 Summary — 8.9 End of chapter assessment question

9 Child Support 142

9.1 Objectives — 9.2 Introduction — 9.3 What sort of children? — 9.4 The Child Support Act 1991 — 9.5 The formula — 9.6 Departure from the formula — 9.7 When is the CSA 1991 not applicable? — 9.8 Summary — 9.9 End of chapter assessment questions

10 The Law Relating to Children 167

10.1 Objectives — 10.2 Introduction — 10.3 What is childhood? — 10.4 Children's rights — 10.5 State intervention — 10.6 Why the Children Act – why? 1989? — 10.7 The Children Act 1989 – key principles — 10.8 Summary — 10.9 End of chapter assessment questions

11 The Private Law Relating to Children 188

11.1 Objectives — 11.2 Introduction — 11.3 The concept of parental responsibility — 11.4 Who has parental responsibility? — 11.5 Joint or individual liability? 11.6 Losing your parental responsibility — 11.7 Private law orders — 11.8 Summary — 11.9 End of chapter assessment question

12 The Public Law Relating to Children 218

12.1 Objectives — 12.2 Introduction — *Part One:* 12.3 Child abuse — 12.4 The local authority's role in child protection — 12.5 The duty to investigate — 12.6 Child protection case conferences — 12.7 Short-term orders — 12.8 Emergency protection orders: s. 44 — 12.9 The guardian ad litem — 12.10 Summary of Part One and case study — *Part Two:* 12.11 Long-term orders — 12.12 The criteria — 12.13 The process — 12.14 The final hearing: what are the options? — 12.15 The consequences of the orders — 12.16 Appeals — 12.17 Summary of Part Two and case study

13 Adoption 277

13.1 Objectives — 13.2 Introduction — 13.3 What is adoption? — 13.4 What are the effects of adoption? 13.5 Who can be adopted? — 13.6 Who can adopt? — 13.7 Who can arrange adoptions? — 13.8 The process of adoption — 13.9 Protection during placement — 13.10 Post-adoption issues — 13.11 Summary — 13.12 End of chapter assessment question

14 The Inherent Jurisdiction 299

14.1 Objectives — 14.2 Introduction — 14.3 What is the inherent jurisdiction? — 14.4 Injunctive or declarative orders — 14.5 Wardship — 14.6 The local authority and the inherent jurisdiction — 14.7 Summary

15 The End 309

Index 310

ABBREVIATIONS

AA 1976	Adoption Act 1976
Agency (the)	The Child Support Agency
CA 1989	Children Act 1989
CSA 1991 and 1995	Child Support Acts 1991 and 1995
CAO	Child Assessment Order
CWO	Court Welfare Officer
DPMCA 1978	Domestic Proceedings and Magistrates' Courts Act 1978
DVMPA 1976	Domestic Violence and Matrimonial Proceedings Act 1976
EPO	Emergency Protection Order
FLA 1996	Family Law Act 1996
GAL	Guardian ad litem
ICO	Interim Care Order
LAB	Legal Aid Board
MCA 1973	Matrimonial Causes Act 1973
MHA 1983	Matrimonial Homes Act 1983

TABLE OF CASES

A (A Minor) (Adoption: Contact), Re [1993] 2 FLR 645   294, 295
A v A (A Minor: Financial Provision) [1994] 1 FLR 657   164
A v A (Minors) (Shared Residence Order) [1994] 1 FLR 669   207
A v Berkshire County Council [1989] 1 FLR 273   302
A v N (Committal: Refusal of Contact) [1997] 1 FLR 533   213
AMT (Known as AC) (Petitioners for authority to adopt SR) [1997] Fam Law 225   281
Ash v Ash [1972] 2 WLR 347   42

B (A Minor) (Adoption), Re [1991] Fam Law 136   290
B (A Minor) (Wardship: Medical Treatment), Re [1981] 1 WLR 1421   302
B (Adoption Order: Jurisdiction To Set Aside), Re [1995] 2 FLR 1   297
B (Minors) (Care: Contact: Local Authority's Plans), Re [1993] 1 FLR 543   272
B (Minors) (Change of Surname), Re [1996] 1 FLR 791   196
Barder v Barder [1987] 1 FLR 18   89
Barnett v Hassett [1981] 1 WLR 1385   101
Baxter v Baxter [1948] AC 274   29
Beach v Beach [1995] 2 FLR 160   80
Berkshire County Council v B [1997] 1 FLR 171   272
Bernard v Josephs [1982] 3 All ER 162   110
Birmingham City Council v D and Birmingham City Council v M
  [1994] 2 FLR 502   256
Brooks v Brooks [1995] 2 FLR 13   82
Buffery v Buffery [1988] 2 FLR 365   44
Burgess v Burgess [1996] 2 FLR 34   78
Burns v Burns [1984] 1 All ER 244   111

C (Interim Care Order: Residential Assessment), Re [1997] 1 FLR 1   265, 266
C, Re [1992] 2 FCR 341   206
Carron v Carron [1984] FLR 805   162
Cleary v Cleary [1974] 1 All ER 498   41
Cooke v Head [1972] 2 All ER 38   109
Coombes v Smith [1986] 1 WLR 808   116
Corbett v Corbett [1970] 2 All ER 33   26
Crozier v Crozier [1994] 2 WLR 444   154

D (A Minor) (Wardship: Sterilisation), Re [1976] Fam 185   302
D, Re [1993] 2 FLR 423   258, 259, 268, 274
D (An Infant) (Adoption: Parent's Consent), Re [1977] 2 WLR 79   281
D v D (County Court Jurisdiction: Injunctions) [1993] 2 FLR 802   232, 235
Dart v Dart [1996] 2 FLR 286   78
Davis v Johnson [1979] AC 264   119
Davis v Vale [1971] 2 All ER 1021   114
DH (A Minor) (Child Abuse), Re [1994] 1 FLR 679   268

Dyer v Dyer (1788) 2 Cox Eq Cas 92   103

E (A Minor) (Adoption), Re [1989] 1 FLR 126   292
Eves v Eves [1975] 3 All ER 768   111

F (in utero), Re [1988] Fam 122   302
F v Wirral Metropolitan Borough Council [1991] 2 WLR 1132   246
Falconer v Falconer [1970] 3 All ER 499   109
Ford v Ford [1987] Fam Law 17   28, 29
Frary v Frary [1993] 2 FLR 696   77
Fuller v Fuller [1973] 1 WLR 730   43

G (A Minor), Re [1997] 2 WLR 747   295
G v G (Ouster: Ex Parte Application) [1990] 1 FLR 395   126
Gascoigne v Gascoigne [1918] 1 KB 223   105
Gillick v West Norfolk and Wisbech Area Health Authority [1986] AC 112,
    [1985] 3 All ER 402   171, 189, 193, 194, 208
Gissing v Gissing [1970] 2 All ER 780   108
Goodman v Gallant [1986] Fam 106   114
Grant v Edwards [1986] 2 All ER 426   112

H (A Minor) (Section 37 Direction), Re [1993] 2 FLR 541   234
H (A Minor) (Parental Responsibility), Re [1993] 1 FLR 484   200, 201, 212
H and others, Re [1996] 1 All ER 1   258, 259
Hanlon v Hanlon [1978] 1 WLR 592   71
Hanlon v The Law Society [1981] AC 124   73
Hardy v Hardy [1981] 2 FLR 321   76
Hirani v Hirani [1982] 4 FLR 232   30
Hodgson v Marks [1972] 2 All ER 684   103
Horner v Horner [1982] 2 All ER 495   123
Horton v Horton [1947] 2 All ER 871   28
Humberside County Council v B [1993] 1 FLR 257   256
Hussain v Hussain [1982] 3 All ER 369   27
Hussey v Palmer [1972] 3 All ER 744   110

J (Minors) (Care: Care Plan), Re [1994] 1 FLR 253   263
J v C [1970] AC 668   182
J v S-T (Formerly J) (Transsexual: Ancillary Relief) [1997] 1 FLR 402   26, 34

K (Adoption and Wardship), Re [1997] 2 FLR 221   297, 304
K v K (Financial Relief: Widow's Pension) [1997] 1 FLR 35   86
Kaur v Singh [1972] 1 WLR 105   29
KDT, Re [1994] 2 FCR 721   206
Khorasandjian v Bush [1993] QB 727   122
Kiely v Kiely [1988] 1 FLR 248   163
Knibb v Knibb [1987] 2 FLR 396   71
Kokosinski v Kokosinski [1980] 3 WLR 55   80, 81

L (A Minor) (Adoption: Procedure), Re [1991] 1 FLR 171   290
Le Marchant v Le Marchant [1977] 1 WLR 559   46
Leadbeater v Leadbeater [1985] FLR 789   75, 78
Livesey (formerly Jenkins) v Jenkins [1985] FLR 813   74, 90
Livingstone-Stallard v Livingstone-Stallard [1974] Fam 47   42
Lloyds Bank v Rosset [1990] 1 All ER 1111   112, 115

M (A Minor) (Care Order: Threshold Conditions), Re [1994] 2 WLR 200 (CA);
    [1994] 2 AC 424 (HL)   257
M (A Minor) (Contact: Conditions), Re [1994] 1 FLR 272   210
M (Care Order: Parental Responsibility), Re [1996] 2 FLR 84   256

M v Birmingham City Council [1994] 2 FLR 141   260
M v M (Child Access) [1973] 2 All ER 81   210
M v M (Financial Provision) [1987] 2 FLR 1   75
Martin v Martin [1977] 3 All ER 762   77
Matharu v Matharu [1994] 2 FLR 597   116
Mehta v Mehta [1945] 2 All ER 690   30
Midland Bank plc v Cooke and Another [1995] 2 FLR 215   115
Midland Bank v Dobson [1986] 1 FLR 171   111
Mortimer v Mortimer-Griffin [1986] 2 FLR 315   71
Mouncer v Mouncer [1972] 1 WLR 321   43

Nottinghamshire County Council v P [1993] 3 WLR 637   215, 234, 245, 261, 308

O (A Minor) (Care Order: Education: Procedure), Re [1992] 2 FLR 7   192
O (A Minor) (Care Order: Procedure), Re [1992] 1 WLR 912   256
O (Care or Supervision Order), Re [1996] 2 FLR 755   268
O (Contact: Impostition of Conditions), Re [1995] 2 FLR 124   211

P (Adoption: Freeing Order), Re [1994] 2 FLR 1000   292, 294
P (Emergency Protection Order), Re [1996] 1 FLR 482   247
Park, Re, [1954] P 112   29
Pascoe v Turner [1979] 1 WLR 431   116
Pettitt v Pettitt [1969] 2 All ER 385   105, 108
Phillips v Peace [1996] 2 FLR 230   155
Polovchak v Meese 774 F 2d 731   172
Practice Note [1978] 2 All ER 1056   126

R (A Minor) (Blood Transfusion), Re [1993] 2 FLR 757   301
R (A Minor) (Wardship: Medical Treatment), Re [1991] 4 All ER 177   301, 308
R (A Minor) (Wardship: Medical Treatment), Re [1992] 1 FLR 190   194
R v Lancashire County Council, ex parte M [1992] 1 FLR 109   283
R v R [1952] 1 All ER 1194   28
R v R [1991] 3 WLR 767   120
Richards v Dove [1974] 1 All ER 888   108
Richards v Richards [1983] 2 All ER 807   120, 125, 128
Rukat v Rukat [1975] 2 WLR 201   46, 86

S (Wardship: Education), Re [1988] 1 FLR 128   305
Savill v Goodall [1993] 1 FLR 755   116
Schuller v Schuller [1990] 2 FLR 193   76
Shephard v Cartwright [1954] 3 All ER 649, HL   105
Singh v Singh [1971] 2 All ER 828   28
State v Ward 28 SE 2d 785 (1994)   12
Summers v Summers [1986] 1 FLR 343   124
Suter v Suter and Another [1987] 2 FLR 232   74
Sutton London Borough Council v Davis [1995] 1 All ER 53   197
Szechter v Szechter [1971] 2 WLR 170   30

T (A Minor) (Care Order: Conditions), Re [1994] 2 FLR 423   263
T (Adoption: Contact), Re [1995] 2 FLR 251   290, 296
T v S (Financial Provision for Children) [1994] 2 FLR 883   163, 164
Tinsley v Milligan [1993] 3 All ER 65   106

Vicary v Vicary [1992] 2 FLR 271   90

W (A Minor) (Contact), Re [1994] 2 FLR 441   210
W (A Minor) (Refusal of Medical Treatment), Re [1992] 3 WLR 758   194
W (An Infant), Re [1971] 2 All ER 49   292
W, Re [1995] 2 FLR 466   301, 304

W v A [1981] 1 All ER 100   196
Wachtel v Wachtel [1973] 1 All ER 829   78
Wagstaff v Wagstaff [1992] 1 All ER 275   76
WB (Residence Orders), Re [1995] 2 FLR 1023   207
Whiston v Whiston [1995] 2 FLR 268   34
WM (Adoption: Non- patrial), Re [1997] 1 FLR 132   284

TABLE OF STATUTES

Adoption Act 1958 281
Adoption Act 1976 278, 288, 290, 297
  s.1 282
  s.6 287
  s.7 284
  s.11 283, 285
  s.11(1) 284
  s.11(4) 283
  s.12 279
  s.12(5) 280
  s.12(7) 280
  s.13 280
  s.13(1) 284
  s.13(2) 284
  s.14 281
  s.14(1B) 281
  s.15 281
  s.16(1) 289, 291
  s.16(1)(b)(ii) 291
  s.16(2) 291
  s.16(2)(b) 292
  s.16(4) 291
  s.18(1) 293
  s.18(2) 293
  s.18(2A) 293
  s.18(3) 293
  s.18(5) 293
  s.18(6) 294
  s.18(7) 291
  s.20 294–5
  s.22(1) 285
  s.27 295
  s.28 295
  s.39 279, 280
  s.42 279, 280
  s.44 279, 280
  s.47 279, 280
  s.72 283
  Sch.2 285
Adoption of Children Act 1926 277

Child Support Act 1991 72, 74, 77, 79,
    142, 143–61, 165, 190, 289, 290
  s.1(1) 144

Child Support Act 1991 – *continued*
  s.1(2) 144
  s.2 148–9
  s.3 144
  s.4 146, 147, 149, 151
  s.4(9) 149, 150
  s.4(10) 149, 151
  s.4B 158
  s.6 146–7, 149
  s.6(2) 147
  s.8 160
  s.8(1) 150
  s.8(2) 150
  s.8(3) 150, 151
  s.8(5) 151, 160
  s.8(5)(b) 151
  s.8(6) 160
  s.8(7) 160
  s.8(8) 160
  s.18(1) 151
  s.44(1) 145
  s.46 148
  s.54 145
  s.55 144
  Sch.1 152
Child Support Act 1995 72, 74, 77, 79,
    142, 143, 158, 190, 289
  Sch.2 158
Children Act 1908 176
Children Act 1948 176, 177
Children Act 1989 145, 161, 163–5, 167,
    172, 174, 178–86, 188, 191, 205, 229,
    287, 288, 301, 303, 304
  s.1 181, 207, 218, 243, 288
  s.1(1) 164, 181, 239
  s.1(2) 181, 183
  s.1(3) 181, 239
  s.1(4) 181, 200
  s.1(5) 181, 184, 185, 195, 207, 211, 239,
    274
  s.2 198
  s.2(1) 197
  s.2(2) 197
  s.2(7) 202

Children Act 1989 – *continued*
s.2(8)   206
s.2(9)   199, 201
s.3(1)   189
s.3(5)   201, 231, 274
s.4   199, 200, 201, 203, 290, 291
s.4(2)   200
s.7   233
s.8   195, 203, 204, 207, 209, 213, 214,
      227, 267–8, 273, 278, 281, 291, 301
s.8(3)   185
s.8(4)   185
s.9   273
s.9(1)   185
s.9(2)   185, 204, 215
s.9(3)   204
s.9(4)   204
s.9(5)   215
s.9(6)   208
s.9(7)   208
s.10   296
s.10(1)   185, 204
s.10(2)   204
s.10(3)   204
s.10(4)   204
s.10(5)   204
s.10(9)   204
s.11(4)   206
s.11(5)   209
s.11(7)   205
s.12(1)   211
s.12(2)   201
s.13   206
s.13(1)   195
s.15   163
s.17   185, 223, 225, 231, 256, 261
s.17(1)   181, 223, 224, 225
s.17(3)   223
s.17(6)   224
s.17(7)   224
s.17(8)   224
s.17(10)   223, 224
s.17(11)   224
s.18(1)   225
s.18(3)   225
s.20   227, 228
s.20(1)   225, 226
s.20(1)(a)   226
s.20(1)(b)   226
s.20(1)(c)   226
s.20(3)   227
s.20(4)   226
s.20(6)   227
s.20(7)   226
s.20(8)   226
s.20(9)   226
s.20(11)   226, 227
s.22   225

Children Act 1989 – *continued*
s.23   225
s.24   225, 227, 228
s.24(1)   225
s.29   224
s.31   253, 256, 272, 293
s.31(1)   252, 261
s.31(2)   252, 253
s.31(2)(a)   258, 260
s.31(3)   252, 260
s.31(5)   252, 268
s.31(9)   252, 253, 254
s.31(10)   252, 253, 255
s.33   269, 270–1
s.33(3)   270
s.33(6)   271
s.33(7)   271
s.34   269, 271–2
s.34(6)   272
s.34(11)   272
s.35   273, 274
s.35(1)(c)(i)   274
s.36   192
s.37   233–4, 264
s.37(4)   234
s.38   256, 264
s.38(2)   264
s.38(6)   265
s.39   273
s.39(4)   273
s.39(5)   273
s.40   275
s.42   248
s.43   241
s.44   243, 244, 253, 304
s.44(1)   241
s.44(1)(a)   241–2, 243, 256
s.44(1)(a)(i)   242
s.44(1)(a)(ii)   242
s.44(1)(b)   239, 242, 243
s.44(1)(c)   239, 243
s.44(2)   241
s.44(4)   244
s.44(4)(c)   246
s.44(5)   246
s.44(6)   245
s.44(10)   244
s.44(13)   245
s.44A   245
s.45   244
s.45(1)   245
s.45(5)   246
s.45(8)-(10)   247
s.46   230
s.46(6)   230
s.46(7)   230
s.47   228–33, 234, 242, 243, 253, 256
s.47(1)   229

Children Act 1989 – *continued*
  s.47(3) 229, 230
  s.47(4) 243
  s.47(6) 232
  s.47(7) 232
  s.47(9) 229
  s.47(10) 229
  s.47(11) 229
  s.91 272
  s.100 305–7
  s.100(2) 305, 306
  s.100(3) 305
  s.100(4) 305, 307
  s.100(5) 307
  Sch.1 163
    para.2 163
    para.4 164
  Sch.2
    para.5 245
    para.7 223
    para.9 223
  Sch.3 192
    Part I 273
      para.4(4) 273
    Part II
      para.6(1) 275
      para.6(3) 275
Children and Young Persons Act 1933, s.1
    191, 193
Children and Young Persons Act 1969
    177, 178–9, 260, 306
Clandestine Marriages Act 1753 12, 18
Criminal Justice and Public Order Act
    1994 120

Divorce Reform Act 1969 38, 44, 45, 51
Domestic Proceedings and Magistrates'
    Courts Act 1978 93, 98, 126–30, 131,
    133, 138, 161, 162
  s.1 95
  s.2 95
  s.2(1)(a) 96
  s.2(1)(b) 96
  s.2(3) 96
  s.3 95
  s.3(2) 96
  s.3(3) 163
  s.3(4) 163
  s.4 96
  s.6 97
  s.7 97
  s.7(4) 97, 98
  s.16 127
  s.16(3) 128
  s.16(3)(b) 128
  s.16(5) 129
  s.16(8) 129
  s.18 127, 129
  s.25 96

Domestic Violence and Matrimonial
    Proceedings Act 1976 124, 125, 126,
    127, 128, 129, 130, 131, 133, 139
  s.1 122
  s.2 122
  s.2(1) 123

Ecclesiastical Licences Act 1533 16
Education Act 1944, s.36 191, 192
Education Act 1993 192
Equal Pay Act 1970 7, 67

Family Homes and Domestic Violence
    Bill 130, 136
Family Law Act 1996 9, 35, 37, 39, 51, 61,
    67, 70, 81, 84, 85, 86, 88, 90, 94, 95, 98,
    101, 118, 122, 130–9, 140, 205
  Part IV 122, 130, 245
  s.1 51–2
  s.2 52
  s.3 53, 59
  s.3(1) 64
  s.5(1) 55, 57
  s.6 53, 54, 55
  s.7 56, 57, 58
  s.7(1) 57
  s.7(3) 57
  s.7(6) 55
  s.7(11) 57
  s.7(13) 57
  s.8 54
  s.8(7)(b) 55
  s.9 58, 63, 74–5, 85, 86, 94
  s.9(2)(a) 85
  s.10 60, 85, 86, 87
  s.10(1) 87
  s.10(2) 87
  s.11 59
  s.14 60
  s.16 83
  s.26-s.29 61
  s.30 99
  s.30(1) 99
  s.30(2) 99
  s.31 99
  s.32 99
  s.33 99, 100, 133–5
  s.33(1) 134
  s.33(3) 100
  s.33(6) 99, 134, 135
  s.33(7) 134
  s.33(10) 135
  s.34 99
  s.35 135
  s.36 135, 136–7
  s.36(6) 136
  s.36(6)(e) 136
  s.41(2) 136
  s.42 130

Family Law Act 1996 – *continued*
  s.42(1)(a) 131
  s.42(1)(b) 131
  s.42(2)(b) 132
  s.42(4) 132
  s.42(5) 132
  s.42(6) 131
  s.42(7) 133
  s.45 137
  s.46 138
  s.47 138
  s.62 131
  Sch.1 58, 59
  Sch.2, para.3 84
  Sch.4, para.2 101
  Sch.6 245
  Sch.8, para.9(3) 81

Guardianship of Minors Act 1971
  s.1 182
  s.1(3) 182

Land Registration Act 1925, s.70(1)(g)
    113
Law of Property Act 1925 107
  s.30 102
  s.51 114
  s.52 102
  s.53(1)(b) 111
  s.60(3) 103
Law of Property (Miscellaneous
    Provisions) Act 1989, s.2 102
Legal Aid Act 1988
  s.13B(3) 61
  s.15(3F) 62
  s.15(3F)(a) 62
  s.15(3F)(b) 62
Legitimacy Act 1976 34
  s.1 198
  s.2 198
  s.2(1) 198
Local Government Act 1970 218
Lord Hardwicke's Act (Clandestine
    Marriages Act 1753) 12, 18

Marriage Act 1836 12–13
Marriage Act 1949 13, 16
  s.3 19
  s.4 20
  s.5 15
  s.6 15
  s.7 15
  s.15 15
  s.16 15
  s.27 14
  s.31 14
  s.32 14
  s.33 14
  s.41 18

Marriage Act 1949 – *continued*
  s.44(3) 17, 18
  s.48 19–20
  s.49 19–20
  Sch.1 24, 280
Marriage Act 1994 17
Marriage Ceremony (Prescribed Words)
    Act 1996 17
Marriage (Prohibited Degrees of
    Relationship) Act 1986, s.1 24–5
Marriage (Registrar-General's Licence)
    Act 1970 16
Matrimonial Causes Act 1973 44, 45, 47,
    49, 51, 57, 60, 63, 67, 73, 77, 80, 82, 84,
    85, 86, 90, 93, 96, 98, 102, 108, 161,
    181, 288
  s.1 40, 95
  s.1(2) 40, 95
  s.1(2)(d) 43
  s.1(3) 46
  s.2 45
  s.3 40
  s.3(1) 40
  s.5 46, 85, 86
  s.10 46
  s.11 23, 33, 38, 39
  s.11(a)(i) 23
  s.11(a)(ii) 25
  s.11(c) 26
  s.11(d) 27
  s.11(e) 31
  s.11(f) 32
  s.12 28, 33
  s.12(a) 29
  s.12(b) 29
  s.12(c) 31
  s.12(d) 31
  s.12(f) 32
  s.13 32
  s.17(2) 35
  s.22 70, 85
  s.22A 84
  s.22B 84, 85
  s.23 34, 68, 69, 82, 93
  s.24 34, 70
  s.24A 70, 71
  s.25 88
  s.25(1) 73, 74
  s.25(2) 73, 74, 77, 79, 93
  s.25(2)(a) 74, 80
  s.25(2)(b) 80
  s.25(2)(g) 80, 81
  s.25(3) 163
  s.25(4) 163
  S.25A 83
  S.25A(2) 84
  s.25B(4) 82
  s.27 93–4, 95
  s.27(6) 93

Matrimonial Causes Act 1973 – *continued*
  s.27(7) 93
  s.28 69
  s.28(1A) 88
  s.28(2) 94
  s.31 87
  s.31(7A) 88
  s.52(1) 162
Matrimonial and Family Proceedings Act
  1984, s.38 302
Matrimonial Homes Act 1967 99, 101,
  125
Matrimonial Homes Act 1983 98, 99,
  101, 102, 126
  s.1 99–100, 125
  s.1(1) 99
  s.1(2) 100
  s.1(3) 99, 100
  s.3 101
Matrimonial Homes and Property Act
  1981 99
Matrimonial Proceedings and Property
  Act 1970, s.37 114

Mental Health Act 1983 31, 273

Offences Against the Person Act 1861
  191, 193

Pensions Act 1995 82
  s.166 82
Police and Criminal Evidence Act
  1984 121
Poor Laws 175
Prevention of Cruelty Act 1889 176
Private International Law (Miscellaneous
  Provisions) Act 1995 27
Protection from Harassment Act 1997
  139

Social Security Administration Act 1992,
  s.78(6)-(9) 98

Trusts of Land and Appointment of
  Trustees Act 1996 102

TABLE OF STATUTORY INSTRUMENTS

Child Support and Income Support
    (Amendment) Regulations 1995   154
Child Support (Maintenance Assessment
    Procedure) Regulations 1992   148
Child Support (Maintenance Assessments
    and Special Cases) Regulations 1992
    155
Child Support (Miscellaneous
    Amendments) Regulations 1996
    148
Children Act Rules   262

Family Proceedings Rules   248
    Sch.2   247

Marriages (Approved Premises)
    Regulations 1995 (SI 1995) (No. 510)
    17

Placement with Parents Regulations 1991
    270

Rules of the Supreme Court   303

CHAPTER ONE

THE FAMILY – WHAT?

1.1 Objectives

By the end of this chapter you should be able to:

■ define the family and distinguish between social and legal definitions of the family;

■ evaluate which definitions are acceptable in law, and which the law seeks to promote;

■ identify social changes, which may impact upon the coverage and remit of the law;

■ draw a hierarchical diagram of the family court structure.

1.2 Introduction

Before commencing your studies on family law, it is essential that you start to think about the basic concepts involved with the topic – what the family is, how the law relates to the family, what other concepts impinge upon the legal definitions. The purpose of this introductory chapter is to get you to think about the social and legal concepts that surround the family. No law can exist in isolation; it must fit into the social structure that created it. How close a fit exists will inevitably be debatable. You will also be reminded in this chapter of the legal institutions that will dispense family justice, and some of the agencies that may also have a part to play.

1.3 Definitions of the Family

We all belong to a 'family', whether we like it or not, but you may have one idea of what your family is, and who comprises your family, and others may have a completely different idea. Distinctions in these definitions may arise due to cultural differences, historical patterns, economic factors and social values, and yet the definitions will all have some form of validity.

ACTIVITY 1

Write down your definition of your family.

Think about who comprises your family – you may wish to write down all the names of those individuals in your family.

If you have a spouse or partner, ask them to do the same and compare your lists. Alternatively, ask a friend to do a list of their family.

What similarities were there?

From doing this activity you may have established that you and your fellow contributor have very similar views on your respective families, or wildly different ones. Generalising, many people will identify their immediate relatives as being 'family' – their spouse, children and parents. This close family is often referred to as the nuclear family, the parents with 2.4 children. However, the family does extend wider than this nucleus, and you may have included grandparents, cousins, aunts, uncles *et al* in your list. Going back to your list, did it make a difference to who was included if you see that person? You may find that you have referred to some of the wider kin but not all, since many people class family in terms of how often they are seen or contacted. Cultural differences may also affect your list, since the western tradition tends to favour the nuclear family rather than the extended family. The Asian community, for example, have a greater sense of the wider kinship, due to their culture. To continue along this theme, try the next activity.

On a separate sheet of paper draw a spider diagram and identify all the different groupings of individuals that may class themselves as a 'family'. You may find that some of the groupings overlap, or fall into more than one category. To help you, there is an example of some of the groupings you may find below.

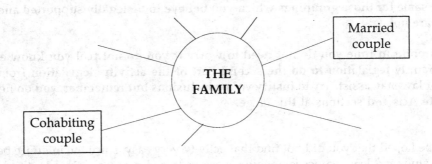

1.4 Social versus Legal

Having drawn your diagram, you should have some of these groups:

(a) married couple with children;

(b) married couple without children (never or grown up);

(c) cohabiting couple (heterosexual);

(d) cohabiting couple (homosexual/lesbian);

(e) cohabiting couple with or without children;

(f) single person (did you define this individual as a family?);

(g) single parent (and who will that single parent more likely be?);

(h) wider blood relations;

(i) relationships by marriage.

Naturally you should have more than this, but this will at least highlight the diversity that is the family.

Whilst you may agree that all the above are a family, your response may depend upon your moral and social standpoint, since not all of the above are seen to be acceptable to society as a family. It follows that, since law is generally seen to reflect the values of society, not all of the above are legally accepted, or legally supported.

ACTIVITY3

With different coloured pens go back to your spider diagram and indicate which of the family groupings listed you believe to be socially acceptable, and which are not.

Again, if you can, get a friend or relative to do the same, and see whether you have a similar opinion.

Do the same for those groupings which you believe to be legally supported and those which are not.

At this point in time you do not need to worry if you do not feel you know enough about family legislation to do the second part of the activity: legislation from other areas of law may assist. Try to justify your conclusions but remember, you do not need to quote Acts and sections at this stage.

It is to be hoped that you did not find that activity very easy, since the interface between social values and legal values is not always exact. It is also compounded by the fact that the law does not really define the family – it merely supports certain types of families – a subtle distinction.

Should the law reflect social norms, or should it be proactive and try to influence the way individuals live their lives? Due to the legislative process it is hard for the law to be proactive, it tends to react to changes that have occurred already. To take an example, you may have highlighted cohabitation as being socially acceptable, but the legal provisions do not provide the same level of support to couples in this type of relationship as to a married couple. Changes are happening as you will learn as you go through this text. You may agree that these changes are limited, and in line with the traditional social norm of the nuclear family which tends to discount the commitment shown by cohabitants. Homosexual relationships may be more acceptable in the social context, but are not supported in the legal sphere. Unmarried fathers may be caring parents, and yet the law does not give them automatic rights over their children. The fact that the law does not support these different family relationships equally may be of concern to you, and this is something you should bear in mind as you complete your studies – does the law meet the needs of individuals or should the law try to support the majority at the expense of the minority?

SAQ 1

Should the law treat every family grouping the same?

Should the same provisions apply equally?

This SAQ is one that you may wish to come back to at different stages in the course, since your views may change. To help you think about the types of issues you could bring into this question, consider the following:

Anne and Paul are married, and have two children under the age of 10 years. They own their own home, which they bought before their marriage and whilst they were cohabiting.

The marriage breaks down irretrievably and they wish to go their separate ways.

In this situation, the law would initially try to support the idea of saving the marriage (one of the principles behind the divorce laws), but if the marriage had clearly broken down, the law would dissolve the marriage and the legal ties. It would allow the couple to claim maintenance from one another for themselves and the children, and it would permit division of the property between them regardless of the legal ownership.

Denise and Bob are not married but cohabit, and they have two children under the age of 10 years. They jointly own their own home, although Denise only holds a 20 per cent share. The relationship has broken down and they wish to go their separate ways.

If you hold the view that the law should treat family groupings equally, then Denise and Bob should have the same sorts of remedies from the law as Anne and Paul. But despite the similarities of their positions, they do not. Neither Denise nor Bob can claim maintenance from the other (they may do so for the children). They may voluntarily divide the ownership of the property differently, but in the event of a dispute resolved by the court, the stated percentage is potentially all that will be obtained. Indeed, the law is not involved with the ending of the relationship at all, as it is when couples are married.

This may seem unfair, but you should be asking yourself, why do people choose not to comply with the 'social norms'? Denise and Bob may have decided to cohabit as they did not want to be forced to abide by legal rules in the event of a relationship breakdown, and have the court decide how their future affairs would be regulated. The couple may have felt that they were perfectly able to decide these things for themselves. They may not have known of the disadvantages to which they would be put by not getting married. If they had deliberately chosen to avoid the legal provisions of marriage, would it really be fair to apply the law regardless?

It is this type of reasoning that will help you appreciate and formulate your views on **SAQ 1**. At the end of the course you should be in a position to argue whether the law is the best machine to adjudicate over such a social and moral creature as the family.

1.5 Prevalent Family Groupings

As you have seen from the above sections, the category of family groupings in the UK is changing. Whilst it is still the case that the nuclear family is seen as the moral 'high ground' and the grouping to which we should all strive, the reality is that the family is more diverse. To enable you to identify the reality of the family in the UK today, complete the following activity.

Look at the statistics from e.g. the General Household Survey in *Cases and Materials* (1.1.1).

What conclusions can you draw from these figures as to the make up of the family today?

1.5.1   HOUSEHOLDS

From the table 'Household estimates and projections 1971–2016 England', it is clear that the number of households is set to increase, albeit not dramatically, over the next couple of decades. The term 'household' is one that should be approached carefully since, as you can see, it is used to cover a wide range of different groupings.

The numbers of married couples are gradually declining, but the numbers of cohabiting couples and lone parents have increased rapidly since 1971. It is strange that there has not been a linked decrease with any other grouping during this period.

Why do you think this is?

Although it is only a hypothesis, it may be suggested that the numbers of cohabiting couples are made up of many young people who previously lived with their (married) parents. Upon reaching maturity, and leaving the parental home, they become a statistic of their own, rather than being subsumed within 'married couples'.

The increase in one person households is also predicted to be high (from 2,944,000 to 8,577,000 between 1971 and 2016). The ageing population will account for much of this increase. However, a more affluent society can enable individuals, who may be in a steady relationship but who prefer to maintain two separate households, to do just that. Today, this is potentially affordable.

Turning to marriages, two main issues can be raised. First, the decrease in the numbers marrying in the 'first marriage' category. For both males and females, there has been nearly a 100,000 decrease in marriages from 1961. You should also have noted the age at which first marriages take place. There has been a gradual decline in 'teenage marriages' and a gradual increase in cohabiting households. It may be indicative of the desire to fulfil a career before 'settling down': however, this hypothesis is difficult to establish on these figures.

Remarriage is, on the face of it, popular, but starting to decrease from its peak in 1988. The massive increase in the numbers of divorced people remarrying, and the decrease in widowed persons remarrying may be accounted for in the increasing number of divorces. As you can see from the statistics on matrimonial suits, the number of decree absolutes in 1968 was 45,036 compared to 162,579 in 1992. If you compare these with the remarriage figures in 1967, 26,700 of men remarried but in 1993 it was 77,000. The threefold increase has almost been replicated.

1.5.2 BIRTHS

The conception rate appears to be somewhat static over the 10 year period illustrated from the first table. In 1994 a slightly higher rate of legal abortion was recorded (the majority being where the conception was outside marriage). However, what all the figures illustrate is the increase in births outside marriage, with a corresponding decrease in births within marriage. A total of 31 per cent of births are now outside marriage. This percentage would be higher if live births were to be considered since the 1994 figures are based on total conceptions and hence include those conceptions which are legally terminated. Joint registrations, i.e. where the father is named on the birth certificate, have also increased significantly. Taken together with the figures for households, the social acceptability of cohabitation, and raising children outside marriage is clear.

1.5.3 ECONOMIC ACTIVITY

The trend for women to enter the work-force is set to continue, if the social trend predictions are accurate.

In so far as the nature of that work is concerned, the perception is that women work part-time. This is true only where women have dependent children, supporting the notion of women as carers. However, of those women working full-time, there are a surprising number with dependent children. The differential between part-time employment of men and women is startling (see the table of gender and age and part-time employment in *Cases and Materials* (**1.1.3**)).

The type of work carried out by the genders still identifies a stereotypical division, with many more women working in the service industry and undertaking secretarial work. In the managerial categories the notion that women may rise to middle or associate level, but not higher management, is borne out. Nineteen per cent of men are classed (in 1996) as managerial/administrative compared with 10 per cent of women.

1.5.4 INCOME

Women, despite the Equal Pay Act 1970, still achieve a lower earnings capacity than men. However, you should have noted the problems with that statement. The figures on relative earnings do not differentiate between the types of employment – i.e. full-time or part-time. If a woman is working part-time, it is highly probable that her earnings will be less than her male partner working full-time.

The reliance on welfare benefits for single parents is to be expected, although political rhetoric does not appear to focus on the 37 per cent of single parents who do not rely on welfare.

Can you think of any reasons why these changes may have come about?

Whilst there are probably many reasons for such changes, some of the crucial ones you should have considered are:

■ the change in women's roles in the economic market. More women are able and wish to pursue a career and hence may not wish to marry. Also it is less stigmatising today for women not to marry;

■ the greater availability of state benefits. Whilst in no way suggesting that this will encourage single parenthood, it does potentially reduce the need for single mothers to give their children up for adoption, thereby increasing the numbers of single mothers;

■ the wider availability of the divorce process. As you will learn later, historically it was very hard for an ordinary person to get a divorce. Nowadays this stumbling block has gone, enabling more marriages to be dissolved;

■ the increasing secularisation of society which to a certain extent will reduce the need to go through a formal (religious) marriage ceremony;

■ changes to the legal structure which help promote diversity.

As you can see, the law is relevant to some of these changes, as are society and social values. This continues to highlight the importance of these latter two concepts in relation to your studies.

1.6   A Change in Direction – Where is the Law Enforced?

If you have already completed a course in the English legal system, you should be able to study this section quite quickly. If not, you may need to do some additional reading. In which case, you will need to go to a library and use a basic textbook.

Obviously, regardless of the definition of the family that you prefer, any law applicable to that family will need to be enforced somehow. To this extent, there is within the traditional court hierarchy, a distinct, family court hierarchy. The emphasis should in many 'family' disputes be to resolve matters outside court. This is something that the legislature is keen to promote – you may recall the media coverage surrounding the passing of the Family Law Act 1996, which will herald the introduction of mediation to resolve disputes, as it is perceived to be more appropriate to the sensitivities of family law, and the nature of family relationships. That said, matters might inevitably need court resolution.

On a separate sheet of paper, draw a diagram showing the courts that have family jurisdiction.

If you have not studied English legal system, this is where you may need to refer to another textbook.

Compare your diagram to the one in *Cases and Materials* (1.2).

Can you think of any reasons why there should be so many courts that have jurisdiction over family matters?

Partly, the division of jurisdiction reflects the *ad hoc* and haphazard way in which the legal system and the court structure developed. It also reflects the historical aim of achieving fairness in access to justice for the lower classes, hence the jurisdiction of the magistrates' court (correctly known in family matters as the family proceedings court) which was often seen as cheaper and more accessible. The courts identified have an overlapping jurisdiction, which can be confusing to the individual who has to make use of the courts' services. Whilst the jurisdiction often overlaps, there may be a difference in the type of remedy that is available. This was more pronounced before the partial implementation of the Family Law Act 1996. The overlapping function can also lead to an unfairness when applying for legal aid funding, since frequently the family proceedings court will not attract assistance as proceedings are seen to be uncomplicated and not worthy of legal assistance. Hence, being familiar with the differences in jurisdiction is essential to advising clients (especially in exam questions!).

As you continue through the course, return to your diagram and add to it, to show the nature of the jurisdiction of each court and to remind yourself of the overlapping nature of the existing court hierarchy.

1.7   Note on Additional Reading

If you wish to read more on family law, the following texts may be useful:

Cretney, S. and Masson, J., *Principles of Family Law*, 6th edn, London: Sweet & Maxwell, 1997.
Bond, T., Bridge, A., Mallender, P., and Rayson, J., *Blackstone's Guide to the Family Law Act 1996*, London: Blackstone Press, 1996.

Journals:

Family Law (published by Jordans, 21 St Thomas Street, Bristol).

Internet Sites:

Family law   http://www.familylaw.co.uk
Lord Chancellor's Department, press releases   http://www.open.gov
House of Lords judgments   http://www.parliament.the-stationery-office.co.uk/pa/id/Ldjudinf.htm

1.8   Summary

In this chapter, you have been introduced to some basic definitions of the family, and have been required to provide your own definition too. By comparing these you should be aware of the diversity of family life that exists currently in the UK. By considering the official statistics from the General Household Survey, you should be familiar with the reality of family life, and this too may be related to the definitions available. You have been introduced to the importance of the social concept of the family, and the bearing that social norms and values have on the interpretation and development of law. Whilst these themes have not been developed fully, you should be able to apply these themes and considerations to the substantive law in later chapters. Finally, you have looked at the court hierarchy with family jurisdiction, and again in later chapters will be able to build on to this aspect, to deepen your understanding of the court structure in this area.

CHAPTER TWO

MARRIAGE – THE STARTING POINT

2.1 Objectives

By the end of this chapter you should be able to:

■ describe the legal rules on the process of marriage;

■ apply the law to client scenarios, and advise on the marriage formalities;

■ advise clients on the consequences of failure to comply with the formalities.

2.2 Introduction

Historically, the law did not involve itself too much in the regulation of marriage. An individual was free to 'marry' merely by the exchange of vows, or by the act of sexual intercourse with their partner. This lack of legal regulation led to the term 'common-law wife', which is still in use today, although having little, if any, legality or rights attached to it. The law did, however, start to become involved in marriage in the eighteenth century, and now legislation provides the rules surrounding the process of marriage. In this chapter you will be looking at the formalities of the marriage process and the potential consequences of failure to comply with the law, hence considering the question of how do you marry, before moving on in the next chapter to look at the issue of who can marry whom.

2.3 Development of the Law

As you have just read, the law has only begun to become involved with the process of marriage in the last 200 years, by laying down requirements on parties wishing to marry. Common-law marriages, which took the form of an exchange of vows (not required to be in a church or religious place of worship), or the act of living together and having sexual relations, were the norm.

Can you think of any problems that may arise from such a form of marriage?

Whilst there may have been advantages to this system, e.g. the lack of expense, the lack of state regulation over what was seen both as a religious issue and also as a personal matter, there have been some problems identified with this common-law system.

Cretney in *Principles of Family Law*, 6th edn, London: Sweet & Maxwell, 1997, identifies them thus:

> The informality permitted by the common law had a number of disadvantages. First, there would often be uncertainty about the validity of a marriage. It was not so much that there might be doubts about the validity of the informal union itself; but rather that indiscreet and quickly forgotten words breathed under the influence of passion would be relied on many years later by one of the parties to a, possibly transient, relationship. The intention underlying such an assertion of an informal marriage might well be to invalidate the other party's subsequent solemn marriage with a third party.
>
> Secondly, hasty and ill-considered marriages were facilitated. The agreement which is all that is necessary to form a valid common law marriage might – as an American writer has put it – have been entered into 'in the privacy of one's own bedroom, in an automobile after a picnic in the country, or after a night's debauch'. In such cases, it seems unlikely that there would be much point in inquiring whether the promises were in the present or future tense.
>
> Thirdly, the creation of such a marriage might have important and undesirable legal consequences. The American case of *State* v *Ward* 28 SE 2d 785 (1994), provides a striking illustration of the potential evil of such 'quickie' marriages: the defendant to a charge of unlawful intercourse with a minor successfully asserted that the complainant was his wife at common law.
>
> It was this third factor which most influenced the call for change in English law. Marriage had important financial consequences, not least that the rich heiress's property immediately vested in her husband. Informality or secrecy made no difference to the validity of the marriage and its possibly devastating effect in terms of the wife's family's property.

Consequently legislation was passed in 1753 to regulate marriage, and the manner in which a marriage could be contracted. Whilst the Act is commonly called Lord Hardwicke's Act, its correct title was the Clandestine Marriages Act 1753, and it succeeded in replacing the common-law marriage with a marriage celebrated in church. Certain pre-marriage formalities were stipulated (such as the calling of banns), and failure to comply with them would result in the marriage being invalid.

In 1836, the Marriage Act was passed, which amended Lord Hardwicke's Act, and introduced the secular procedure for marriage. This therefore meant that couples could legally marry, but without having to go through a Church of England ceremony. This secular ceremony was not to be as simple as the common-law exchange of vows, since the Act again specified the formalities to be met before the marriage would be acceptable in law. This dual system of marriage, and in particular, the dual system of pre-marriage formalities, is still with us today. The legislation has however been amended, and the relevant law is contained in the Marriage Act of 1949 (as amended).

2.4   The Formalities of Marriage

Within this heading, there are different areas to be considered, namely the pre-marriage requirements, the solemnization of the marriage, and consent.

If you are married, write down all the things that you had to do before the marriage ceremony, in order to 'get to the church on time'. If you are not married, ask someone you know who is.

How long was your list? If you are married, did thinking about all the organisation of the wedding bring back good or bad memories? Today, the actual process of getting married can be fraught with stress, since generally so much has to be arranged. Did your list include such matters as getting the wedding outfits, the choosing of the rings, arranging the reception? If it did, then you probably had a very traditional wedding, with the normal type of anxieties. However, the issues identified in this list have nothing to do with the legality of the process, they are little more than the social etiquette that is attached to the wedding ceremony. The legal formalities refer to the giving of notice of the forthcoming ceremony and other prerequisites, and these will differ according to the type of ceremony you have, i.e. a Church of England ceremony, a purely secular or civil ceremony, or a religious ceremony (other than C of E).

As you go through the next few sections, draw up a table on a separate sheet of paper to highlight the differences between the different types of ceremony and their respective formalities.

2.4.1   PRE-MARRIAGE REQUIREMENTS

2.4.1.1   Civil marriages and marriages other than in accordance with the Church of England

A secular marriage, as well as a marriage which is conducted under the auspices of a religion other than the Church of England, must only be performed after the necessary forms of notice have been given and the relevant superintendent registrar's certificate or licence issued.

Read ss. 27, 31, 32 and 33 of the Marriage Act 1949 in *Cases and Materials* (2.1.1.1).

What types of notices and prerequisites are required for the different types of marriage certificate or licence?

You should have identified that there are two types of marriage covered by these sections:

■   marriage under a superintendent registrar's certificate without licence;

■   marriage under a superintendent registrar's certificate with licence.

The former is the more usual route to take and is used in the majority of non-Anglican weddings. In 1992, of the 156,967 civil marriages, approximately 129,000 were subject to the superintendent registrar's certificate and approximately 27,000 to the certificate and licence. For this type of ceremony, you should have noted down that the requirements are that: the parties have resided in the district where notice is given for a period of at least seven days; they have declared that there are no lawful impediments to the marriage; they meet the residence requirements and the relevant fee is paid. Once the notice and the declarations have been given to the superintendent registrar, notice will be posted in a marriage notice book available for public inspection. A total period of 21 days will have to pass from the posting of the notice, before the certificate authorising the marriage ceremony can be issued.

For the second form of marriage, these requirements are slightly different, in that the residence requirement only applies to one of the parties, and is extended to 15 days prior to the giving of the notice. The waiting time before the marriage can take place is reduced to one day, and no notice of the wedding is posted for public inspection. Naturally a fee is payable, and this is higher than the fee for the certificate without licence.

2.4.1.2   Anglican or Church of England marriages

The formalities relating to these weddings are linked with religious tenets. It is possible that some of these requirements will be changed in the near future, perhaps due to their 'old-fashioned' nature.

ACTIVITY 10

Read ss. 5, 6, 7, 15 and 16 of the Marriage Act 1949 in *Cases and Materials* (2.1.1.2).

What type of notices and prerequisites are required for an Anglican ceremony?

Again you should have identified that there are two types of marriage permitted:

■ marriage after publication of banns;

■ marriage under common licence.

The former is, again, the commoner and also the cheaper! The requirements are for the banns to be published for three consecutive Sundays in the parish churches where the parties reside (having at least 15 days residence), and in the church where the marriage will be conducted, if different. Publication means that the banns are both entered into a written register and also read out in church itself. Once they have been published, then the marriage ceremony can be conducted immediately. It should be noted that there are plans for this type of preliminary to be changed, with the proposal that the reading of banns be removed.

The second form of notice is rarer, and has, again, different requirements. There is still the residence requirement, but in relation to only one of the parties and it is still 15 days. Rather than the registering and reading out of the banns, one of the parties is required to swear an affidavit stating that there is no impediment or legal reason why the couple should not marry. There is no waiting time, and once the licence is granted, the marriage can be conducted.

SAQ 6

What is the purpose of giving notice? Do you think the types of notice indicated above are effective?

According to the Efficiency Scrutiny of the Registration Service (1985), the Register Office notice board is normally used by those tradespeople who have an interest in weddings, e.g. the photographer, the chauffeur, the florist etc. The real purpose of giving notice and having the forthcoming marriage publicly displayed, is to enable anyone who knows of any objections to the marriage to bring those objections to the notice of the registrar. The same is true of the calling of banns. In reality this is not likely to occur, since many individuals would never think to view the notice board (when did you last do so?) nor go to church. Also, with a more 'mobile' population it is not as common for individuals to be well known in an area.

2.4.1.3   Other forms of notice

The above notice requirements may not be suitable for all situations, and there do exist forms of 'emergency notice' provision to deal with 'deathbed' weddings, or 'prison' weddings. Under the Marriage (Registrar-General's Licence) Act 1970 it is possible to obtain a licence to marry away from a Register Office if one of the parties is seriously ill and not likely to recover, or if one of the parties cannot be moved to a place where marriages can be conducted. If the same situation is relevant to an Anglican ceremony, then under the Ecclesiastical Licences Act 1533, the Archbishop of Canterbury is able to grant a licence to permit a marriage at any time of day, whether or not in a church. It has been commented on by Cretney at page 24 that this procedure is often used to permit marriages in college chapels, or churches where the parties have no connection, and hence cannot use the traditional notification procedures.

2.4.2   THE MARRIAGE CEREMONY

2.4.2.1   Introduction

Whilst only two forms of notification procedure exist, there are four main types of ceremony that are permitted in English law.

Write down the four categories which you think exist.

Two of the categories should have been easy to identify, namely the civil ceremony, and the Anglican ceremony. The others are religious ceremonies, not according to the rights of the Anglican Church, and marriages according to Jewish or Quaker traditions.

2.4.2.2   The civil ceremony

After the civil preliminaries, a marriage can take place in any Register Office, subject to certification, albeit that the office where one of the parties resides is often preferred. The marriage ceremony will need to be conducted by an authorised person, and will need to take place between the hours of 8 a.m. and 6 p.m. In addition, the marriage should take place with 'open doors', meaning that any member of the public may enter (under the Marriage Act 1949). The parties to the marriage must, at some point during the ceremony, declare that they know of no impediment to the marriage, and also make the 'required declaration'.

Can you think what the 'required declaration' is?

Even if you have not attended a civil marriage, the same type of declaration must be made in religious marriages. The parties are required to call upon the persons present at the ceremony to witness their contract to one another. The precise wording is set out in s. 44(3) of the Marriage Act 1949 and is in *Cases and Materials* (2.1.2.1). You will also find extracts from the Marriage Ceremony (Prescribed Words) Act 1996 at the same point, which allows for another form of wording to be adopted.

Can you think of any reason why the changes in wording have been brought about?

You may have found this a hard question since the changes are very slight, and in reality seem to do nothing more than modernise the language used. By so doing, the wording is more readily understood, and perhaps may be thought to be more appropriate to the individuals concerned, but other than this, there seems to be no clear reason for introducing this choice.

2.4.2.3 Alternative venues for the ceremony

In addition to the changes to the wording used in the ceremony, recent changes have occurred with regard to the place where a civil marriage can be carried out. The Marriage Act 1994 amended the Marriage Act 1949, to enable marriages in 'approved premises' (see *Cases and Materials* (2.1.2.2)). These are premises approved for the purposes of a marriage ceremony by the relevant local authority.

The Marriages (Approved Premises) Regulations 1995 (SI 1995 No. 510) set out the process for the application and registration of other 'premises'.

Look at the extracts from the 1995 Regulations in *Cases and Materials* (2.1.2.2) and make a list of the basic requirements for registration.

A marriage will not be permitted anywhere, for example, there must be a roof, it must be a permanent structure, or be permanently moored if a boat. You should also have noted that there must be a separate area for the ceremony, away from the reception. The criteria that the premises are a 'seemly and dignified venue' are perhaps a little subjective, since each individual is likely to have their own view as to what is seemly. The changes do however mean that individuals have a greater scope for marrying in surroundings that they feel to be appropriate, and perhaps far more attractive. In *Cases and Materials* (2.1.2.2) you will find a short extract from *The Times*, and a short extract from *The Sunday Times*, which indicate how popular these alternative venues are, and also how far removed from a Register Office they can be.

However, you should also note some of the potential problems.

Look at the report 'Encounter at station not so brief' in *Cases and Materials* (2.1.2.2)

Can you spot the issue that Cretney has highlighted in the short extract from *Principles of Family Law* in *Cases and Materials* (2.1.2.2)?

To answer this, you would need to recall some of the requirements for a marriage ceremony, and in particular that it be conducted with open doors. If guests have to go through customs before they can witness the marriage, then is it truly open to the public? Return to *Cases and Materials* (2.1.2.2) to see how Cretney phrases it.

2.4.2.4 The Anglican ceremony

The nature of the ceremony is very similar to that in the Register Office, with the obvious emphasis on the religious nature of the ceremony. There must be a qualified clergyman to conduct the ceremony, before witnesses, with open doors, and between the specified times. Again, the prescribed words and declarations must be made, although there is little scope to amend them as with civil ceremonies.

2.4.2.5 Other religious ceremonies

This category will incorporate those individuals of the Roman Catholic faith, Sikhs, Hindus and Muslims. Before the ceremony, the civil preliminaries must be carried out. Thereafter the ceremony may be carried out in accordance with the relevant religion. The law requires that the building is one which is a place of meeting for religious worship (s. 41, Marriage Act 1949). In addition, there must be an authorised person in attendance – this may in fact be the registrar but is more commonly a priest or minister of the necessary faith. Regardless of which religion is involved, the wording in s. 44(3) of the Marriage Act 1949 must be said at some stage in the ceremony.

2.4.2.6 Jewish and Quaker marriages

For some reason, these two faiths were exempted from the provisions of the Marriage Act 1753. Hence today the only requirements are for couples to comply with the civil notification procedure.

2.5 Registration

Formal registration of the marriage is necessary to enable the parties to have proof of their status. As you will see during the rest of this programme, many rights and obligations, both of the parties to one another and of the state, are dependent upon the status of a married person. The marriage register must be completed and signed by witnesses. A copy of this is provided to the couple.

2.6 Consent

This is a topic to which you will return in the next chapter when considering the legal status of a marriage. At this point it is necessary merely to note that marriage is, in effect, a contract between the two individuals concerned. As such, it is a very simple contract and most individuals are deemed capable of entering into it. The idea that individuals need to be of a certain age to contract holds true for marriage: it is not permissible to marry under the age of 16. If a young person between the ages of 16 and 18 wishes to marry, they can do so only with the consent of their parents (those who hold parental responsibility) or their guardian. However, if this consent is not given, or the consent is fabricated, it is still a valid marriage. If you wish to look at the full definitions with regard to who can consent, you should look at the extracts from s. 3 of the Marriage Act 1949 (as amended) in *Cases and Materials* (2.2).

2.7 Consequences of Non-compliance with the Formalities

What do you think the consequences should be if the required preliminaries have not been complied with?

You may have decided that if the preliminaries were ignored then the marriage should be invalid, and hence have no legal consequences. Alternatively, you may have looked at the nature of the requirements and decided that they were not really significant and hence failure to comply should not result in the marriage being deemed invalid. Unfortunately the legislation is not so clear cut.

Read ss. 48 and 49 of the Marriage Act 1949 in *Cases and Materials* (2.3).

On a separate sheet of paper, write down the situations in which a marriage will be treated as valid regardless of breach of the formalities, and the situations in which a marriage will be invalid (or void).

Your lists should look something like this:

VALID	VOID
Breach of residence requirements	No notice to the registrar
Lack of consent of parents/guardians if party below 18 years	No certificate issued or void
Building not registered as a place of religious worship	No licence issued (where necessary)
Building not the parties usual place of worship	Married in a place not specified on the certificate
	Building not an approved place
	In the absence of an authorised person or registrar.

Did you notice the caveat to the invalid or void marriages? If not, go back to the section and try to spot it.

You should have noticed the phrase, 'If any persons knowingly and wilfully intermarry . . . the marriage shall be void'. This means that it is only where a marriage is carried out with the parties knowing that they have not fulfilled the relevant preliminaries that the marriage is not valid. It is not clear from the legislation whether or not both parties should know of the defect, although most writers (for example Cretney and Hayes & Williams, *Family law; principles, policy and practice*, 1995) do speak in plural terms, suggesting that both parties should know.

Section 4 of the Marriage Act 1949 requires that the marriage is conducted between 8 a.m. and 6 p.m. What is the consequence for the marriage if it is conducted at 6.05 p.m.?

If you have gone back to the sections in **Activity 14** (*Cases and Materials* (**2.3**)), you would not have received much assistance. With regard to certain of the formalities, the law is not clear as to the effect of failure to comply. The hours for marriage are one such formality. Others that fall into this 'vague' category include the requirement for open doors, and the need to make the required declarations.

2.8   Summary

In this chapter you have looked at the means by which a marriage can be conducted and legally formed. You should now be familiar with the requirements to notify of an impending marriage ceremony, and the purposes for which this notice is given. The ability in today's society for this notice to achieve its aims is an issue you should be able to discuss. The actual process of the marriage ceremony itself, who may conduct it and where, is another area which you should feel comfortable discussing. Linked to this, the consequences for ignoring the legal requirements should be clear. You should also be in a position to suggest why there have been calls for reform in this area, since this is relevant to the End of Chapter Assessment Question.

2.9   End of Chapter Assessment Question

'[M]any of the procedures [relating to marriage] are unnecessarily complex and restrictive': Government Green Paper Cm 531, *Registration: A Modern Service*.

Discuss the validity of this statement.

See *Cases and Materials* (2.5) for an outline answer.

CHAPTER THREE

NULLITY AND JUDICIAL SEPARATION

3.1 Objectives

By the end of this chapter you should be able to:

■ explain the importance of ss. 11 and 12 of the Matrimonial Causes Act 1973;

■ analyse and discuss the meanings within the legislation;

■ apply the law to problem scenarios, and advise hypothetical clients;

■ identify areas where the law may be capable of change and the nature of those changes;

■ explain the relevance of judicial separation to ending a marriage.

3.2 Introduction

In 1995 only 516 marriages were brought to an end by the use of nullity, compared with 153,337 divorce petitions (Judicial Statistics 1995, HMSO). Consequently you may be wondering why you need to study this area of law. Whilst nullity, in particular, is little used to bring a marriage to an end, it is important in understanding the legal rules surrounding marriage itself, and the question of 'who can marry whom?'. In addition, nullity illustrates the historical difficulties of obtaining a divorce, which in reality is only a recent option. Judicial separation is also a little used provision, but does retain relevance for certain individuals in society.

3.3 Void versus Voidable

In **Chapter 2** you have already come across the term 'void' in respect of a marriage – did you understand what it meant? Do you know what voidable means?

Write down what you understand to be meant by these terms. You may be assisted by other legal courses which you have already completed.

In reality, marriages fall into three categories:

■ those that are *valid*, and can only be brought to an end through divorce or judicial separation;

■ those that are *void*, and have therefore never existed as a valid marriage, indeed in law, no marriage has been created; and

■ those that are *voidable*, which will be seen in law to be valid although due to an irregularity the marriage may be set aside and declared no longer in existence.

You will see during this chapter that the distinctions between void and voidable marriages, in so far as the consequences are concerned, are not that great.

3.4 Void Marriages

Read s. 11, Matrimonial Causes Act 1973 in *Cases and Materials* (3.1).

Using a separate sheet of paper, list the reasons when a marriage will be deemed to be non-existent in the eyes of the law.

Try to write a definition or short explanation for each reason you have listed, and then compare this with the discussion below.

You should have found six reasons or grounds for a marriage being void.

3.4.1 THE PROHIBITED DEGREES

The first to consider is that the 'parties are within the prohibited degrees of relationship' (MCA 1973, s. 11(a)(i)). You may not have been able to define this very easily. There are two types of prohibited degrees within the law, and they clearly reflect the question 'who can marry whom?'. The first category is the prohibited degrees of consanguinity, i.e. relationships by blood. The second category is the prohibited degrees of affinity, and these are relationships created by marriage.

On a separate sheet of paper, write down whom you think will be prevented from marrying whom in these two categories.

When you have done this, compare your list with that in the Marriage Act 1949, sch. 1, which you will find in *Cases and Materials* (3.1.1).

How well did you do?

For revision purposes, you may find it useful to draw a family tree to show these relationships and the prohibitions.

The justifications for these restrictions span a variety of considerations. As you may know, the potential for genetic defects in offspring is greater the closer the blood link between parents. Genetically therefore, marriage within the prohibited degrees of consanguinity may increase the risks from inherited disease. The morality and social policy considerations of marrying a member of your close family are also relevant, especially in the degrees of affinity where step-parents/children and other affines are concerned. It would not be acceptable in the majority of circles for a child to be raised by someone acting as a parent and then for those two to subsequently marry, and create a totally different relationship.

Do you think the same prohibitions should apply if the step-parent and child had not actually lived in the same household in a parent/child relationship?

Clearly here there is less of a 'family' relationship and so you might agree that the law should treat this case differently, and yet the degrees of affinity have only been relaxed in the recent past. There are now limited situations where marriage across the degrees is permissible.

Read s. 1 of the Marriages (Prohibited Degrees of Relationship) Act 1986 in *Cases and Materials* (3.1.1).

Write down the effects of this legislation.

You should have discovered that the prohibition would be relaxed:

■ where both parties are over 21 (in all cases);

■ where the marriage is between step-parent/child and the child had not been treated as a child of the family before reaching the age of 18;

■ where the marriage is between an individual and their parent-in-law, or child-in-law and the respective (intervening) spouses are dead.

3.4.2   THE AGE OF THE PARTIES

The terms of this restriction are not difficult to understand, but the rationale is less clear. It would appear that social mores affect this principle. You may not be aware that in the early part of this century it was permissible for a girl to marry at the age of 12 (this age was raised in 1929), something that would seem quite unacceptable today. The fact that there is a minimum age for marriage does not seem too important, with only a minority of individuals marrying in their teens.

If a child of 16 or 17 wished to marry, this is permissible, subject to the consent of their parents (or persons with parental responsibility). However, in the event that this consent is not forthcoming, the court can be asked to consent instead. If this is not done, and the child lies about their age, or the validity of the consent, then the marriage is still valid in law. No challenge may be made, regardless of the breach of requirements.

3.4.3   THE DISREGARD OF CERTAIN FORMALITIES

You should recall the situations and the types of breach that will invalidate the marriage.

Write down what you can remember from the previous chapter on this issue. Once you have completed your answer/notes, go back to Chapter 2 and refresh your memory.

3.4.4   ALREADY LAWFULLY MARRIED

As with MCA 1973, s. 11(a)(ii) this prohibition should not cause too many problems. The restriction on marriage is in connection with the second marriage – the first will remain valid (always assuming it was valid to start with). As you may be aware, if this situation does arise, a criminal charge of bigamy may result.

3.4.5   THE PARTIES ARE NOT RESPECTIVELY MALE AND FEMALE

This again would appear to be an uncontroversial aspect of the legislation since it reflects the notion of marriage being the union of one man and one woman. In reality, there has been continued debate on this provision and the issue of what is meant by 'male' and 'female'.

Read the extracts from *Corbett* v *Corbett* [1970] 2 All ER 33 in *Cases and Materials* (3.1.2). Why do you think that the marriage was not upheld?

When you have considered this, read the extracts from *J* v *S-T (Formerly J) (Transsexual: Ancillary Relief)* [1997] 1 FLR 402 (in *Cases and Materials* (3.1.2). Are there any distinctions?

From these cases, you will have seen that the situation of transsexuals who wish to marry is somewhat difficult. Whilst the prohibition on marriage in MCA 1973, s. 11(c) reflects the notion of an individual's 'gender', i.e. their maleness or femaleness, the courts have interpreted this in terms of an individual's biological sex. Not only that, but the determination on that sex is made at birth. A transsexual who completes reassignment surgery and who has all the outward attributes of their new 'gender' can therefore not marry as that gender. In *J* v *S-T* (a case to which you will return), the reassignment was not complete. If the law were to be changed to enable transsexuals to marry as their new gender, it is debatable whether an individual in the situation of J would be assisted.

Do you think this prohibition should continue, or should transsexuals who have completed re-assignment be permitted to marry?

As you will see as you continue through this course, there are many areas where reviews of the law are being made, or called for, due to what is happening in society and the changes in patterns of living. If you believe that marriage is a public sign of an individual's commitment to their partner, then you may agree with the latter part of the above statement. If you favour the more traditional and religious based concept of marriage, you may disagree. By only accepting the concept of marriage between two different genders (which is indicated by the question), you would still be supporting a narrow construct of marriage. Perhaps you should consider the position for homosexual and lesbian couples. Should the law restrict their rights to form a legally accepted relationship, i.e. one which gives them rights and responsibilities?

3.4.6 POLYGAMOUS MARRIAGES

The restriction on polygamous marriages would appear to overlap with that of bigamy, and this is true to the extent that both concern marriages to more than one person. However, polygamy is not automatically a criminal offence, in other words, a polygamous marriage may be valid in England and Wales.

Read the case extracts from *Hussain* v *Hussain* **[1982] 3 All ER 369 in** *Cases and Materials* **(3.1.3) which considers the interpretation of s. 11(d). Write down what you think this case establishes.**

Now read s. 5 of the Private International Law (Miscellaneous Provisions) Act 1995 (*Cases and Materials* (3.1.3)). How has this section affected the decision in *Hussain*?

Section 11(d) of the MCA 1973 often causes confusion, and yet is now not a complicated provision. The key issue to deciding whether or not a marriage will be void for polygamy is where the parties are domiciled. If the country of domicile permits polygamy (for example Pakistan), then as long as all parties are domiciled within that jurisdiction, there will be no question of the marriage being invalid. If one of the parties is domiciled in England and Wales, under the unamended provisions of s. 11(d) and the precedent in *Hussain*, if the non-English domiciled party could validly take another spouse, the marriage would be potentially polygamous, and therefore void. The amendment made by the 1995 Act is to remove the potentially polygamous criteria. Now, if both parties are unmarried, even if the non-domiciled party could take a second spouse, the marriage will be valid in English law. If, however, one of the parties were already married, then the marriage would be void for polygamy.

3.5   Voidable Marriages

Read s. 12, MCA 1973 in *Cases and Materials* (3.2).

Using a separate sheet of paper, write down the situations when the law will declare a marriage voidable.

Write down a brief definition or explanation for each of the reasons you have listed, and then compare them with the following discussion. You should note that the reasons for which a marriage may be annulled under s. 12, theoretically, must exist at the time of the marriage. You may wish to reflect upon this and the accuracy of this ideal when looking at the individual definitions.

3.5.1   INCAPACITY TO CONSUMMATE/WILFUL REFUSAL TO CONSUMMATE

Although these two categories are separate, their similarities mean that it is easier to consider them together.

Read *R* v *R* [1952] 1 All ER 1194 in *Cases and Materials* (3.2.1). How would you define the term 'consummation'?

From this case you should realise that the condition of consummation is one that requires sexual intercourse to take place between the parties. Intercourse does not have the same definition as it would in criminal law for the purposes of rape. Sexual intercourse must be 'ordinary and complete'. A marriage will be consummated regardless of whether or not ejaculation occurs, and does not depend upon the use of contraception: what is at issue is not the ability to conceive, but the ability to have sexual relations.

Incapacity to consummate can be due to the 'defects' of either party and an individual can rely on their own incapacity but it is always for the petitioner to prove that incapacity exists. The common perception of incapacity would relate to physical difficulties in consummating the marriage. This does not have to be the case, and psychological aversion can suffice. You may find the case of *Singh* v *Singh* [1971] 2 All ER 828, illustrative of this point, and extracts are in *Cases and Materials* (3.2.1).

By contrast, for wilful refusal to be proven, the petitioner must prove that the respondent has reached a 'settled and definite decision without just excuse' (per Jowitt LC in *Horton* v *Horton* [1947] 2 All ER 871, at page 874) not to have intercourse. The assessment of the settled decision is a question of fact for the court and the extracts from *Ford* v *Ford* [1987] Fam Law 17, in *Cases and Materials* (3.2.1) will illustrate the courts' approach.

What do you think is meant by 'just excuse'? Can you think of an example?

As you will have seen from *Ford*, the failure to consummate the marriage whilst still in prison, would have equated to a just excuse: it was a valid reason for not having intercourse. Other cases have highlighted that refusal to have intercourse unless a condom was used does not equal wilful refusal (*Baxter* v *Baxter* [1948] AC 274). The failure to arrange a religious wedding, even though a civil marriage has taken place, however does equal just excuse (*Kaur* v *Singh* [1972] 1 WLR 105 and extracted in *Cases and Materials* (3.2.1)).

Would it matter if the parties had had intercourse prior to the marriage?

Given that the focus of both s. 12(a) and (b) of the 1973 Act is on the ability of the couple to have sexual intercourse it would be logical to answer this question in the affirmative. However, what is at issue is whether or not this marriage has been consummated and therefore the ability or desire of the parties prior to the ceremony is irrelevant.

In connection with this area of the MCA 1973, an article entitled 'Wilful Refusal to Consummate: Just Excuse' from *Family Law* has been extracted in *Cases and Materials* (3.2.1) which you should read once you are happy with the basic concepts.

3.5.2 CONSENT

The legal requirements for consent cover three main areas, as you should have identified.

Starting with unsoundness of mind, the first thing you should be aware of is that this is not automatically the same as mental illness, although it may include it. The real concern here is that due to the individuals' mental incapacity they are unable to enter a contract, as marriage is a contract. The level of understanding and therefore capacity that is needed is quite low, since marriage is a simple contract (per Hodson LJ in *Re Park* [1954] P 112 at page 136).

Turning to duress, this is not a clear-cut concept, with a variety of approaches being taken by the courts as to what actions will constitute duress, and hence vitiate consent.

ACTIVITY 24

Read the extracts of *Szechter* v *Szechter* [1971] 2 WLR 170 and *Hirani* v *Hirani* [1982] 4 FLR 232 in *Cases and Materials* (3.2.2). How did the courts interpret 'duress' in these two cases? Which interpretation do you believe is the most appropriate?

In the former case you should have seen that the court's view was that to establish duress, the petitioner had to show that their will had been overborne by genuine and reasonably held fear that was caused by an immediate threat to life, limb, or liberty. In the case of *Hirani*, the interpretation of duress was that it will be found where pressure, of whatever kind, had been such as to destroy the reality of the consent given to the marriage.

If you did not pick up on these two interpretations, go back and read the extracts again.

Of the two interpretations, the latter is preferable since it looks at duress in a more common-sense way, and focuses on the subjective element of consent. You should note that both *Szechter* and *Hirani* have been followed in subsequent cases but, given the timing of the cases, the approach in *Hirani* is suggested to be the current law.

Mistake is the final reason for obviating consent to marriage.

SAQ 15

Can you think of situations where you might make a mistake that would vitiate consent?

There are two types of situations where a mistake might occur. You may have thought of a situation where you do not realise that what you are doing is getting married. In a case in 1945 (*Mehta* v *Mehta* [1945] 2 All ER 690) the petitioner wrongly believed that they were going through a ceremony of religious conversion. This mistaken belief was held to vitiate consent.

Alternatively, you may have considered the situation where you wrongly believe your spouse to be a millionaire, when in reality he/she is a pauper. In this case, if it is merely a mistake as to the attributes of the person you marry, you cannot plead mistake. If, however, you marry Tom, believing him to be Fred, his twin brother, mistake would be a valid claim.

3.5.3 MENTAL ILLNESS

Again, the mental capacity of one of the parties to the marriage is the main issue here.

What are the differences between this ground and s. 12(c) of the MCA 1973?

There are two main distinctions between s. 12(c) and (d) that you should have identified. Sub-section (d) refers to the suffering of a mental illness within the meaning of the Mental Health Act 1983. If you have studied medical law, you will have an idea what the 1983 Act means by mental illness; if you haven't studied medical law, don't worry. The important point is that in (d), the mental illness is more specifically defined, (c) just refers to unsoundness of mind, a much wider and potentially vague concept. The second distinction which you should have noticed is the consequence of the mental illness. In (d) it makes the party 'unfitted for marriage', whereas (c) is simply looking at consent. An individual may have a mental illness, but still be capable of giving consent. After the marriage it may be found that such an individual is 'unfitted', and the marriage can be avoided.

3.5.4 VENEREAL DISEASE

Do you think that s. 11(e) is still an appropriate reason to avoid a marriage?

This reason for avoiding a marriage is little used, and is perhaps anachronistic given the ability of medicine to cure venereal disease. Today, the subsection has generated debate in relation to HIV/AIDS and whether this would be within the terms of the provision.

Do you think these diseases would be covered?

No cases on nullity seem to have focused on HIV/AIDS to date. The problem would be that HIV itself is not really a disease, it is a virus, and also both HIV and AIDS are deemed to be blood disorders, and not VD. To a degree this would make sense since HIV can be transmitted in manners other than sexual contact. Given this doubt it may be preferable for an individual to seek a divorce rather than use nullity.

3.5.5 EXISTING PREGNANCY

A marriage may be avoided under this ground under s. 11(f), MCA 1973. The presence of this ground for annulling a marriage is rooted in history, when fraudulent or wilful concealment of a relevant fact was ground for annulment. If a wife was pregnant by another man and had not revealed this to her husband before the marriage it did not amount to fraud or concealment and hence would not enable the husband to end the marriage. An existing pregnancy would also not be sufficient to enable the husband to divorce the wife. Consequently, the law had to be changed to ensure that men who had been deceived into marriage could break those legal ties — hence the provision now found in s. 12(f) of the 1973 Act. Today it seems more to highlight the potential discrimination in the law: do you think a wife could petition for nullity because her husband had caused another woman to become pregnant before the marriage?

3.6 Bars to the Annulment

Read s. 13, MCA 1973 in *Cases and Materials* (3.3).

How does this affect an individual's ability to get the marriage annulled?

This section does, to a degree, temper the effects of s. 12. The basic premise is that if an individual is seeking to set their marriage aside as voidable, then if that individual had known it would be possible to set the marriage aside, had conducted themselves in a manner which suggested they did not intend to set the marriage aside, and it would be unjust for the court to set the marriage aside, the court can refuse to make the order.

In addition, you should have noted that if the nullity petition is brought under the consent, mental illness, VD or pregnancy grounds, the proceedings must be commenced within three years of the marriage. Also, if the petition is brought under the VD and pregnancy grounds, the petitioner must satisfy the court that they did not know of the illness/pregnancy at the time of the marriage.

3.7   Who can Apply for the Marriage to be Annulled?

From all you have read, who do you suppose can apply to have a marriage annulled, under s. 11 or s. 12 of the MCA 1973?

If you looked back at the sections, you will probably have noticed that s. 12 indicates who can petition on which ground, but s. 11 is silent on the matter.

Where a marriage is void, the number of potential applicants is much wider. It includes not just the parties to the marriage, but any other interested individual (e.g. a child) who may wish to have the marriage set aside. This can happen, not just in the parties' lifetime, but also posthumously. A reason why this might occur is in relation to rights of inheritance.

If the marriage is voidable, then only the parties to the marriage can annul it, and only in accordance with s. 12. You should therefore go back and highlight who can petition on which ground. So, for example, under incapacity to consummate, either party can petition, and an individual's own incapacity can be relied on.

On a separate sheet of paper write a list indicating who can use which of the s. 12 grounds, and compare it with the list in *Cases and Materials* (3.4).

3.8   Consequences of Nullity

Apart from the obvious consequence that once a marriage is annulled it will be brought to an end, other consequences flow.

3.8.1 PARTIES' RIGHTS; VOID MARRIAGES

Where the marriage is void, e.g. has never been valid, it may still give the parties rights. If any children are born to the parties, then if one of the parties reasonably believed the marriage to be valid, the child will be treated as being legitimate (Legitimacy Act 1976, s. 1). When a marriage is ended, there are inevitably financial considerations. The ability to seek financial remedies is not restricted to divorce, but can also be extended to nullity (ss. 23 and 24, MCA 1973). The willingness of the court to do so will depend on the reason for declaring the marriage to be void.

Read the extracts from *J* v *S-T* [1997] 1 FLR 402 in *Cases and Materials* (3.5.1). You should already be familiar with the facts.

Write down what you think is the ratio of the case.

In this case, the court followed a previous ratio in *Whiston* v *Whiston* [1995] 2 FLR 268, which indicated that a party to a marriage who had deliberately misled the other party (in *Whiston* as to the fact that they were not already married, and in *J* as you have seen, to the fact that they were male) should not be permitted to benefit from their actions.

You will also find extracts from *Whiston* in *Cases and Materials* (3.5.1). Read them, and try to decide if the two cases are reconcilable.

This is an issue which you may like to come back to once you have studied the next three chapters when you will be able to provide a more detailed analysis.

A major factor you should have identified is that in *Whiston*, the 'wife' had been guilty of bigamy, and so the court felt it was not permissible for her to benefit from her crime. In *J*, had any such crime occurred? It is arguable that the crime of perjury had been committed in the signing of the marriage register in the male name. However, if *J* had truly believed himself to be male, is that perjury? In any case, is it a crime against the wife?

3.8.2 PARTIES' RIGHTS: VOIDABLE MARRIAGES

Where the marriage is voidable, the same consequences will apply. However, this is due to the fact that the marriage is valid unless and until it is annulled.

3.9 Judicial Separation

Judicial separation operates as a sort of halfway house between marriage and divorce. It does not totally rescind the marriage contract, but merely absolves the parties from certain requirements, e.g. living together. The grounds for seeking an order currently are the same as for a divorce (see **Chapter 4**) albeit that under s. 17(2), MCA 1973, the court does not have to consider the question of irretrievable breakdown. As with divorce, when the law changes with the implementation of the Family Law Act 1996, so the grounds for seeking a separation order (as it will be called) will change (see **Chapter 5**). If a couple uses judicial separation, there are certain advantages or consequences:

- a petition can be brought at any point in time during the marriage;

- ancillary relief can be sought;

- the parties do not have to cohabit;

- the parties are not free to remarry another person;

- for intestacy purposes the judically seperated spouse is treated as being dead.

3.10 Summary

The annulment of marriage is, at best, the confirmation of necessary rules relating to marriage and, at worst, the continuation of a set of anachronistic provisions with little if no real role to play in marital law. With the forthcoming changes to divorce under the provisions of the Family Law Act 1996, nullity may be an area of increasing interest to couples wishing to legally end their relationship. When studying **Chapter 5** you may wish to consider in more detail the reasons why this may occur. As you have seen, there exist a number of reasons or grounds for annulment, some which may continue to be highly relevant, others less so. You should be familiar with their definitions and the consequences of a petition.

Finally, you should return to your court hierarchy (see **1.6**), and add nullity to it (and ancillary matters). These petitions will be within the jurisdiction of the county court.

3.11   End of Chapter Assessment Questions

To ease you in gently, here are a selection of smaller advice and essay type questions rather than one long question.

1. Alfred has been undergoing medical treatment for clinical depression. The drug regime has made him intermittently 'hazy' and he has difficulty in understanding or making sense of things. Last week Alfred went through a Register Office wedding with Bernadette. After the ceremony, they booked in to a hotel nearby, and the marriage was consummated. They have not lived together beyond that first night. Alfred has now sought your advice on bringing the marriage to an end.

2. To what extent can an individual marry whomsoever they wish, wherever they wish?

3. Andre is married to Steffi and the marriage took place eight months ago. Shortly after the marriage Andre confessed he was bisexual. Due to this, Steffi insisted that Andre must have an HIV test. This has been returned with a positive result. No sexual intercourse has taken place. Advise Andre who wishes to set up home with Phillip and to relinquish all his marriage ties.

4. Four years ago Paramjit and Ravi married in their local temple, the marriage having been arranged by their respective families. The couple had not met prior to the ceremony. Ravi was not keen on the prospect of marrying, but due to her age at the time (28) her parents were constantly telling her of the shame she was bringing on the family. The marriage has never been a happy one; Ravi has never felt able to have physical contact with Paramjit, and sexual intercourse has never taken place. Again, due to the family concerns she agreed to be artificially inseminated and has borne one child, Amandeep, now eight months old.

    Advice Ravi on her chances of bringing the marriage to an end.

See *Cases and Materials* (3.7) for the outline answers.

CHAPTER FOUR

THE LAW ON DIVORCE –
THE MATRIMONIAL CAUSES
ACT 1973

4.1 Objectives

By the end of this chapter you should be able to:

■ explain the current provisions and ground for divorce;

■ evaluate the effectiveness and any problems with the provisions;

■ advise hypothetical clients as to their rights.

4.2 Introduction

As you may be aware, the law on divorce is currently undergoing change, with a new Act, the Family Law Act 1996, coming into force in the near future: it is anticipated that the provisions affecting divorce will be in force sometime in 2000. Given that the new Act is not yet in force, it is necessary for you to know the current law, and the nature of the changes. In this chapter you will consider the existing law, and in **Chapter 5** you will move on to the Family Law Act 1996.

By having two different schemes, it is an ideal opportunity to theorise, since until there is any case law on the new system, it is not exactly clear what will happen and how.

4.3 A Historical Perspective

As you will recall from **Chapter 1**, the number of divorces currently granted annually are in excess of 153,000 (Judicial Statistics 1995, Lord Chancellor's Department). This statistic is seen as being detrimental to the stability of family life, and indeed detrimental to the family *per se*. The ability to seek a divorce, for the majority of couples who wish to do so, is a relatively recent development. Historically, divorce was available only to the few, those rich enough to obtain a Private Act of Parliament, and was often only an option for the male partner. In 1857 the concept of judicial divorces was introduced, being available where one party to the marriage was guilty of adultery, and the petitioning spouse was free from any guilt. A move away from only adultery as a basis for divorce came in 1937, with a widening of the categories, although all were a 'matrimonial offence' such as cruelty, desertion, insanity or adultery. The modern law stems from the Divorce Reform Act 1969, which has been re-enacted in the Matrimonial Causes Act 1973, and this Act was intended to move away from the idea of a matrimonial offence as a basis for bringing the marriage to an end.

Following the full introduction of the Divorce Reform Act 1969, the number of divorces increased although not immediately. However, as you can see from the table on matrimonial suits in *Cases and Materials* (1.1.1), there was over a threefold increase in decrees granted between 1968 and 1978. The Law Commission has pointed out that whilst it may be easy to blame the changes to the divorce laws for increasing marital breakdown, these factors are not necessarily linked.

Read the extracts from the Law Commission Discussion Paper (No. 170), *Facing the Future – A Discussion Paper on the Ground for Divorce* in *Cases and Materials* (4.1).

The increasing number of divorces does not predicate that marriage is unpopular, albeit (as you saw in **Chapter 1**) that marriage for the never married category of individuals is decreasing.

What form of living do you think the 'never married' are adopting?

As you will recall from **Chapter 1**, the idea of cohabitation has gained prevalence and this may be a reason for the drop in this group's marriage figures. The fact that individuals will divorce and then remarry also supports the concept of serial monogamy; a term to indicate the increasing numbers that will take one or more partners in succession.

4.4 The Basic Presumptions of the Modern Divorce

The forerunners of the 1969 Act were the reports entitled *Reform of the Grounds for Divorce: The Field of Choice* (Law Commission No. 6, 1966) and *Putting Asunder*, produced by a committee set up by the Archbishop of Canterbury and also published in 1966.

Read the extracts from the reports in *Cases and Materials* (4.2).

Write down the main purpose of a 'good divorce law'.

As you should have seen, the main planks upon which the new law was to be built was that the law should 'buttress, rather than undermine, the stability of marriage' and 'enable the empty shell of a marriage to be destroyed with the maximum fairness and the minimum bitterness, distress and humiliation'. To achieve these ends the legal basis upon which a divorce should be granted were to be changed.

Do you think any law can achieve these aims?

You will return to this sort of question when you consider the Family Law Act 1996, so briefly note down your response on a separate sheet of paper and keep it somewhere safe.

Return to the extracts from the Law Commission Paper No. 6, 1966, and consider the summary of the proposals. Which do you think is the most practical? Does this accord with the proposal you think Parliament adopted?

The Commission put forward several options for reform:

■ removing the references to matrimonial offences and replacing the ground with 'irretrievable breakdown' either with or without the need to carry out a thorough inquest into the breakdown;

■ allowing divorce by consent, noting problems where children are involved;

■ allowing divorce where there has been a minimum of six months' breakdown, but this was perceived to be an *additional* ground to the existing one.

Several safeguards were listed, and if you haven't picked up on them, go back to *Cases and Materials* (4.2) and look at them.

4.5 The Grounds for Divorce

The method adopted by Parliament in 1969, and subsequently re-enacted in the MCA 1973 was, in reality, a mixture of the two approaches in the preceding reports.

Read ss. 1 and 3 of the MCA 1973 in *Cases and Materials* (4.3). What is the ground for divorce, and what is/are the restrictions on the granting of an application for a divorce?

The first thing you should have noted is that there is only one ground on which a divorce can be granted, namely that the marriage has broken down irretrievably.

Does this ground indicate that any party is at fault?

In its attempt to move away from the idea of matrimonial offences, the ground for divorce was intended to be 'fault free' and, notionally, irretrievable breakdown does achieve this. However, what restrictions did you note? There are two major inroads into the idea of dissolving the 'empty shell' of a marriage: in s. 3(1) the prohibition on being able to seek a divorce until the marriage has existed for at least one year; and in s. 1(2) the need to prove irretrievable breakdown by reference to one or more of five facts.

4.5.1 THE FIVE FACTS

You should have noted down the five facts when you did the last Activity; if not, write them down in the space below and also write a definition for each one. Go back to your list once you have finished this next section.

4.5.1.1 The respondent has committed adultery and the petitioner finds it intolerable to live with the respondent

This fact, as you will see, involves the proving of two distinct elements:

■ the fact of adultery;

■ the fact that there is a level of intolerability.

The first is easily defined – there must be an act of sexual intercourse between the respondent and another person, not being the respondent's spouse. Intercourse does not have the same definition as in nullity proceedings, and all that is required is some degree of penetration.

SAQ 24

Is this definition adequate?

The idea of adultery comprising sexual intercourse, is a very common-sense approach, but the definition ignores the fact that sexual conduct less than intercourse may be just as distressing to the petitioner, and yet he/she would not be able to petition. Also, the definition applies only to heterosexual intercourse, and therefore there would be no means of redress through this fact for the petitioner if his/her partner had had a homosexual/lesbian relationship.

Turning to the second element, intolerability, this is a subjective issue in that the MCA 1973 states that 'the petitioner finds it intolerable'.

ACTIVITY 33

Read the extract from the Law Commission Paper 1988 in *Cases and Materials* (4.3.1.1). What does this tell you about the second element?

From this little bit of reading, you should have seen that intolerability is not linked to the act(s) of adultery. The fact that no link is needed between the two aspects of the adultery fact has led to criticism of the provision. You may wish to look at the case of *Cleary* v *Cleary* [1974] 1 All ER 498, a short extract from which is in *Cases and Materials* (4.3.1.1), on this issue.

4.5.1.2 The respondent has behaved in such a way that the petitioner cannot reasonably be expected to live with the respondent.

This is commonly called the unreasonable behaviour fact.

Why is this shorthand term inaccurate?

When looking at the words used it is, or should be, clear, that it is not the behaviour that is intended to be unreasonable, but the expectation of cohabitation. There are, again, two conditions to be satisfied:

■ that there has been some form of 'behaviour';

■ that it is unreasonable for the petitioner to continue living with the respondent.

With regard to the first condition, almost all types of behaviour will have been cited by a petitioner somewhere at some time. In general, behaviour such as violence and excessive drinking are the ones that spring to mind, but the continued occurrence of minor or trivial incidents will often be sufficient. In the case of *Livingstone-Stallard* v *Livingstone-Stallard* [1974] Fam 47 the court had to consider the parties' methods of washing their underwear under the behaviour element.

Turning to the unreasonableness of cohabitation, you are again looking at a type of subjective test – it is what is *reasonable for this petitioner* – but with aspects of objectivity. The test was formulated in *Livingstone-Stallard* (at page 54) thus:

> Would any right-thinking person come to the conclusion that this husband has behaved in such a way that this wife cannot reasonably be expected to live with him, taking into account the whole of the circumstances and the characters and personalities of the parties?

Can you see the two aspects of the test?

To see how the courts use this test, look at the extracts from *Ash* v *Ash* [1972] 2 WLR 347 in *Cases and Materials* (4.3.1.2).

4.5.1.3 The respondent has deserted the petitioner for a continuous period of two years

Desertion is an infrequently used fact. For desertion to be proved it requires the respondent's withdrawal from the state of marriage, without just cause. Hence there needs to be a mental withdrawal from the marriage which in most cases (although not necessarily in all) is accompanied by a physical withdrawal. If the respondent has a reason for not being with the petitioner, for example if he/she is imprisoned, or has to work abroad for a lengthy period, then desertion will not be proven.

The desertion fact overlaps greatly with s. 1(2)(d) of the MCA 1973, and it is generally the case that the separation fact will be used in preference.

4.5.1.4 The parties have lived apart for a continuous period of two years preceding the presentation of the petition and the respondent consents

This fact is similar to the desertion fact, except that consent is required.

There is still a requirement of withdrawal from the marriage – the separation – which must last for two years and it is possible for parties to be living in the same house, but to be separated from each other. This reflects the common economic reality that it is often hard for couples to move out physically from the matrimonial home, but it can cause problems. If the parties share any community of living, then they will not be deemed to have separated.

Read the extract from *Mouncer v Mouncer* [1972] 1 WLR 321 in *Cases and Materials* (4.3.1.3) and contrast it with the case of *Fuller v Fuller* [1973] 1 WLR 730 in *Cases and Materials* (4.3.1.3).

Did you see the difference in approaches? You may feel that the Mouncers should have succeeded in their petition since, as the court indicated, they had lived in the way they did purely for the interests of the children.

4.5.1.5 Separation for five years without consent

This fact is basically the same as the separation in **4.5.1.4**, with the exception of the time period and the absence of consent. The purpose of the longer period is to prevent unilateral divorce being too easy.

4.6 Relationship between the Ground for Divorce and the Facts

Without returning to the start of the chapter, write down the ground for divorce and how you think/remember the ground and facts interrelate.

You should have remembered the ground is 'irretrievable breakdown of the marriage' and that proving one of the five facts evidences that breakdown.

What would be the position if you could not prove a fact to the court's satisfaction, but still felt your marriage had broken down irretrievably?

Having thought about the question, turn to the extracts from *Mouncer v Mouncer* (*Cases and Materials* (4.3.1.3)) and *Buffery v Buffery* [1988] 2 FLR 365 (*Cases and Materials* (4.4)) and see if you agree with the courts' views.

It does seem somewhat unfair that a marriage may be accepted as having broken down, and yet cannot be ended due to the failure to prove the fact.

Does this accord with the principle of the MCA 1973 and the forerunning Divorce Reform Act 1969?

4.7   Which Facts are most Commonly Used?

Which of the facts do you think are most commonly used to base a petition upon?

Might there be a difference in relation to the gender of the petitioner, or the socio-economic group to which the couple belongs?

Again, you should have marshalled your thoughts on this question, and once you have, turn to the statistics extracted in *Cases and Materials* (4.5). Look also at the Government and the Law Commission Discussion Paper extracts at *Cases and Materials* (4.5).

How did you fare? Do the statistics surprise you? Does the evidence from the statistics accord with the principle of the MCA 1973 and the Divorce Reform Act 1969?

4.8 Bars to Divorce and Stopping the Clock

Can you remember the first principle of a good divorce law? If not, go back to the beginning of the chapter and refresh your memory.

The manner in which the stability of marriage is promoted is in s. 2, MCA 1973 which you should now read: see *Cases and Materials* (4.6).

How does the section support marriages?

The key to supporting marriages is to be found in the ability to attempt reconciliation, and to stop the divorce fact clock running. The way the section works differs for each fact, so for example with adultery, a petition must be lodged within six months of the petitioner's knowledge that the respondent has committed adultery. This clearly goes to the root of the intolerability criterion, for if cohabitation continues, it cannot be intolerable. For behaviour, the length of continued cohabitation after the behaviour complained of would affect the assessment of the reasonableness of continued cohabitation. For the other three facts, the reconciliation provisions will stop the clock for a maximum of six months, albeit that the time spent attempting reconciliation will not be taken into account in computing the length of desertion or separation.

Read ss. 5 and 10, MCA 1973 in *Cases and Materials* (4.6).

How does this affect the potential petitioner and respondent?

The conditions in these sections relate only to petitions under the separation facts. In effect, only s. 5 can prevent the divorce going ahead; s. 10 is in reality a delaying tactic. For s. 5 to operate, it must be shown that there will be a resulting 'grave financial or other hardship' if the divorce is granted. The hardship must relate to the divorce. Where financial matters are concerned, often an arrangement can be made; see for example *Le Marchant* v *Le Marchant* [1977] 1 WLR 559 in *Cases and Materials* (4.6).

Where 'other hardship' is concerned cases often reflect religious factors, but the courts' attitude is such that this will be insufficient to meet s. 5; see for example *Rukat* v *Rukat* [1975] 2 WLR 201 which is in *Cases and Materials* (4.6).

4.9   The Divorce Process

Very few divorce petitions are defended (approximately 600 defences are laid) but almost all are disposed of before trial. A process called the special procedure, which is in effect purely a documentary system, deals with the majority of cases. The petitioner files his/her petition, to which the respondent files an answer; this normally consents to the allegations made by the petitioner. The documentation will then be put before a district judge who 'checks' that everything is in order. This is partly to satisfy the courts that the ground and fact relied upon have been established as is required by s. 1(3), MCA 1973.

Do you think a thorough investigation into the allegations will be made?

In checking the paperwork, it is unlikely that anything other than procedural errors will be spotted, and no real investigation will take place. This reliance on the special procedure, and the failure of the court to meet its obligation in investigating the truth of the statement of irretrievable breakdown has caused concern. Indeed it is one of the reasons for the forthcoming changes to divorce law.

Read the comments of the Law Commission in Discussion Paper No. 170 in *Cases and Materials* (4.7).

4.10   Other Problems

You will be introduced to the Law Commission's view on the defects with the MCA 1973 scheme for divorce in **Chapter 5**. However, in addition to the problems with the special procedure, you should have noted the failure of the legal provisions to meet the objectives of a good divorce law. If the intention had been to remove the concept of fault and blame, and to dissolve marriages with the minimum of distress and bitterness, why were three of the old matrimonial offences retained? Also, why must there be a link? If a marriage has broken down irretrievably it is right to bring it to an end regardless of how the breakdown occurred. The attempts to achieve reconciliation are weak, with no emphasis placed upon them, and with no obligation on any one involved in the process to raise the issue. You may have identified more problematic issues in the MCA 1973 provisions: see if they are included in **Chapter 5**.

4.11   Summary

In this chapter you have been introduced to the current scheme for divorce which is considered to be problematic – hence the forthcoming changes in the Family Law Act 1996. You should now be able to advise potential and hypothetical clients on their rights to divorce, but should also be able to discuss the legal provisions on a more academic and theoretical basis. To make sure that you can do, try the following End of Chapter Assessment Questions.

Finally, go back to your court diagram (**1.6**), and highlight the courts with jurisdiction for divorce. These are the county court, if a designated divorce court, and the High Court Family Division.

4.12   End of Chapter Assessment Questions

1. Joyce and Ralph married 10 years ago and approached their relationship on an 'open marriage' basis. Consequently both partners have had casual relationships outside the marriage. Last year Ralph began to have a change of heart, and decided that he would not participate in any such casual relationships. Joyce did not concur with this decision and has continued to act in the same way, much to Ralph's disgust. Recently he learnt that for the last seven months Joyce has been having an affair with Anne-Marie.

 Advise him on his rights to divorce. Is there any way that Joyce could prevent it?

2. Peggy and Tony married 15 months ago and cohabited for two months before Tony left the matrimonial home. He has recently contacted Peggy and asked to give the marriage a second chance. Advise Peggy how this would affect her potential rights to seek a divorce.

3. Evaluate the effectiveness of the divorce provisions in the Matrimonial Causes Act 1973.

See *Cases and Materials* (4.9) for outline answers.

CHAPTER FIVE

THE FAMILY LAW ACT 1996 AND DIVORCE

5.1 Objectives

By the end of this chapter you should be able to:

■ outline the changes to the legislative provisions for divorce;

■ apply the law to hypothetical scenarios;

■ explain possible problems inherent in the new scheme;

■ evaluate the effectiveness of the changes;

■ compare and contrast the new legislation with the previous provisions under the MCA 1973.

5.2 Introduction

You have just finished considering the existing legislation in relation to divorce. Now you will be looking at the future provisions, which are anticipated to come into force in 2000 after a series of pilot schemes have been concluded. In this chapter you will be introduced to the key changes, possible interpretations of the new provisions and some of the potential defects of the new scheme.

5.3 Why the Change?

Using your work from Chapter 4, list (on a separate sheet of paper) the defects to be found in the existing MCA 1973 divorce provisions.

Now look at the extracts from *Family Law: The Ground for Divorce* (Law Com No. 192), paragraphs 2.7 to 2.20 in *Cases and Materials* (5.1) and add to your notes.

Using the headings from the report you should have a list, albeit somewhat expanded, like this:

■   the law is confusing and misleading;

■   it is discriminatory and unjust;

■   it distorts the parties' bargaining powers;

■   it provokes unnecessary hostility and bitterness;

■   it does nothing to save the marriage;

■   it can make things worse for the children.

From this long list of criticisms the Commission concluded that it 'would amount to a formidable case for reform'. This is at odds with an earlier comment in the report in para. 2.4 where it was stated that 67 per cent of the people questioned in a public survey 'found divorce under the present law "acceptable"'. Surely this must raise the question, 'Why the change?'. Perhaps the prevalence and general acceptance of divorce is of concern; you may recall the phrase 'family values' that was used in political rhetoric in the 1990s. Also, there were concerns expressed as to the cost to the state through legal aid payments for divorcing couples and the cost through the welfare benefits system. Regardless of the reasons, change is imminent and the reforms must be considered.

5.3.1   OPTIONS FOR REFORM AND BASIC PRINCIPLES

What do you think the various options for reform would be? If you were a Law Commissioner, what would you suggest?

Ultimately there were perceived to be three possible options for reform:

■   retention of a 'mixed' system along the present lines, perhaps with some modification;

■   divorce after a fixed minimum period of separation;

■   divorce after a fixed minimum period for reflection and consideration of the arrangements, referred to as 'divorce by a process over time'.

Of these three, the last was the preferred option. How did that compare with your ideas?

The aims of the law were also set out in the Report and, as you will see below, have been incorporated to a degree in the legislation.

Read the aims of the law as established by the Commission in paragraphs 3.1 to 3.4 in *Cases and Materials* (5.1.1).

Do they look familiar? Do you agree with the Commission's views as to how they differ?

Unlike the MCA 1973 (and the Divorce Reform Act 1969) which had similar principles to underpin the legislation, but with nothing in the Acts themselves, the Family Law Act (FLA) 1996 has incorporated some of the principles in the Act itself.

Read s. 1 of the FLA 1996 and summarise its requirements. It can be found in *Cases and Materials* (5.1.1).

You can see how the general aims have been introduced. The section also illustrates the other consideration which appears to have guided the reforms, namely cost reductions.

Who do you think will be affected by these principles and how will they work?

The focus of the section is on the court and any person exercising functions under or as a consequence of the Act. Whilst this will clearly affect the court and the judiciary, it will also affect lawyers and other professionals involved in matrimonial disputes. As you will see shortly, the FLA 1996 will increase the role of mediators in the divorce process, and they too will be obliged to consider the principles of s. 1. The matters to be borne in mind will also potentially introduce difficulties and conflicts. To what extent will a solicitor be required to encourage the supporting of a client's marriage and give referrals to counselling when consulted on divorce? Will it require all professionals to become ex officio members of Relate? It is debatable to what extent marriages can be saved: did the aim really work in the preceding legislation and to what degree will including it specifically in the Act make a difference? In dealing with how broken down marriages can be ended, does the Act take too rosy a view, in highlighting the fact that issues should be dealt with in a manner that will promote as good a continuing relationship as possible? Do couples want to continue a relationship? This summary ought to have given you an idea of the uncertainty, and the debate that exists in relation to s. 1, FLA 1996. Think about the issues yourself, and try to formulate some ideas of your own.

5.4   The Divorce Process

The numbering of the sections in the FLA 1996 is somewhat idiosyncratic. Therefore you will not be studying the sections in a logical progression by number, but in a progression stage by stage through the process.

5.4.1   THE ORDERS AVAILABLE

Read s. 2 of the FLA 1996 in *Cases and Materials* (5.2.1).

What orders are available to a couple wishing to end their legal relationship? Are these any different from the MCA 1973?

As you will note, there is little change in the actual result of the legal process. A couple may obtain a divorce to end the marriage, or a separation order to separate legally, i.e. a judicial separation. What has changed is the terminology, orders rather than decrees. The intention is to make the Act more 'user friendly'.

5.4.2 WHEN WILL THE ORDERS BE GRANTED?

Look at s. 3 of the FLA 1996 in *Cases and Materials* (5.2.2).

Write down the prerequisites that must exist before an order can be made.

There are four main requirements:

- the marriage has broken down irretrievably;

- the requirements of s. 8 are complied with;

- the requirements of s. 9 are complied with; and

- the application has not been withdrawn.

In addition, you should have noted down the effect of s. 3(2), i.e. that a divorce can be prevented under s. 10. You will look at s. 10 in due course, but for now, just be aware that it operates in a similar way to s. 5, MCA 1973.

5.4.3 IRRETRIEVABLE BREAKDOWN

This remains the sole ground for divorce or a separation order. The requirement to link irretrievable breakdown to a 'fact' has, however, now gone. The primary means to prove irretrievable breakdown is that a substantial period of time has elapsed. This reflects the reasoning of the Law Commission in paragraphs 3.26, 3.27 and 3.35, extracted in *Cases and Materials* (5.2.3).

Do you agree that this is the only means to prove irretrievable breakdown?

When you study s. 6 of the FLA 1996, you may wish to revise your opinion, since you will see that the Law Commission's ideas have not been followed exactly.

5.4.4   THE INFORMATION SESSION

Read s. 8 of the FLA 1996 in *Cases and Materials* (5.2.4).

What does this require?

The actual consequences and requirements of s. 8 are not that clear, unless taken as a whole with the rest of Part II of the Act. The statement referred to is a statement of marital breakdown (s. 6), and is the second stage in the process. The first stage, the information meeting, must take place at least three months before the statement is filed but there is no minimum duration of marriage specified before this meeting can take place. The purpose of the meeting is to give the individual contemplating divorce an opportunity to obtain information on the process, to give details of marriage guidance/counsellor services, to encourage attendance at such services and to enable couples to reconsider the decision to separate.

Information sessions do not have to be attended by both parties to the marriage, only one need do so.

Is it consistent with the idea of saving the marriage for only one of the couple to attend?

If only one party attends an information meeting, there is no obligation to tell the other party. Hence the situation may arise where one party is convinced they wish to divorce, and so does not take up counselling services, without even giving the other the opportunity to do so.

The section sets out the basic information that needs to be imparted, and covers issues such as mediation, counselling, children and their welfare, financial matters, legal aid and legal services.

The format of the session, and the identity of the individuals who will hold the information sessions, is not yet known. Pilot studies are being held to evaluate the most appropriate schemes. You will find details of the pilot schemes in *Cases and Materials* (5.2.4) extracted from the Law Society's *Gazette*. Note the reference to the possibility of solicitors acting as information givers.

Does this suggestion, i.e. solicitors acting as information givers accord with s. 8(7)(b)?

It is interesting to note that this requirement to attend information sessions was not mooted by the Law Commission in their Report (Report No. 192, *The Ground for Divorce*). The Law Commission proposed a comprehensive information pack to be given out by the court when the statement was filed.

5.4.5 THE STATEMENT OF MARITAL BREAKDOWN

Read ss. 5(1), 6 and 7(6), FLA 1996 in *Cases and Materials* (5.2.5) and the Law Commission's comments on this issue. Write down a list of the key elements.

You should also look back to 5.4.3 above.

What have you noticed with regard to the ground for divorce? Whilst the intention was for irretrievable breakdown to be the sole ground for divorce, you can now see that, in proving this, an individual must have filed a correct statement – there are therefore still conditions attached.

The main requirements of s. 6 for the statement are:

■ it cannot be filed unless the marriage has existed for at least one year;

■ it can be made by one or both of the parties to the marriage;

■ it must state that the parties are aware of the period of reflection and consideration;

■ it must state the parties wish to make arrangements for the future.

The statement will not include details of why the marriage is perceived to have broken down; this is deemed to be contrary to the policy of reconciliation and supporting the marriage even at a stage where one or both parties feel it is at an end. In debate in the Lords, the Lord Chancellor stated:

> [the statement] should not contain allegations, and so on, against the other party to the marriage, because that is not likely to be conducive to healing the relationship,

and

> One of the most important aspects of this Bill . . . is the opportunity, even at the late stage when someone is contemplating divorce, of a period . . . of consideration and reflection. You cannot have such a genuine period if the parties are already committed to a situation in which it is said, 'this marriage has already irretrievably broken down'. (Hansard, 11 January 1996, vol. 568, No. 24, Col 310 and 348.)

Do you agree with the Lord Chancellor's views?

If the statement has been made by one party only, it must be served on the other party. This may be the first time that the latter party has become aware of the situation, although it is to be hoped that some preliminary discussion will have taken place. The difficulty with this notion is that it takes a favourable view of human nature and presumes that couples will have recognised the marriage has problems. In any event, the party making the statement may well have already decided that the marriage is at an end, which is why the filing of the statement has taken place.

5.4.6 THE PERIOD OF REFLECTION AND CONSIDERATION

Having filed a statement, the parties will then enter their period of reflection and consideration, to continue to attempt to reconcile and to make arrangements for the future.

Read the rest of s. 7 of the FLA 1996 in *Cases and Materials* (5.2.2). What are the principal objectives within this period, and how long will it be?

As you can see, s. 7(1) sets out the main objectives of reconciliation, and making arrangements. The parties will have a period of nine months in which to do this (s. 7(3)) and this period will commence 14 days after the statement was filed. The position is slightly different if children are involved, as here the period will be extended by a further six months (s. 7(11), (13)).

Do you think these main objectives are compatible and achievable in the time period?

Read the opinion of the Law Commission, in *Cases and Materials* (5.2.6), as to the purpose of the period of reflection. Has the law implemented the Commission's ideas?

The extension of the period where children are concerned seems somewhat illogical and is certainly contrary to the Commission's initial intentions. The reasoning is unclear; the amendment was made in parliamentary debate, and was carried by a handful of votes. Presumably it was done to enable parties to reflect upon the consequences for the children, and also to give them more time to make arrangements. However, it was recognised that 'allowing proceedings to drag on, with all the inevitable uncertainty, can be very harmful to children as well as potentially to the parties' (Gary Streeter, Official Report (HC), 17 June, 1996, col 603).

In any event, the period for reflection can be extended, where the parties have served notice that a reconciliation is being attempted. This works in a similar way to the reconciliation provisions in the MCA 1973.

If an application for divorce has not been made within a year of the end of the period for reflection and consideration, then the parties must start again, as they must if the interruption for reconciliation exceeds 18 months (see ss. 5 and 7).

It is also difficult to predict how effective the period will be in addressing reconciliation versus arrangements. How long will couples be expected to take to reconcile before realising that it is not possible? Will couples try to reconcile on Monday to Wednesday, make arrangements Thursday to Saturday and have a day of rest from negotiations on Sunday? Also, is it fair to make couples wait if they have made their arrangements in less than a month?

5.4.6.1 Financial arrangements

During the s. 7 period, couples must make their future arrangements as explained above. These relate primarily to financial matters, and have to be sorted out before an order can be made. The nature of arrangements will be returned to again in subsequent chapters, but you need to know the basics now.

Read s. 9, FLA 1996 in *Cases and Materials* (5.2.6.1).

What does this require?

Under the provisions of this section, before an order can be put into effect, the parties must be able to provide the court with:

■ a court order, either by consent or otherwise;

■ a negotiated agreement detailing financial arrangements;

■ a declaration by both parties stating they have made their arrangements;

■ a declaration by one party, and not objected to by the other, that they have no assets and that no arrangements need to be made.

Under the terms of sch. 1 to the FLA 1996, it is not necessary for the order or agreement to have been put into effect; what is essential is that the arrangements are made (sch. 1, para. 5).

There will be further procedural requirements put into place to deal with s. 9, since the court will need certain information when dealing with arrangements under the section. So, for example, where the arrangements are as a result of negotiation, the negotiation must have taken place through mediation, or through a third party. You will find this and other requirements/conditions in sch. 1 to the Act, extracts of which are in *Cases and Materials* (5.2.6.1).

Even the first listed item presents difficulties since, as you will learn later, no court may make a financial order before a divorce is granted, other than an interim order. This raises the question of whether this will be adequate for the court's purposes – to what extent will an interim order be continued after divorce? Naturally, exceptions exist to this restriction, and these are in sch. 1 (paras 1 to 4).

Look at sch. 1 in *Cases and Materials* (5.2.6.1) and note down the exemptions.

Do you think they are workable?

5.4.6.2 Arrangements for children

In ensuring that future arrangements have been made, the court must have regard to s. 11, FLA 1996.

Read s. 11 in *Cases and Materials* (5.2.6.2).

Note down the issues to which the court must have regard, and remember to cross-reference this with your notes to Chapter 11 on private law relating to children.

5.4.7 THE APPLICATION

Write down the requirements of s. 3 before the court can grant an order.

When you have done this, go back to s. 3 in *Cases and Materials* (5.2.2), and check to see how well you remembered the section.

Once the parties have complied with the requirements in s. 3(1), then the court has to make the order requested.

Does the court have the same powers as it had under the MCA 1973 to accept that a petitioner has proved irretrievable breakdown, but still not grant a divorce?

The degree to which the court must make the order is conditional on the correct procedures being followed and correct documentation being provided over the correct time scale. Thus it would still be possible for the court to refuse to make the order even though the marriage was over.

5.4.8 PREVENTING THE ORDER

As you may recall, a divorce order can be prevented by the application of the other spouse under the provisions of s. 10.

Read s. 10 in *Cases and Materials* (5.2.7) together with the subsequent extract from the Law Commission. Does this differ from the MCA 1973 at all?

The provisions were included as you have read to protect the minority of applicants, but the justification in particular relating to pensions does not really play any part. The FLA 1996 includes potential changes to the field of pensions, and in any event pensions can be earmarked on divorce. You will look at pensions and how they are accounted for in ancillary matters later.

5.5   Mediation

The introduction of mediation is central to the conceptual changes to be brought about by the FLA 1996, and the promotion of party-led resolution of issues. The information session will need to impart details of mediation to the potential applicant, and the courts themselves may adjourn proceedings to permit mediation (or reconciliation) to occur (s. 14).

The process of mediation is to enable the parties to resolve disputes and make arrangements themselves, with a third party acting to facilitate communication. The mediator should not suggest or recommend any form of resolution to the problem.

5.5.1   WHO WILL NEED TO USE MEDIATION?

In theory, everyone involved in family matters should be directed to mediation to deal with disputes. However, the FLA 1996, whilst it permits the court to adjourn for mediation, focuses on those individuals who will be assisted by the legal aid fund for the divorce process. Sections 26 to 29, FLA 1996 operate as amending sections to the Legal Aid Act 1988.

Read the extracts from ss. 26 to 29 in *Cases and Materials* (5.3.1), and write down what you think they mean, and the effect they will have.

There are a number of things you should have picked up from these extracts. Mediation services will be contracted out by the Legal Aid Board (LAB), and any group/service provider will have to comply with the terms of the LAB's own code of practice, which at the time of writing is in draft format only. The LAB will pay for mediation, where a client is financially eligible, and eligibility is assessed in accordance with the financial criteria for civil legal aid. Merit, the other half of the civil legal aid test, is not applied in the same way. The mediator will decide the suitability of mediation to the individual case, if you hadn't noticed this, re-read the substituted s. 13B(3) of the Legal Aid Act 1988.

Do you think this is a valid way of assessing the 'merits' of a case for mediation?

The code of practice will highlight those cases where mediation is deemed to be inappropriate, for example due to the risk of violence. It is also crucial for the parties to enter the process willingly if mediation is to work. However, you should have highlighted the importance of the substituted s. 15(3F). This provision will restrict the availability of legal aid for legal advisers. Under the new provision if a client is seeking state funding, they must first have their case assessed for suitability for mediation (s. 15(3F)(a)). If mediation is deemed suitable, the client should be advised on whether to apply for mediation (s. 15(3F)(b)). The wording of s. 15(3F)(b) does not therefore preclude a client attending a meeting for assessment, being found suitable for mediation, but deciding not to pursue that course and continuing to seek legal aid for legal representation. However, given that the Legal Aid Board will consider the reasonableness of the individual's decision not to seek mediation in the face of the mediator's view that the case is suitable, it seems unlikely that many clients will be able to avoid mediation. This has given rise to concerns, in that through the working of the legal aid scheme, there will be a two-tier system: one for those who can pay privately and need not go to mediation, or even attend a session (subject to the court directing them to consider it), and those who are reliant on state funding, who will have to go if the mediator has assessed the case as suitable. It is also worrying that the mediator, the person whose income depends on the provision of mediation services, is the person who assesses suitability. Despite the presence of the code, it must surely be questioned whether this amounts to a potential conflict of interest.

This area is quite complex. Take a break, and then come back to this issue. Try to recall what the changes, and some of the criticisms, are. When you have done this, re-read the sections and text, and make sure you really do understand it.

5.5.2   THE ROLE OF LAWYERS

As you will have seen from the above text, the role for lawyers in family disputes may in future be reduced. If legally aided clients are to be channelled into mediation as a first option, where will this leave solicitors? Arguably, legal advice will still be required.

Why can this be argued?

The function of mediation, to try to achieve a voluntary arrangement, depends on the willingness of the parties to co-operate. Even if this willingness is present, total agreement is not always going to arise, or the talks may break down.

Read the extract from Nigel Shepherd's article in *Family Law* (February 1996) in *Cases and Materials* (5.3.2). What chance of success does he hold out for mediation?

As you have just seen, mediation, even where the parties want to mediate, does not guarantee it will work. In the event of failure, parties may well turn to the traditional source of advice and assistance, the lawyer. If legal aid has been granted for the mediation, which doesn't succeed, do you think the Legal Aid Board will give assistance for legal advice, or might it be suggested that the parties have not tried hard enough?

Even if agreement is reached lawyers will still be needed. Whilst many legal practitioners are seeking to become qualified mediators, it is still the case that most mediators have no legal qualifications at all. If an agreement is made through the parties' mediation sessions, this can be classed as an agreement for s. 9, FLA 1996 purposes. As you will learn when you look at financial arrangements later, the courts are required to take into account certain factors when dealing with ancillary arrangements. The question is, to what extent will mediators make these factors known to the parties? Will parties find an agreement being thrown out when the application is made to divorce? Will parties be able to re-open a negotiated agreement if they later find that they could have got more? To prevent these potentially drastic situations arising, it can be argued that it is appropriate for legal advice to be sought alongside the mediation.

Why might this not be possible?

You should be able to answer this quite easily. It might not be possible to access legal advice purely due to the inability to pay, especially if the clients are making a contribution to costs for mediation purposes. Can you also see how this reference to mediation (and the lack of legal advice) may create the two-tier service for divorcing individuals?

Perhaps the justification is purely cost driven. It was suggested in *The Guardian*, 1 March 1994, that the 'typical mediated divorce cost £557 – a third of the average divorce legal aid bill'. If this is the case, i.e. that mediation will remain cheaper, what better way to reduce the amount of legal aid spent? The backlash may be an increase in litigation after divorce, relating to failure to meet the legal considerations in the MCA 1973 on financial issues.

Now read the extracts from the article by Professor Cretney, 'Lawyers under the Family Law Act' [1997] Fam Law 405 in *Cases and Materials* (5.3.2).

Do you agree with his views?

5.6   Summary

You have now finished a very difficult chapter, since you are dealing with areas of law that are untested, and unclear in modes of operation. This will give you scope to theorise and suggest your own opinions as there is no case law to contradict you. However, you must always justify your views. You should now be able to discuss the major changes in the law, the lack of fault in divorce, the increased time for the process to be completed, and the increased importance for mediation, together with some of the criticisms that can be levelled at the changes. To consolidate this learning, try the End of Chapter Assessment Question.

5.7 End of Chapter Assessment Question

This is a longer question, and one that necessitates a good understanding of the divorce laws.

'Evaluate the effect of the Family Law Act 1996 on divorce.'

See *Cases and Materials* (5.5) for an outline answer.

CHAPTER SIX

PROPERTY AND FINANCE ON DIVORCE

6.1 Objectives

By the end of this chapter you should be able to:

■ explain the nature of the orders that can be made on divorce, both for property and finance;

■ list the criteria and factors that the court will have to consider when making orders;

■ provide an analysis of those criteria;

■ apply the law to hypothetical problems;

■ highlight and discuss any defects or criticisms of the legal rules.

6.2 Introduction

The granting of a divorce does not end the legal relationship between a spouse and their partner. The existence of children, and jointly held assets will ensure that further contact or legal action is needed. As you have learnt in the last chapter, the scope and timing of financial claims will change under the FLA 1996. The fundamental principles will remain. In this chapter you will be considering the nature of the orders that can be made, and the principles upon which any orders will be made. Rather than go through the principles separately in relation to the existing law and the new law, you will be looking at the law in parallel. Remember, in this chapter you are learning the rules with regard to spouses and not children, the legal provisions for children will be discussed in **Chapter 9**.

It is important to approach this chapter in stages. Do not try to study it all at once, as it is quite long, and also contains some complex concepts. It is crucial that you understand a topic before you move on to the next.

6.3 The Concept of Maintenance

Before you start to study the nature of the orders that can be made for financial and property assets when a couple divorce, it is perhaps wise to think about why these orders are needed. The law operates on the basis that there is a mutual obligation on spouses, and ex-spouses, to maintain one another. The extension of the obligation after divorce may strike you as strange: if the obligations arise from the entering into of a marriage contract, surely they should end when that contract is ended?

Can you think of any reasons why the obligations should be extended?

If you consider the marriage contract purely from a contractual position then, arguably, the maintenance that is sought equals the damages that could be claimed when a contract is brought to an end early. However, the notion of maintenance also illustrates the unequal status of women in society, especially those women with childcare responsibilities. Women who marry, and have children, will often (although not always) face a loss of marketability in employment terms, a career may have been broken, or entirely given up on marriage. Despite the Equal Pay Act 1970, women's salaries are still consistently lower than men's and this will inevitably place them at a disadvantage after divorce. If a couple do have children, the law places an obligation upon the parents to care, or to pay for care for them. The societal constraints within the family see the mother as the primary carer and the man as the breadwinner and the mother will often retain this primary carer role after any separation. If unable to work as well, she will need some form of support. Politically it is not acceptable for that 'provider' to be the state.

6.3.1 AMENDMENTS TO THE MCA 1973

The concept of permanent maintenance, whilst being in accordance with the above hypothesis, is equally one which the law is loath to accept, unless necessary. The MCA 1973 was amended in 1984 to introduce the 'clean break' provisions, which you will look at later. These provisions exist to cause the court to reflect upon the possibility of ex-spouses gaining independence financially from one another after the divorce, in other words trying to move away from the idea of a long term right to be maintained. The courts do not impose clean breaks in all cases, the reality of the situation is always considered.

6.3.2 THE ORDERS AVAILABLE

The orders that can be sought under the MCA 1973 fall into financial and property orders. The FLA 1996 will make some minor amendments to the orders, but the primary changes will be to the timing of the orders. You will be introduced to the changes later in the chapter.

A mixture of financial and property orders are the norm.

6.4   Financial Orders: s. 23

Read s. 23, MCA 1973 in *Cases and Materials* (6.1). What orders can be made under this section?

You should have noted down that there are six types of orders under this section, albeit that some overlap, and also that some are in relation to children. The orders fall into three categories:

■ periodical payments;

■ secured periodical payments;

■ lump sum orders.

6.4.1   PERIODICAL PAYMENTS

Periodical payments are the most common form of maintenance that is awarded. This form of maintenance covers the situation of regular payments of specified amounts from one spouse to the other. These payments may be substantial, or only a nominal figure (such as 5 pence per annum). An order which is nothing more than nominal will enable the recipient to return to court for an increase in the amount in the event that their situation changes. If the payments are just 'periodical', then if the payer fails to comply with the terms of the order the payee must seek to enforce the order through court action. If the order is secured, as in the second category, in the event of non-payment, the payee has a means to secure payment. This is because a secured periodical payments order will require the payer to set aside a capital fund, which may comprise shares or other forms of interest-bearing capital, but could even be property such as a home, to act as a 'pot' into which the payee can dip if the payments are not made as ordered.

How long do you think a periodical payments order will last?

There are a variety of potential cut-off points for periodical payments. The most drastic is where either party dies. If the order has been secured, whilst the order may not extend beyond the death of the payee (the recipient) it may in fact extend beyond the death of the payer. This does in fact make sense since the 'pot' will still exist, and is likely to be in the hands of trustees.

The order will also end on the remarriage of the payee, and this is a factor to be borne in mind when advising clients. The same is not true of cohabitation and it has been suggested that it will result in a 'disincentive to marriage' (Professor Cretney, *Principles of Family Law*, 6th edn, page 413). In addition, there may be a detriment to the payee and any children from the first marriage if a second marriage results in an overall lower standard of living. In this case, the only option would be to endeavour to increase maintenance for the children. If cohabitation is favoured as a means to avoid the provision, the payer may seek to vary the order in any event, to reflect the changed situation. Regardless of marriage or cohabitation, it could be argued that this merely continues to highlight the attitudes of society to the roles and dependencies of men and women.

You may also have mentioned clean breaks in the duration of the order. A clean break may not have to be effective immediately, and can be deferred. In this situation it will end at the time specified in the order itself.

All of these rules will be found in s. 28, MCA 1973 which you will find in *Cases and Materials* (**6.1.1**).

6.4.2 LUMP SUM ORDERS

An applicant can only seek one lump sum order.

Given the above statement, why does the MCA 1973 refer to sums in s. 23?

Lump sums can be useful where a couple has substantial financial assets, and these sorts of payments promote the idea of a clean break. A court may order the payment of a lump sum, and dismiss periodical payments if the lump sum could generate sufficient income on a regular basis. The ordering of a lump sum does not have to be to the exclusion of periodical payments however; it may be appropriate in a particular case to order both.

When lump sum orders are made, the court has the power to direct that payments be made in instalments, hence the reference to 'orders' in the section. This might be suitable where the payer is likely to have difficulty raising sufficient capital immediately. An instalment order may also be useful to take into account future realisation of assets, such as a pension, which may account for a large sum. If instalments are ordered, then there is a power to ensure the payments are secured.

An advantage for the client is that the lump sum, once made, is virtually irrevocable, and the remarriage of a party will not affect the payment made.

6.4.3 MAINTENANCE PENDING SUIT

Under s. 22, MCA 1973 (which is subject to amendment by the FLA 1996), an order for maintenance can be sought prior to the divorce being made. This is useful if the couple has separated, and one individual is not in employment, or if so, has a lower income than is needed. The court can only make periodical payments under this section, highlighting that the order is intended to be a temporary one, pending final resolution during the divorce process. Section 22 (in its unamended format) is in *Cases and Materials* (6.1.2). Whilst the order will not last beyond the granting of the divorce, the amount of the maintenance may be influential in any final settlement.

6.5 Property Orders: s. 24

Read ss. 24 and 24A of the MCA 1973 in *Cases and Materials* (6.2).

What orders can be made under these sections?

Again, as with s. 23 your list should have several orders on it. Once more, ignore the provisions relating to children. You should have noted the following orders:

■ property transfers;

■ property settlement;

■ sale of property;

■ variation, extinguishment or reduction of interest in an ante- or post-nuptial settlement.

6.5.1 TRANSFERS AND SETTLEMENT OF PROPERTY

In the majority of marriages, the home will be the largest asset that is possessed by the couple. On divorce, the court, as you have seen under s. 24, has considerable powers to reorder the ownership of family property or even to order its sale. The order made will depend on the individual circumstances. It is obvious that one household is unlikely to become two in an easy way, and the occupation of the family home is that which will inevitably result in loss to one party. The need to house children will weigh heavily on the court's mind when deciding on the appropriate order.

6.5.1.1 Types of property adjustment orders

Write down the types of adjustment to property ownership that the court may wish to carry out. Also list any advantages or disadvantages that you perceive to be relevant.

This activity will have been easier if you have studied land law. If not, it is to be hoped that your common sense will have been useful. Taking the types of arrangements in no particular order:

(a) The court might order an immediate sale of the property concerned. This can be coupled with an order that the proceeds of sale be divided between the parties. Whilst this has the advantage of promoting a clean break for the couple, it can only be used in limited situations. To start, you should have noticed from s. 24A, it can only arise as part of other orders – the court must be making a secured periodical payment order, or a lump sum order, or a property adjustment order. Both parties need to be in a position to secure alternative housing; this is especially so if there are children involved, and so invariably there will need to be sufficient equity, or other capital available.

(b) The court may transfer ownership of property completely to one party. To reflect the potential loss of a large asset, there may be compensation in the form of reduced maintenance or a lump sum payment back or a charge being placed on the property.

To see how these options work, read the cases in *Cases and Materials* (6.2.1.1) of *Hanlon* v *Hanlon* [1978] 1 WLR 592, *Mortimer* v *Mortimer-Griffin* [1986] 2 FLR 315 and *Knibb* v *Knibb* [1987] 2 FLR 396.

There are advantages to these orders, in that they will achieve certainty, and will enable a clean break to be achieved in so far as housing is concerned. However, there are difficulties:

■ the introduction of the Child Support Acts in 1990 and 1995 has meant that it is impossible to offset maintenance for children against a capital transfer;

■ the party gaining the property may not be in a position to pay back a lump sum, or may be unable to get a loan or mortgage to do so;

■ the party in receipt of the charge back will have to wait,· potentially, some considerable time before being able to benefit from the property.

(c) The court may settle the property on one party until a specified event occurs and establish the division of proceeds when this event happens. This often used to be set at the date that any children of the family reach 18 years or leave full-time education. Orders of this type are called Mesher orders. Whilst it is common for a Mesher order to reflect the children's situation, the specified event may be the wife's subsequent cohabitation or marriage, or death if neither of the former occurs. As you can see, this is quite a flexible order, but have you thought of any disadvantages?

You should already have listed some disadvantages if you identified item (c) as a possible option. Can you think of any more?

A major criticism of the Mesher order, and one of the reasons why it has lost favour with the courts, is the fact that it merely delays the time when the parties will have to consider rehousing themselves. If the order is to last until the children reach 18, and then the property is to be sold, the wife may find herself, literally, without a roof over her head, if the equity is insufficient to rehouse her. In addition, by virtue of the time delay, she may be unable to obtain work or a mortgage. The order also ignores the fact that many children do not leave home when they reach 18 and the home may still be needed for the wife and children. If the event specified is cohabitation or re-marriage, it may be the case that the new partner is not financially able to support the wife, and possible family. Again, this would seem unfair for a wife to have to support the children still, but with the loss of the property. Finally, you should have noted that the Mesher order does not accord with the principle of the clean break. Some of these disadvantages were raised in *Hanlon* v *Hanlon*. The effects of the order as perceived by Ormrod J are in *Cases and Materials* (6.2.1.1).

The impact of the Child Support Acts (CSA) 1991 and 1995 has again affected the potential use of this order. It has been suggested that the Mesher order may come back into favour since it can run alongside the continuing obligation to children under the CSA 1991 and 1995. Given the inability to utilise clean breaks to offset child maintenance, the Mesher order may be preferred.

6.6 How Will the Court Reach its Decision?

The court will need to have regard to the criteria set out in the MCA 1973 itself, which you will study very shortly. But the court operates in a pragmatic manner, and as you have seen from the types of orders that can be made, can act without necessarily having regard to who owns what in a legal sense.

The best explanation given on the court's approach was by Lord Denning MR in *Hanlon* v *The Law Society* [1981] AC 124 where he stated (at page 147):

> [The law] takes the rights and obligations of the parties all together and puts the pieces into a mixed bag. Such pieces are the right to occupy the matrimonial home or to have a share in it, the obligation to maintain the wife and children, and so forth. The court then takes out the pieces and hands them to the two parties – some to one party and some to the other – so that each can provide for the future with the pieces allotted to him or to her. The court hands them out without paying any too nice a regard to their legal or equitable rights but simply according to what is the fairest provision for the future, for mother and father and the children . . .

6.6.1 THE CRITERIA TO BE TAKEN INTO ACCOUNT

When the court is making decisions with regard to property and financial claims, the MCA 1973 provides a checklist of factors to assist the court's decision. However, the factors are not prescriptive, nor is the list exhaustive. You should also remember that it is more often the legal advisers who will be considering the checklist, since the court's role should be kept to the minimum. The Solicitors Family Law Association's Code of Practice works on the basis that the legal adviser will endeavour to deal with matters in a non-antagonistic and non-confrontational manner. Court action is perceived to heighten feelings and often to be contrary to the clients' needs – it does not promote good future relationships. This is not to say that court action should never arise, in some cases the only option will be to go to court.

Read s. 25(1) and (2), MCA 1973 in *Cases and Materials* (6.3.1). Summarise the factors that the court will take into account.

SAQ 49

From your initial reading, are there any factors that you think are unnecessary?

If so, why do you believe that they are not needed?

6.6.2   SECTION 25(1): AN OVERVIEW

This subsection reflects the non-exhaustive nature of the following list in s. 25(2). It also highlights the importance of children of the family, and this again can be linked into the priorities of the Child Support Acts 1991 and 1995, which include the duty of a parent to maintain his/her child. It also emphasises the notion that a parent may be able to divorce his/her spouse, but not his/her child. However, you should note that the child's welfare is not the court's paramount consideration, but only the first consideration. To see how this can affect the courts reasoning, see the extracts of *Suter* v *Suter and Another* [1987] 2 FLR 232 in *Cases and Materials* (**6.3.2**).

6.6.3   RESOURCES AND EARNINGS

As you will have seen, s. 25(2)(a) relates to the resources that each party to the marriage has, whether it be income or property, or earning capacity, or resources that the parties will conceivably have in the future. Whilst the current assets and earning capacity should be easy to establish, subject of course to the party's co-operation, the future earning capacity requires a court to gaze into its crystal ball.

Dealing first with disclosure, and the establishing of existing financial and property assets, parties are under a duty to make a full disclosure of assets, and it is not just in contested cases that this must take place, but also where the court is being asked to endorse an agreement by way of a consent order. The most commonly cited case on this is *Livesey (formerly Jenkins)* v *Jenkins* [1985] FLR 813, which was decided by the House of Lords. You will find extracts from this in *Cases and Materials* (**6.3.3**).

SAQ 50

How will the FLA 1996 and in particular s. 9 affect this principle?

It is common sense to say that parties need to state clearly what assets they have, before the court can divide them up between the parties involved. However, in the absence of clear rules under the FLA 1996, it is not certain how courts will assess agreements made by the parties under s. 9 in order to obtain a divorce. As you will remember from **Chapter 5** (and if you can't, go back and re-read the relevant sections), under s. 9 the parties must have made arrangements for the future during the period of reflection and consideration. Any arrangements in regard to financial matters may be:

■ by consent, and subject to a court order ratifying the agreement;

■ by order of the court, and not made by consent (although this is unlikely to be the preferred option);

■ by negotiation through a third party;

■ by the parties simply stating they have made their arrangements; or

■ by the parties stating they have no assets and no arrangements to be made.

Under this multifaceted scheme, and especially in the absence of legally trained mediators, it is potentially going to be far easier to 'hide' assets or fail to disclose relevant matters. It is suggested that the court will not have time to conduct a thorough investigation into all financial arrangements put before it – a rubber stamp exercise akin to the existing special procedure for divorce is more likely – and hence it may become common practice for litigation to arise, after divorce, for failure to disclose. If this does occur, whilst the legal profession may lose out in the divorce process itself, they may more than make their money in the disputes that arise later on!

Looking now at the crystal ball gazing that the court will undertake, this primarily affects women, who may be expected to return to the work force. However, you should not disregard the potential increases in men's salaries through promotion etc.

How feasible is it for women to return to work in today's economic climate?

The courts appear to recognise the difficulties for a woman when it comes to returning to the workplace given the nature of the economy, both in terms of availability of employment and the income that a woman can generate, but still feel able to make judgments on quantification of earnings. The cases of *Leadbeater* v *Leadbeater* [1985] FLR 789 and *M* v *M (Financial Provision)* [1987] 2 FLR 1, extracted in *Cases and Materials* (**6.3.3**), illustrate the courts' reasoning. Statistically, more women will work on a part time basis than men, with the resultant reduction in earning capacity and long term benefits. This is especially so if the woman has care of any children. A factor that seems to be ignored by the judiciary (perhaps because the majority of judges are men, one could suggest), is the difficulty of working as a single parent. Many employers do not operate on a sufficiently flexible basis to accommodate employees' needs for time off work to deal with children's illnesses, or school holidays.

To see that men will be affected by these principles, read the extracts from *Hardy* v *Hardy* [1981] 2 FLR 321 in *Cases and Materials* (**6.3.3**).

Crystal ball gazing may also include examining aspects of potential inheritance for one of the parties. If it is expected that a party will inherit property or assets in the near future, the court may take this into account. This also raises the issue of what resources can be considered. What should happen if a marriage has broken down several months or years earlier, and then one spouse inherits after the breakdown, but before a divorce?

Should 'after-acquired' assets be made available for the (ex) spouse?

It may seem a little unfair to take account of a windfall gained after breakdown, after all this is not a matrimonial asset. Unfortunately for the recipient, the courts can take into account any resources, whether gained pre- or post-breakdown, if obtained before the ancillary proceedings.

In *Cases and Materials* (**6.3.3**), read the extracts from *Wagstaff* v *Wagstaff* [1992] 1 All ER 275 and *Schuller* v *Schuller* [1990] 2 FLR 193 which both illustrate this principle.

6.6.3.1   New partners

To what extent do you think the court will take into account the earnings of a new partner when dealing with ancillary matters?

Would the court's views be the same if the new partner had no earnings and a second family (i.e. children) existed?

These questions highlight another problematic area for the courts, advisers, and the individual when the question of maintenance is considered and the different scenarios above will result in different answers.

With regard to new partners, on a general level the courts will take into account any assets or earnings that they possess when deciding on maintenance for the first spouse. However, this is not to say that a second partner will be made to *pay* maintenance to the former spouse. The courts approach the matter by asking, 'to what extent does the second partner's financial situation free up the income and assets of the spouse?'. To give you an example, in the case of *Martin* v *Martin* [1977] 3 All ER 762, the husband had commenced cohabitation with another woman, the intention being to marry. He lived in his new partner's council house, the tenancy of which could be transferred to them jointly. When the ancillary matters were decided, the court took account of the availability of accommodation for the husband and treated it as a resource of his own. Consequently the wife was awarded a life interest in the former matrimonial home.

It is potentially easier for the courts to assess resources where the asset in question is property as opposed to earnings. Whilst the court can consider a new partner's financial status, this new partner cannot be compelled to give precise details of their economic position. They cannot be forced to swear an affidavit but may be required to give evidence in court. The danger of new partners making no disclosure is that the court will make assumptions about the wealth or otherwise of the partner.

Read the extracts of *Frary* v *Frary* [1993] 2 FLR 696 in *Cases and Materials* (6.3.3.1) to see how this works in practice.

The second question in **SAQ 53** leads into the second consideration in the checklist in the MCA 1973, s. 25(2), namely the financial needs of the parties.

6.6.4   THE FINANCIAL NEEDS, OBLIGATIONS AND RESPONSIBILITIES

These three categories are not synonymous, but all have to be balanced in so far as is possible. The main need in the majority of cases will be to rehouse the parties and to ensure that the children are adequately provided for. Immediately you should be thinking of **SAQ 53**, i.e. what is the position if there are two families? As you will learn later, the CSA 1991 and 1995 may make an important inroad here. The MCA 1973 and its interpretation by the courts, would permit the man 'to maintain his newly formed family and . . . although the first wife has a claim for adequate support the second marriage will result in a reduction in his capacity to support her' (Cretney and Masson, *Principles of Family Law*, 6th edn at page 445). It is suggested, however, that whilst the needs of, and obligation to, a new family may result in a reduction in maintenance to the first wife, it may not significantly reduce the maintenance payable to the children under the CSA 1991 and 1995.

6.6.4.1   What is the test of 'need'?

Should a party's needs be assessed on a subjective basis or an objective one?

For the purposes of the MCA 1973 the needs of a party will be considered in a subjective way, i.e. what does this party need, having regard to the financial status of the parties? Need is therefore treated in a relative manner. Two leading cases on this issue are *Leadbeater* v *Leadbeater* [1985] FLR 789 (*Cases and Materials* (**6.3.4.1**)) and *Dart* v *Dart* [1996] 2 FLR 286 (*Cases and Materials* (**6.3.4.1**)) both cases dealing with wealthy couples.

Even where the couple is of more modest means, the matter will still need to be assessed on a subjective basis, albeit that more notice will need to be taken of the actual financial standing of the couples in question.

6.6.4.2   How are needs calculated: what is the starting point?

It is all very well stating that the courts will assess the different needs of the parties, but how is this done – what is the starting point for their assessment?

The extracts from *Dart* v *Dart* may have given you a clue, but what do you think is the starting point?

To assist you further to assess whether your answer to SAQ 55 matches that of the court, read the extracts from the case of *Wachtel* v *Wachtel* [1973] 1 All ER 829 in *Cases and Materials* (6.3.4.2).

Also consider the approach that was taken in *Burgess* v *Burgess* [1996] 2 FLR 34 (*Cases and Materials* (6.3.4.2)).

The latter approach highlights the fact that whilst it is often advantageous to have some sort of starting point in the assessment of needs and division of assets, the court cannot fetter itself by applying a blanket formula. You may wish to make a note of this in order to compare this with the assessment of child support under the CSA 1991 and 1995, where a strict formula is applied.

6.6.5 SECTION 25(2)(c), (d) and (e): THE STANDARD OF LIVING, THE AGE OF THE PARTIES, THE DURATION OF THE MARRIAGE AND PHYSICAL AND MENTAL DISABILITIES

These three criteria can be taken together, since they are not problematic. Indeed, these should have been identified by you as being potentially unnecessary when you first considered the s. 25 checklist. However, by specifically raising them as considerations, it ensures that relevant factors are not overlooked by the courts.

6.6.5.1 The standard of living

It has long been recognised that normally one household cannot be divided into two and still result in the parties enjoying the same standard of living. The courts are only required to see what standard of living was in existence during the marriage, and this will affect the consideration of the party's relative needs under MCA 1973, s. 25(2)(b).

6.6.5.2 Age of the parties and duration of the marriage

Again, you should now see how these two considerations reflect other factors in the checklist. The age of the parties and the duration of the marriage will affect the assets that they have available, and will also reflect their ability to seek employment, rehouse themselves and settle their needs.

6.6.5.3 Physical or mental disability

If one party has either a physical or mental impairment, the same arguments as in section 6.6.5.2 will arise. The individual's ability to become more self-sufficient may be limited, and their needs may be considerably greater. Therefore, this factor could easily be subsumed into the others.

6.6.6 CONTRIBUTIONS MADE TO THE MARRIAGE

SAQ 57

What sort of contributions will be relevant here?

The subsection itself (s. 25(2)), will help you in answering this SAQ, since it is stated within it. The MCA 1973 refers to contributions to the welfare of the family and these will include looking after the home and the family. Principally this is directed at the 'housewife' who should not be at a disadvantage from not taking part in the public economic sphere. As Lord Simon of Glaisdale expressed it: 'The cock bird can feather his nest precisely because he is not expected to spend most of his time sitting on it' (*With All My Worldly Goods*, 1964, Holdsworth Club).

Once more, there is an overlap between this factor and s. 25(2)(a) and (b). Whilst the subsection highlights time spent caring for the family, it is arguable that other contributions, perhaps helping build up a family business, can be included under this head. In many cases however, this type of action would also be referred to under the next subsection.

6.6.7   THE CONDUCT OF THE PARTIES

Under the MCA 1973, as originally enacted, conduct would be taken into account when it was such that it would be inequitable to disregard it.

 SAQ 58

When would that be likely to happen? What sort of conduct would it be?

Both positive and negative conduct has been considered by the courts under s. 25(2)(g). In *Wachtel* v *Wachtel* it was held that conduct would only be taken into account to reduce a financial award if the conduct were 'both obvious and gross' (per Lord Denning at page 835, see extract in *Cases and Materials* (**6.3.5**)). The difficulty for the courts would otherwise be that a full investigation into who was responsible for the breakdown, or whose conduct was worse, would be needed. This would be contrary to the ethos of the MCA 1973 and 'fault free divorce'. It is not the case that only conduct leading to the breakdown of the marriage will be considered. In *Beach* v *Beach* [1995] 2 FLR 160 the husband's reckless dissipation of assets was classed as 'conduct that was inequitable to disregard'. The case is extracted in *Cases and Materials* (**6.3.5**).

Positive conduct is also capable of consideration, since that too may be inequitable to disregard. Here, the links with the contribution to the family welfare can be seen.

 ACTIVITY 63

Read *Kokosinski* v *Kokosinski* [1980] 3 WLR 55 in *Cases and Materials* (6.3.5) and note down the principles and reasoning of the court.

6.6.8 THE FAMILY LAW ACT 1996

The wording of s. 25(2)(g), MCA 1973 will, once the FLA 1996 is brought into force, be changing subtly.

Read the amendments to be made by virtue of sch. 8, para. 9(3) of the FLA 1996 in *Cases and Materials* (6.3.6).

Will this make any real difference to the way in which courts assess ancillary matters?

The main shift in emphasis will be to widen the scope for consideration. Under the initial wording, conduct during the marriage was the focus of attention. Some cases, such as *Kokosinski*, did adopt a more flexible approach. Now, it is legitimate to have regard to negative and positive conduct whenever occurring, which is potentially fairer to cohabitees who later marry. This view may be at odds with the previous Lord Chancellor, Lord Mackay of Clashfern, who stated that 'The role in ancillary relief proceedings has not changed and there is therefore no question, as has been suggested in some quarters, of conduct being introduced through the back door' (Weekly Hansard, 27 June 1996, no. 1672, col. 1113).

In addition, the continued ability of the courts to take notice of conduct may be at odds with the principles of the 1996 Act itself. As you should recall, the FLA 1996 is premised on a 'no fault' basis. Conduct, especially where that conduct is negative, is not in keeping with this philosophy. It is also strange that there will be a difference in emphasis on conduct between those who use mediation, and those who prefer to use the courts.

6.6.9 THE LOSS OF FUTURE BENEFITS, ESPECIALLY PENSIONS

The matrimonial home is normally perceived to be the biggest matrimonial asset that a couple will possess. Today, with the growth of company pensions and private pensions, more couples will find themselves with another major asset, i.e. a pension. Albeit the subsection does not concentrate purely on pensions, these provide the focus of this section.

How might a court deal with potential loss of a benefit such as a pension?

Under the MCA 1973 (as unamended), the loss of benefit could be dealt with by compensating the loser in another manner. Lump sum orders should spring to mind as possible remedies. This might not be an option in a particular case if, for example, the husband does not have sufficient capital assets to meet the lump sum order. The making of a property transfer order, giving all the equity in the home to the wife, may also be possible. But what of the husband's ability to rehouse himself? In some situations the compensation has taken the form of an annuity. It has therefore not been easy to make adjustment for loss of pension rights.

6.6.9.1   The Pensions Act 1995

Until the introduction of this Act and its amendments to the MCA 1973, the scope for the courts to intervene with pension rights *per se* was limited. A pension fund had been divided between divorcing spouses in the case of *Brooks* v *Brooks* [1995] 2 FLR 13, but the circumstances of the fund itself had been unusual in this case. This uniqueness had enabled the court to hold the pension fund as being a post-nuptial settlement, and hence capable of reallocation under the MCA 1973. The headnote of the case is in *Cases and Materials* (6.3.7.1).

Read the amendments to the MCA 1973 made by virtue of s. 166, Pensions Act 1995 in *Cases and Materials* (6.3.7.1). (Note: not all of the section is extracted.)

What will this allow?

In addition to the continued powers of the court to make adjustment for pensions in the ways outlined earlier, the 1995 amendments will introduce the concept of pension 'earmarking'. Under s. 25B(4) of the 1973 Act, if the court makes a s. 23 order, it can require the pension fund trustees or managers to make payments from the fund to the non-fund holder. These payments may be either periodical, or a lump sum, and are dependent on the types of pension fund benefits for the pension holder. In effect this power permits the court to divide future pension benefits between the parties, albeit only one has contributed. Problems will no doubt arise. What will the situation be if the pension holder dies before the other ex-spouse, and in particular, dies before the pension has 'kicked in'? Can the court do anything if the fund holder simply stops paying in to the fund, and starts another pension fund elsewhere? Can the fund holder prevent the court taking the pension value as a whole if a large proportion of the fund was built up prior to the marriage?

6.6.9.2 Pensions and the Family Law Act 1996

Read s. 16 of the FLA 1996 in *Cases and Materials* **(6.3.7.2). What will this do when it is brought into force?**

Under this section the concept of 'pension splitting' is introduced. This differs from 'earmarking' in **6.6.9.1** in that the pension fund will be split into shares, and allocated to each party. Splitting pensions in this manner would prevent some of the problems identified in **6.6.9.1**. A split pension may be transferable to other pension providers, it will not disappear on the death of the fund holder and provides fairness in that contributions after divorce will benefit the individual making the payments. Pension splitting, whilst on the statute book, is not anticipated to be feasible for some time, since additional legislation will be required to provide the courts with the mechanisms to create the split.

Pensions will no doubt continue to cause debate for some time within divorce, but you may wish to reflect upon them in the context of the divorce process. If you were divorcing, and were negotiating with your spouse to reach your financial arrangements, would you know the value of your pension? Would you think about bringing it into the calculations? Unless mediators, and non-legal advisers are trained to inform couples about these types of issues, it is possible that individuals may lose out in the future financial stakes, or may find the court rejecting their agreement, merely prolonging the process or creating additional antagonism between the couple.

For more information on the concepts of earmarking and splitting, you will find two articles from *Family Law* extracted in *Cases and Materials* (**6.3.7.2**).

6.6.10 THE CLEAN BREAK

Read s. 25A of the MCA 1973 in *Cases and Materials* **(6.3.8). Write down what you think this section tries to achieve and how.**

As you have seen in **6.3.1**, these provisions were introduced due to the need to encourage ex-spouses to be independent and also self-sufficient after divorce. When a court is exercising its powers under the MCA 1973, it is under a duty to consider if financial obligations can be ended immediately or at some time in the future. This fits with the notion that a divorce should end the empty shell of a marriage, and allow the individuals to move on to another life, without any ties from the relationship. Some of the orders you have studied in this chapter are naturally suited to this concept.

Go back and highlight the orders meeting the clean break principle.

If the court does not feel that the parties can be financially independent, despite the wide range of orders available, it may believe that this independence will be possible in the future. Consequently the court can, under subsection (2) of s. 25A, make an order for a specified period of time. At the end of this period the payments may end automatically, without the possibility of seeking a continuance. The court can, and will, impose a prohibition upon the right to obtain a continuation of the order. In some cases this prohibition is not placed on the order. If so, a further application for maintenance can be made.

6.7   When Will the Orders be Made?

Under the current process, financial and property orders are normally made after the decree of divorce has been made absolute (final). These ancillary proceedings may take quite some time to conclude in comparison with the speed with which an agreed divorce can be granted. Under the FLA 1996 the position will be different. As you know (or should do by now), the parties must make their arrangements before a divorce order can be granted. The court can be asked to validate any voluntary agreement, by way of a consent order. However, if no consensus can be reached, the court may be asked to make a decision using the MCA 1973 provisions discussed above.

The court can intervene, and make a financial or property order at the 'appropriate time'. This is defined in sch. 2, para. 3 (which introduces s. 22A to the MCA 1973) to the FLA 1996 as being:

■   after a statement of marital breakdown has been filed but before a divorce or separation order has been applied for;

■   when an application for a divorce or separation order has been made;

■   after a divorce order has been made; and

■   when a separation order is in force.

As you can appreciate, this is very similar to the existing MCA 1973 provisions. However, when the court is dealing with applications after the filing of the statement of marital breakdown, but before the application for an order of divorce/separation, it can only make an interim order, and may only make a financial adjustment order. This is set out in the amendments to the MCA 1973 in s. 22B, the text of which is in *Cases and Materials* (6.4).

SAQ 60

Does this raise any problems?

A couple of issues arise in relation to this provision. First, the ability to seek a court order (even if interim) after the statement of marital breakdown has been filed is clearly needed, and as it stands, is the same as the existing s. 22, MCA 1973. However, if maintenance has not been paid voluntarily, necessitating the application, then there is little chance of the couple reaching an agreement to put before the court on the divorce application.

Secondly, if no agreement can be reached, will the interim order of the court be sufficient to meet the requirements of s. 9, FLA 1996? Section 9(2)(a) refers to a court order (whether by consent or otherwise), clearly suggesting that contentious proceedings can take place. But as only an interim order can be made, does this order settle the financial arrangements? It can be argued that the answer to this question is, 'No'. Under the FLA 1996 only *financial* matters will be dealt with, as the question of property cannot be considered at an interim stage (s. 22B). Also, it is debatable to what extent the court will consider issues such as pensions prior to the making of the application for divorce.

If an interim order will not be sufficient, the applicant for the divorce must consequently try to fit the case into one of the exceptions to s. 9, and pursue a final order after the making of the divorce order. The exception in sch. 1 is the only realistic option in such circumstances.

6.8 Preventing or Delaying the Divorce

6.8.1 PREVENTING THE DIVORCE

Under both the current MCA 1973, and the new FLA 1996 provisions, there will be a possibility that the divorce will not be granted, or that it will be delayed.

ACTIVITY 69

Read s. 5, MCA 1973 (*Cases and Materials* (4.6)) and then look at s. 10, FLA 1996 in *Cases and Materials* (6.5.1). Highlight the differences between the two Acts.

The two Acts are quite similar in effect when looking at hardship to the respondent. Both give the court power to refuse to grant the divorce if the making of the order would result in 'financial or other hardship' to the respondent. Hardship in both cases includes the loss of acquiring a benefit which may have been obtained if the marriage had not been dissolved. This is a factor that fits in nicely with the consideration of loss of pension rights looked at earlier. The hardship that will be suffered must, under both pieces of legislation, be such that the courts believe it to be wrong to dissolve the marriage.

However, the Acts are different in the sense that the MCA 1973 will only apply where the petition has been lodged on the basis of five years' separation. The FLA 1996, based as it is on the fact that no 'facts' need to exist, does not restrict the situations where the respondent can try to stop the divorce. In addition, you should have noticed that the 'nature' of hardship to be suffered is subtly different. Under the MCA 1973 the respondent must suffer 'grave' hardship, whereas for the FLA 1996 it is 'substantial' hardship.

Finally, the MCA 1973 reflects only the position of the spouses. The FLA 1996 by contrast, enables the court to consider the position of the children to the marriage, potentially increasing the number of divorces that will be delayed.

The number of situations when a divorce will be prevented are small. The courts have consistently stated that the hardship must relate to the ending of the marriage, not the fact of separation. When considering hardship, other than financial, there is again a reluctance by the courts to refuse to make the order. Religious grounds are often cited in this respect, but due to the links with the dissolution of marriage, and the availability of judicial separation/separation orders, the marriage can be ended to a degree, if not totally.

To illustrate how s. 5 of the MCA 1973 works, re-read the extract from *Rukat v Rukat* [1975] 2 WLR 201 (*Cases and Materials* (4.6)); and look at *K v K (Financial Relief: Widow's Pension)* [1997] 1 FLR 35 (*Cases and Materials* (6.5.1)) and make notes on this latter case.

6.8.2   DELAYING THE DIVORCE

You have already seen some means by which a divorce can be delayed in the FLA 1996, i.e. by one party failing to co-operate in the process of settling arrangements in the period of reflection. If one of the exceptions applies to the process under s. 9, then the divorce will not be delayed. Other than s. 10 above, the FLA 1996 does not contemplate a delay of proceedings, other than at the parties' request, normally for reconciliation to take place. Under the MCA 1973, however, the parties may delay the procedure (note: it is only a delaying tactic) by virtue of s. 10.

ACTIVITY71

Read s. 10, FLA 1996 in *Cases and Materials* (6.5.1). Do you think this is helpful?

Certainly the powers under s. 10(1) can be very useful if a consent order has been made, albeit very often any misinformation will cause the individual to seek to vary the actual order rather than rescind the decree. You may feel that s. 10(2) does not add much to the existing provisions, and in one sense this is correct. There will, in all likelihood, be an application for ancillary relief in any event. However, the advantage is in continuing in the status of spouse. As you know, the majority of financial claims are dealt with after the divorce has been granted, and consequently the individuals do not have the status of a spouse. In the absence of this status, and a court order for ancillary relief, if the one party dies there will be the loss of widows' pension rights etc. The ability to 'hold up' the divorce may also encourage realistic bargaining on the part of the couple.

As with most areas of matrimonial law, there is an element of discretion in s. 10, in that the court may grant the order if it believes the decree to be desirable in all the circumstances.

6.9 Variation and Appealing of Orders

Variation and appeal of orders is often a possibility in family proceedings, although the ability to do so will reflect the imposition of a clean break, and also the nature of the orders made. The law as set out in s. 31 of the MCA 1973 will be changed a little after the introduction of the FLA 1996 but not drastically.

SAQ 61

What factors may cause an individual to seek a variation in an order, or an appeal?

Two types of situation may give rise to the wish to change the order made:

■ a change in circumstances; or

■ a lack of full and frank disclosure.

6.9.1   VARIATION

The ability to make any variation will depend on the initial order. In reality the court will not vary lump sum orders, nor property adjustment orders as a matter of course albeit that these orders may be appealed against.

Periodical payments can be varied, and for this reason it is often tactically useful to get a nominal periodical payment that may be revived at a later date if circumstances change. If the order was specified for a fixed period of time, as can be done under the clean break provisions, the court may be prevented from reopening that arrangement. When granting the initial order, the court can include a restriction in the order to prevent any orders being made after the expiry of the fixed date. This is by way of a s. 28(1A) direction. For the individual paying maintenance, it will be in their interests to ensure that this restriction is included in the order.

The criteria to be considered by the court when faced with a variation application, are all the circumstances of the case with first regard being the welfare of children under 18. However, the courts in practice will take into account all the factors of s. 25, MCA 1973 anew.

The court is also limited under the MCA 1973 as to the orders that can be imposed on a variation application. Whilst under s. 31(7)(a), it can consider making a clean break arrangement, it cannot replace periodical payments with lump sum orders. This will change when the FLA 1996 comes into force, when a new s. 31(7A) will be included in the MCA 1973 to allow courts to vary periodic payments by way of a lump sum or property adjustment order.

6.9.2   APPEALS

The parties to the proceedings will have the right to appeal against the decision made, although any client wishing to do so will need to be advised of the costs involved in so doing. Only if it is clear that the appeal is warranted should it be attempted. Appeals will lie from the county court to the Court of Appeal.

Put the appeal route on your court hierarchy diagram.

Appeals may be based on either a change in circumstances or fraud. The latter is more likely to be successful since once a couple has divorced, a party should not be in a position to rely on the other's good (or bad) fortune. Regardless of the reasons for seeking the appeal, there is only a limited time in which to do so before leave of the court is required.

ACTIVITY73

Read the case extracts of *Barder* v *Barder* [1987] 1 FLR 18 (*Cases and Materials* (6.6.1)) and write down the conditions that will need to be satisfied before the court will grant leave to appeal.

You will have noted from this case the type of change in circumstances that may lead to an appeal against an order being successful. The conditions that need to be satisfied before leave will be granted are:

■ the basis or fundamental assumption underlying the order had been falsified by a change of circumstances;

■ such change had occurred within a relatively short time of the making of the original order;

■ the application for leave was made reasonably promptly; and

■ that the granting of leave would not prejudice unfairly third parties who had acquired interests for value in the property affected.

To be successful, all must be satisfied.

SAQ 62

Would these same considerations apply if the reason for seeking leave to appeal were the failure to disclose information fully?

Whilst it would be beneficial to have guidelines into the granting of leave in the event of fraudulent behaviour by one spouse, it would not be practical to adopt the above. The fraudulent act or failure to disclose may not be established for some time. This would contradict the second principle as set out in *Barder*. Also the non-fraudulent party may not be in a position to act upon the fraud if insufficient evidence existed or was available to them.

ACTIVITY74

You have already reflected upon non-disclosure in this chapter. If you are not clear on the scope of non-disclosure, and more importantly, the impact of the FLA 1996, go back to 6.6.2.1 and refresh your memory. In addition to the case of *Livesey*, read the extract from *Vicary* v *Vicary* [1992] 2 FLR 271 in *Cases and Materials* (6.6.1) which deals with fraudulent conduct.

6.10   Summary

In this chapter, you have covered a great deal of ground. The information itself is not complicated, although you may feel it is having read so much! It is important to realise that where financial settlements are concerned, the prime objective is to reach a suitable agreement without the need to go to court. This meets both the objectives of the FLA 1996, but will also achieve a better relationship between the parties, and also a reduction of costs. When advising clients, you should always keep the s. 25 factors in mind, but the approach must be holistic. You cannot focus purely on one or two of the factors to the exclusion of others – the approach is of the net effect to the couple. Matrimonial assets that once kept *a* family are unlikely to keep *two* families. You should also remember that unless the parties are very well off, no situation will be ideal and invariably both parties will lose out. Finally, in your revision of this topic, be sure to highlight the differences between MCA 1973 pre FLA 1996 and post FLA 1996. The changes are subtle, but may give rise to considerable legal argument.

6.11   End of Chapter Assessment Questions

1. To what extent will s. 25(2), Matrimonial Causes Act 1973 become irrelevant after the coming into force of the Family Law Act 1996?

2. In June 1996 Jayne (32) walked out on her husband, Trevor (45), taking their daughters, Abigail (8) and Lucie (6) with her. She moved back into her parents' home. The cause of the split was Trevor's increasingly violent behaviour and his chronic alcohol dependence. Jayne did not seek any maintenance since at that stage she was in full time employment. She filed a statement of marital breakdown at the local county court in September 1996. She has now been made redundant but due to having been with the company for less than two years has received no redundancy pay.

    Advise her on her rights to maintenance for herself and the children.

    (You may prefer to leave the question of the children until after **Chapter 9**, when you will have considered the law in depth. The answer to this question does, however, talk about child maintenance.)

See *Cases and Materials* **(6.8)** for outline answers to these two questions.

CHAPTER SEVEN

PROPERTY AND FINANCE WITHOUT DIVORCE

7.1 Objectives

By the end of this chapter you should be able to:

■ describe the legislative provisions for obtaining maintenance in the absence of a divorce;

■ evaluate the effectiveness of the provisions;

■ advise hypothetical clients as to the preferred options;

■ discuss the rules relating to occupation of property by virtue of spousal status;

■ outline the factors used by the courts to assess property ownership rights within equity.

7.2 Introduction

Having spent time looking at what happens after divorce, you will now turn to the position of couples who may part and lead separate lives, but who do not wish to take proceedings for divorce or separation. Indeed, some couples may utilise the legal provisions to obtain maintenance or property rights without thinking about separating at all. The rules in relation to property, both occupation rights and ownership will be discussed. Many of these property provisions (in particular the equitable rights) referred to in the latter half of the chapter, will be equally relevant to cohabitees.

7.3 Maintenance without Divorce

As you will recall from **Chapter 6**, there is a common law duty of a spouse to maintain the other spouse and it is this duty which has been relied upon to form the basis of the existing laws on maintenance in divorce. However, what happens if a couple does not wish to divorce, but the parties merely prefer to live apart? Should the same rules apply, or should the law recognise this as a different category, and provide other remedies? Is it practicable for spouses to seek to enforce the common law duty whilst still living with their partner, or do you think that this would create too much antagonism?

In fact the law treats the question of maintenance outside divorce in only a slightly different manner. The issue of property is, by contrast, more akin to land law principles than it is to matrimonial law. If a couple has not separated, there is nothing, legally, to prevent property claims being made under land law, as long as the criteria for the application can be met.

7.3.1   CLAIMING MAINTENANCE

Spouses are able to seek maintenance under two statutes, the Matrimonial Causes Act (MCA) 1973, with which you are already familiar, and the Domestic Proceedings and Magistrates' Courts Act (DPMCA) 1978. Neither of these Acts is available to cohabitees, and this is an important fact to remember. The general thrust of both Acts is the same, but there are a few crucial differences that are relevant when advising clients on their rights of action.

7.3.1.1   The MCA 1973

Read s. 27, MCA 1973 in *Cases and Materials* (7.1.1.1) and write down when this section can be used, the criteria for assessment, and the nature of the orders that are obtainable.

As with the rest of the MCA 1973, this section can be used to obtain support for children; however, this will be covered in **Chapter 9**.

The section allows maintenance to be sought where the other party has 'failed to provide reasonable maintenance for the applicant'. This is the sole trigger factor. When assessing what reasonable maintenance is, you should have written down that the criteria are in fact the same as for any other maintenance under the MCA 1973. Consequently, all you have learnt in **Chapter 6** is relevant here. A major difference to be aware of is that the courts are only reflecting upon the maintenance situation under s. 27; the holistic approach which takes in property requirements does not automatically apply. If couples are separating without divorce or judicial separation, and they wish to deal with the matrimonial home, land law principles will become applicable.

The types of orders that can be granted, again, are very comparable with those under s. 23, MCA 1973. The court can make a periodical payments order, which may or may not be secured, or a lump sum order (s. 27(6)). There is no set limit on the amount that may be awarded, the court will assess the 'reasonableness' purely on the s. 25(2) factors. In addition, lump sum orders may be made, again with no limit as to amount (s. 27(7)).

How long should these orders last?

Would your answer differ if an order were sought whilst the couple lived together, as opposed to if the couple had separated?

The orders that can be made under s. 27 may be for any term that the court may specify. Hence, the notion of fixed term payments is clearly anticipated. If a spouse is merely trying to force the other into paying maintenance, a short term order may be appropriate. In any event, the court may be loath to grant an unlimited duration order if the parties are still cohabiting, but a long term order is not outside the realms of possibility. If an unlimited term order is made, the only restrictions on duration are set out in s. 28(2).

Read s. 28(2), MCA 1973 in *Cases and Materials* (7.1.1.1).

Can you write down any other situations in which the order will be brought to an end?

Clearly, the remarriage of one of the parties will not be the only situation where a s. 27 order can be ended. The couple may resume cohabitation, or maintenance may be paid more willingly and apply for the termination of the order, one of the parties may die or, perhaps less tragically, the couple may divorce and another order made in those proceedings. You should note that the divorce of a couple which has obtained a s. 27 order does not automatically end that order. This will potentially benefit couples under the FLA 1996 as the Act has not amended this provision of the MCA 1973. A couple could therefore obtain a s. 27 order before filing the statement of marital breakdown and, due to the timing, this order would not automatically have to be an interim award. A knock-on effect from this would be that the parties have made their financial arrangements for the purposes of s. 9, FLA 1996. They would be in difficulty if property existed, which would not be covered by s. 27.

If this argument is not clear in terms of the relationship and focus of the FLA 1996, return to Chapter 5, or your own notes, to refresh your memory.

7.3.1.2   The DPMCA 1978

This is the alternative source of remedies for spouses to seek maintenance where a divorce is not contemplated. Indeed, this Act is only applicable where spouses are currently cohabiting or are separated.

Read ss. 1, 2 and 3 of the DPMCA 1978 in *Cases and Materials* (7.1.1.2).

On a separate sheet of paper, list the trigger criteria for this Act, the factors that the court will take into account when making an order, and whether there are any limitations on the orders that can be granted.

The DPMCA 1978 is a more limited source of remedies for a married couple, as your lists should show, when compared with s. 27, MCA 1973. In s. 1, you will have read that there are three trigger criteria for spouses (don't forget you will deal with children in **Chapter 9**):

■ a spouse has failed to provide reasonable maintenance to the applicant;

■ a spouse has behaved in such a way that the applicant cannot reasonably be expected to live with them; or

■ a spouse has deserted the applicant.

What will happen to these trigger criteria when the FLA 1996 comes into force?

When looking at this list, you should be able to see that the criteria are a mixture drawn from other statutory provisions. The first is the same as in s. 27, MCA 1973, and the second and third are drawn from s. 1, MCA 1973, the facts upon which a divorce order can be based. However, the FLA 1996 will be repealing the facts in s. 1(2), MCA 1973 and, consequently, to ensure comparability across statutes, all but the first criterion in the DPMCA 1978 will be repealed too.

When the magistrates are assessing whether to make the order, s. 3(2), DPMCA 1978 sets out the factors to be borne in mind. These will be familiar to you by now – you've seen them before so nothing more will be said about them.

The scope for making orders is where the constraints of this Act become apparent. Your list should refer to ss. 2(1)(a), (b) and 2(3). A court may make both periodical payments and lump sum orders. However, the court can only make *unsecured* periodical payments, whilst those under s. 27, MCA 1973 may be *secured*. Additionally, the magistrates' powers only extend to the making of a lump sum to a total of £1,000. There is no such restriction for the MCA 1973 and the county court.

Now read ss. 4 and 25, DPMCA 1978 in *Cases and Materials* (7.1.1.2). What limits with regard to duration of orders are placed on the magistrates' court?

The restrictions included within s. 4 are the same as for s. 27. It is interesting that the magistrates' orders can survive divorce when the input this court has into divorce *per se* is very small. Section 25 is more in keeping with the lower status of the court, and its power to bind. Unlike the MCA 1973 however, any order made for periodical payments will cease if the couple remains in, or recommences cohabitation for a period in excess of six months. This restriction is probably more in line with your answer to **SAQ 63** in **7.3.1.1**. It is a very logical approach – if the parties are living together, the state should not have to intervene in this way, and it should be for the individuals themselves to sort out their financial affairs.

Can you think of any other reasons (apart from the nature and duration of the orders) why you may advise an individual to use either the MCA 1973 or the DPMCA 1978 to seek maintenance?

These are the types of questions that you will need to reflect upon if you intend to work within the law. Where an individual has options of venues for legal proceedings, it is for the legal adviser to inform on the best option for that particular client.

The advantages of using the magistrates' jurisdiction are that the court is generally quite quick to deal with the application, the court is often easier to access since there are more magistrates' courts than county courts, and the application will result in lower costs for the client. However, a disadvantage of the magistrates' courts is that legal aid may not be granted for the application since it might be perceived to be a simple application where no legal assistance is warranted.

7.3.1.3 Other orders in the magistrates' courts

In addition to the orders available under s. 1, DPMCA 1978 criteria, the magistrates have a slightly extended jurisdiction by virtue of ss. 6 and 7.

Read ss. 6 and 7, DPMCA 1978 in *Cases and Materials* (7.1.1.3). How do these sections extend the jurisdiction?

Taking s. 6 first, you should have noted that this provides the magistrates with the power to make consent orders. Without this section, a consent order could not be made under the DPMCA 1978. The court is not required to go behind the agreement, merely to consider whether the making of the order is contrary to the interests of justice. By implication, this would involve some investigation to ensure that any provision was reasonable.

Section 7 is a very useful section. Under this provision the couple must have been living apart for more than three months. The court can make an order, without consent, where one party has paid sums of maintenance to the other voluntarily over that period. The aggregate amount of maintenance will dictate the amount that can be ordered (subject to s. 7(4)).

A husband has paid to his wife the following amounts:

Month 1 – £500
Month 2 – £300
Month 3 – £400

How much may the court order by way of maintenance?

The maximum award would be £400 per month, which is the total amount divided by 3, being the period over which voluntary payments have been made.

The proviso in subsection (4) is important. If the aggregate in this question had been £600, the magistrates may feel that £200 per month is not a reasonable provision. If so, they can treat the application as made under s. 2, and hence increase the amount awarded.

7.3.2 THE WELFARE STATE

In addition to the above Acts, the influence of the social security legislation may be felt. In the event of a couple separating, and maintenance being unforthcoming, one party is potentially reliant on welfare benefits. If this is so, under the Social Security Administration Act 1992, s. 78(6) to (9), the non-claiming spouse will be classed as a 'liable relative' and thus 'liable to maintain his wife [and any children of whom he is the father]'. The same applies to a wife. The Benefits Agency may 'persuade' the claimant to apply for maintenance under the MCA 1973 or the DPMCA 1978. Alternatively the Agency may contact the liable relative directly to request 'voluntary payments' to be made. If no maintenance is paid, the Secretary of State has the right to apply in the magistrates' court for an order against the non-claiming spouse.

It was explained earlier that the MCA 1973 and the DPMCA 1978 are not applicable to cohabitees who separate, or who do not maintain each other: the same is *not* true of the social security provisions. A partner in a heterosexual relationship who wishes to seek benefit may be prevented from doing so if the Benefits Agency believes he/she is living in the 'same household' as their partner. Only one partner in this sort of couple can claim benefits. The social security legislation implies a dependency between cohabitees, but if benefits are paid to one partner, that partner cannot legally be 'forced' to hand over any money to the partner unable to claim. This is a clear illustration of how the law currently treats cohabitees differently, and here may arguably be acting in a discriminatory manner.

Whilst you need to know these distinctions, detailed knowledge of welfare benefits is beyond the scope of this text.

Return to your court hierarchy diagram, in 1.6, and add the jurisdiction discussed above to it.

7.4 Occupation Rights and the Matrimonial Home

The right to occupy the matrimonial home is not the same as the right of ownership, which we will look at later. For many spouses, occupation rights will be bound up with their right of ownership, if the matrimonial home is legally jointly owned. However, it will still be the case that some spouses do not have rights of ownership. This section will consider the Matrimonial Homes Act (MHA) 1983, and the Family Law Act 1996, since the latter in effect repeals the MHA 1983, and re-enacts it in the same terms.

For those of you who have studied land law and trust law, much of this will be familiar territory. However, you should not ignore this part of the chapter – you may have forgotten more than you thought!

7.4.1 THE MATRIMONIAL HOMES ACT 1983

This Act codifies the Matrimonial Homes Act 1967 and the Matrimonial Homes and Property Act 1981. When the FLA 1996 comes into force, ss. 30 to 34 will substantially re-enact the MHA 1983, with minor changes to terminology. The basic rights of a spouse and their remedies will remain.

Read s. 1(1), MHA 1983 and s. 30(1) and (2), FLA 1996 in *Cases and Materials* (7.2.1). Do you see how similar they are?

The rights that are granted by these sections are those of 'occupation' and not of ownership. The occupation derives purely from the status of marriage, and will only arise where one spouse has no ownership rights but the other spouse does. These ownership rights may be either legal or beneficial (i.e. those ownership rights that exist behind the legal title and arise from principles of equity).

The rights to occupy under the Act mean that the spouse with no ownership rights can remain in the property and cannot be evicted by the owning spouse unless the court orders otherwise; or gives the non-owning spouse the right to be admitted into the property (if already evicted) subject to the agreement of the court.

7.4.1.1 Criteria for the court

When considering the making of orders under the Act, the courts are directed to consider the factors in the MHA 1983, s. 1(3). When the FLA 1996 is in force, the criteria will be found in s. 33(6).

Read s. 1(3), MHA 1983 and s. 33(6), FLA 1996 in *Cases and Materials* (7.2.1.1) and list the distinctions.

The factors that the court will take into account in respect of the existing s. 1, MHA 1983 are:

- the conduct of the parties in relation to each other and otherwise;

- their respective needs and financial resources;

- the needs of any children; and

- all the circumstances of the case.

The factors in relation to s. 33, FLA 1996 are all the circumstances of the case including:

- housing needs and resources of the parties and any children;

- financial resources of the parties;

- the effect of the order, or decision not to make the order, on the health, safety and well-being of the parties or children; and

- the conduct of the parties to each other and otherwise.

These lists, are surprisingly similar in their effect. The only change in emphasis within the FLA 1996 is the reference to the effect of the order in terms of health and well-being. However, arguably this would have already been included within the 'circumstances of the case' by the MHA 1983.

7.4.2 THE ORDERS THAT CAN BE MADE

The orders that are available are, in effect, very similar to the orders under domestic violence legislation, and you will cover them in detail in **Chapter 8**. The nature of the orders is set out in s. 1(2) and (3), MHA 1983, to be replaced with s. 33(3) FLA 1996.

Read s. 1(2) and (3), MHA 1983 and s. 33(3), FLA 1996 in *Cases and Materials* (7.2.1 and 7.2.1.1).

Remember to link this with domestic violence later on in your studies.

7.4.3 PROTECTION OF RIGHTS

Do these provisions protect occupation rights? Are these rights enforceable against third parties?

The ability to occupy premises by virtue of status is, under common law, a personal right that can be enforced only against the other spouse. This would have the consequence of making the wife's position insecure against third parties. To overcome this difficulty the MHA 1983 (and the FLA 1996) provide that a spouse with occupation rights can register this right against the title of the property. If the land is registered, the spouse can place a notice on the Register. If the land is unregistered, the rights of occupation can be secured by way of a Class F land charge. Only one property may be subjected to a charge, so if two or more houses exist, a choice will need to be made before registration occurs (s. 3, MHA 1983 and sch. 4, para. 2, FLA 1996).

SAQ 68

Would this provide protection against the mortgagee who grants a mortgage on the completion of the purchase?

The difficulty for a non-owning spouse in the common situation where property is purchased by way of a mortgage is that the mortgagee will have no notice of the wife's right to occupy. She will not be in occupation at the time the mortgage is completed hence her rights are not capable of overriding, or binding, those of the mortgage company. The registration of a charge or notice will only be effective against later creditors.

ACTIVITY 85

Read the case extracts of *Barnett* v *Hassett* [1981] 1 WLR 1385 in *Cases and Materials* (7.2.2). The fact that the case was decided under the Matrimonial Homes Act 1967 is of no significance.

Will this be the common situation when charges or notices are registered?

The practicality of the registration of charges is unclear, and the use of the legislation to obtain part of the proceeds of sale should be rare. It is true to say that, in a failing relationship, it will be normal for a non-owning spouse to protect rights of occupation by registration. This will hopefully prevent or discourage the owner from selling the matrimonial home or from asking the non-owning spouse to leave the premises.

7.4.4 TERMINOLOGY

Under the MHA 1983 the ability to secure occupation of the matrimonial home is referred to as a 'right of occupation'. The terminology will change under the FLA 1996, and a spouse's right to occupy will be termed 'matrimonial home rights', which in turn may result in an occupation order, if legal proceedings need to be taken to enforce those rights.

7.5 Rights of Ownership

At **7.4** above we concentrated purely on occupation, which may be nothing more than a temporary right. The right of ownership is clearly of greater significance.

Why are rights of ownership better than rights of occupation?

Owning property, whether by way of a joint tenancy or a tenancy in common, is a more permanent arrangement (if you do not know the differences between these types of ownership, see the explanations in *Cases and Materials* (**7.3**)). Alongside the ownership rights will run rights of occupation. An owner has a stake in the equity (profit) that is built up within the asset. In times of falling house prices, this benefit may become the detriment of a share in negative equity. As an owner, a sale of the property may be requested, or even ordered by the court under the terms of the Trusts of Land and Appointment of Trustees Act 1996. If you have studied land law, you may be more familiar with s. 30, Law of Property Act 1925 – this was repealed by the 1996 Act which came into force on 1 January 1997.

A legal interest in land generally has to be created by a deed. Any other interest in land, which primarily will be an equitable interest, must be created by a written contract signed by all parties (Law of Property (Miscellaneous Provisions) Act 1989, s. 2). Both legal and equitable interests give rights of ownership.

However, within the matrimonial sphere, the situation will sometimes arise where one party has no legal or equitable interest in accordance with the above principles. If this is the case, a non-owning spouse may utilise the law of trusts to seek ownership rights through the means of a resulting trust. The same will be true for cohabitees who do not jointly own property. The question of who owns property is perhaps less significant for married couples who, as you have learnt, have the MCA 1973 to fall back on if they divorce. Cohabitees have to rely on property law, which is less flexible in its approach.

7.6   Resulting Trusts

Whilst you are focusing on resulting trusts purely from the matrimonial perspective, knowledge of the concept is essential.

7.6.1   VOLUNTARY TRANSFERS OF PROPERTY

Where property is transferred without any consideration, in other words there is no 'bargain', the question arises as to whether there is a presumption of resulting trust. This works on the basis that if a person gives property away the reason behind it must be that the 'donor' intends to retain the beneficial ownership – who in their right mind would give their property away?

There is a distinction to be drawn here between land and pure personalty.

Look at s. 60(3) of the Law of Property Act 1925 in *Cases and Materials* (7.4.1).

You will see that a voluntary conveyance of land does not give rise to a presumed resulting trust merely because it is not expressed to be conveyed for the use or benefit of the donee. There must be some evidence that a gift was not intended.

In *Hodgson* v *Marks* [1972] 2 All ER 684 Mrs Hodgson was an 83-year-old widow who took in a lodger, Mr Evans who gained her trust and affection, so much so that she allowed him to supervise the investment of her money. Mrs Hodgson's nephew was suspicious of Mr Evans and tried to persuade her to get him to leave. She decided to protect Mr Evans by transferring the house to him on the oral agreement that she would continue to be the beneficial owner. The nephew's suspicions proved to be well founded as Mr Evans, who was registered as absolute owner, sold the property to Mr Marks, a bona fide purchaser for value without notice. We thus have two innocent parties, albeit one rather foolish.

The court decided that Mrs Hodgson remained beneficial owner. Evidence of the oral agreement was permissible and, as a resulting trust it did not matter that the agreement was not reflected in writing to satisfy the Law of Property Act 1925. She thus had an overriding interest which was effective against Mr Marks.

It is true to say that where a voluntary transfer of personalty is concerned the presumption of resulting trust is raised.

7.6.2   PURCHASE IN THE NAME OF ANOTHER

Where you pay for property transferred into someone else's name, it will be presumed that the legal owner holds on resulting trust for you.

The classic statement comes from Eyre CB in *Dyer* v *Dyer* (1788) 2 Cox Eq Cas 92:

> The clear result of all the cases, without a single exception, is that the trust of a legal estate, whether freehold, copyhold, or leasehold; whether taken in the names of the purchasers and others jointly, or in the names of others without that of the purchaser;

whether in one name or several; whether jointly or successive – results to the man who advances the purchase money.

Therefore, according to this principle, into whoever's name the property is transferred the beneficial interest results to the person who paid the money. This will also cover cases where, perhaps, several people have contributed and the property is transferred into the name of one, or some of them. The property is held for the contributors beneficially in the proportions in which they provided the purchase money.

The point about a presumption is that it is just that. It is presumed that a resulting trust reflects the intention of the donor or payer. Unlike the automatic resulting trust, however, it may be that the presumed resulting trust is no such thing – the presumption can be rebutted. Very often the presumption of resulting trust will give way to fairly slight evidence to the contrary.

Today is your birthday. The postman has delivered several packages for you. Do you hold the contents of these packages on resulting trust for the senders?

The answer is surely not! The fact that it is your birthday and the packages are, presumably, accompanied by a card wishing you a happy birthday, will clearly rebut any initial presumption of resulting trust.

7.6.3 THE PRESUMPTION OF AN ADVANCEMENT

As you have seen, a presumed resulting trust can be rebutted by evidence, sometimes slight, that a gift was intended by the donor. The presumed resulting trust can also be rebutted by the presumption of advancement. This is where the donor is presumed to have intended a gift. The presumption of advancement will arise when transfers are made between persons in particular relationships where equity recognises that the donor is under an obligation to support the donee.

This all sounds very technical, i.e. that the presumption of resulting trust may be rebutted by the stronger presumption of advancement. What it boils down to is, where does the burden of proof initially lie? Where there is a presumption of resulting trust it is for the donee, initially, to show that the real intention was to make a gift. Conversely, where the presumption of advancement arises it is for the donor to show that he or she intended to retain the beneficial interest in the property.

Where, then, will there be a presumption of advancement?

7.6.3.1 Transfers to a wife

Where a husband transfers property to his lawful wife the presumption of advancement is raised: it is presumed that the husband intended his wife to take the property beneficially. As with much in property law, these presumptions developed when society was very different. It has not been long, in legal terms, that married women have been allowed to hold their own property. As women have become more financially independent and are often equal partners as far as family finances are concerned, the presumption of advancement between husband and wife is nowhere near as strong as it was.

Read Lord Diplock's statement in *Pettitt* **v** *Pettitt* **[1969] 2 All ER 385 in** *Cases and Materials* **(7.4.2.1).**

Having read that the presumption of advancement is much weaker between husband and wife you must remember that it does still exist. It may be rebutted fairly easily if both parties are available to give evidence, but it will be useful if they are not. Perhaps the most important thing is to remember that, although the presumption is raised, it is likely to be the starting point when considering a transfer of property. It is only in the absence of evidence as to the parties' intentions that you will have to rely solely on a presumption.

In this context the presumption will be raised only by transfers from a husband to his lawful wife. The presumption is relevant to personalty and the matrimonial home. It covers gifts made before marriage but the specific marriage must be contemplated and it must, in fact, take place! There will be no presumption of advancement where a man transfers property to his mistress or, indeed, where a wife transfers property to her husband.

7.6.4 REBUTTING THE PRESUMPTIONS

In many cases simple evidence that a gift was or was not intended will be both available and sufficient; you are looking for the intention at the time the transfer took place. The statement of principle used by the courts (in *Shephard* v *Cartwright* [1954] 3 All ER 649, HL) comes from Snell's *Principles of Equity*, 29th edn, p. 180:

> The acts and declarations of the parties before or at the time of the purchase, or so immediately after it as to constitute a part of the transaction, are admissible in evidence either for or against the party who did the act or made the declaration; subsequent acts and declaration are only admissible as evidence against the party who made them and not in his favour.

In other words, you cannot change your mind. It is what has happened at the outset which will determine how the transfer is treated.

Therefore, if you intend a gift – fine; if you intend to remain beneficially entitled – so be it. But what if your reason for transferring the property was less than honest? Can you use your illegal or fraudulent intent to rebut, say, the presumption of advancement?

The answer is no. A transferor cannot have it both ways.

For example, in *Gascoigne* v *Gascoigne* [1918] 1 KB 223 a husband took a lease of land in his wife's name and used his money to build a bungalow on the land. The property was put into the wife's name, with her knowledge, as he was in debt and wanted to protect the property from his creditors. When the danger from the creditors had passed he claimed that the property was held by his wife on resulting trust. His evidence to rebut the presumption of advancement was evidence of the scheme to defraud creditors. The court was quite appreciative of his dilemma. As against the wife the husband claimed the property was his; as against his creditors it was hers. Both claims could not coexist; the court said the property was hers. In this case evidence of the unlawful purpose was not admitted. In subsequent cases judicial notice of illegality has been taken and the transferor has not been allowed to benefit from the illegal purpose lying behind the transfer.

The fact that an illegal purpose underlies a transaction may be irrelevant; the point is that the illegal purpose of the transferor cannot be used as evidence to rebut a presumption.

In *Tinsley* v *Milligan* [1993] 3 All ER 65 two lesbian women were buying a house. It was agreed that the property should be conveyed into the name of the plaintiff to enable the defendant to continue to claim housing benefit. This claim was fraudulent and continued for some years. The parties separated and the plaintiff left. The defendant subsequently ceased to make her fraudulent claim and 'made her peace' with the authorities. The plaintiff sought to evict the defendant who, in her turn, claimed that the house was held for them both equally. The House of Lords held that the transaction gave rise to a resulting trust, the defendant was entitled and, as she did not have to show why the property was transferred into the plaintiff's sole name, the illegal purpose was irrelevant to the claim.

Consider beneficial entitlement in the following situations:

■ **Jack transfers property to his wife Jill.**

■ **Jill transfers property to her husband, Jack.**

■ **Jack transfers property to trustees on trust for Jill for life.**

Did you decide that in the first case Jill is entitled because advancement is presumed, and in the second case Jill is entitled because Jack is presumed to be a trustee for her, as advancement only works in one direction?

In the third case there is a resulting trust after Jill's life interest because the beneficial interest has not been completely disposed of.

7.6.5 OWNERSHIP OF THE MATRIMONIAL HOME

Who owns the matrimonial home? As you will recall, the first step is to look at the deeds. If the property is conveyed to partners jointly at law and in equity then there is no problem. What if the property is put into the name of one partner? Then, as we have seen, if both parties have contributed to the purchase price the legal owner will hold the property on trust for both in proportion to the respective contributions.

Do you see a possible problem with this state of affairs?

As we have seen, if the non-owner has contributed to the purchase price there will be a 'purchase money resulting trust' and the legal owner will hold the property for each partner beneficially in the proportions in which the purchase money has been provided.

A non-owner may acquire an interest in the home if it is conveyed into the name of one partner only due to:

■ a declaration of trust in favour of the non-owner; or

■ the fact that purchase monies may have been provided by the non-owner.

You will remember that, if it is to be valid and enforceable, a declaration of trust of land must be evidenced in writing. In the second case, hard cash must have been contributed to the acquisition of the property.

SAQ 72

Consider human relationships and think about how couples manage their finances. Think, also, about how property is regarded by partners when the relationship is working. What problems can arise?

For many couples, who owns what is irrelevant until the relationship breaks down – when it becomes a matter of the utmost importance to both. Living with your partner involves an emotional rather than a business relationship. If you were to consider buying property to share, as a matter of convenience, with a friend, you would look on the purchase as a business enterprise. You would sort out how the property was to be held, whether you were the joint tenants or tenants in common in equity, what would happen if one of you wanted to leave etc. In other words, you would cover most, if not all, of the angles. Consider, now, acquiring a property in which you propose to live with your lover. For whatever reason, the home is conveyed into the name of your lover. Both of you regard it as 'our' home but you have never talked about the 'ins and outs' of ownership. Your lover pays the mortgage and you pay household expenses. After an argument, you leave the home. Will you be able to claim a share in the property? Where was your contribution to the purchase price?

You can see the sort of problem that can so easily arise. When people decide to share their lives the concept of sharing does not, necessarily, extend to their property. As you have seen, sharing at this point involves payment of, or towards, the purchase price. This insistence on 'direct contributions' causes both difficulty and hardship.

SAQ 73

Suppose that a couple share in the sense that they divide their expenses. Perhaps he deals with the mortgage and council tax whilst she pays for food, clothing, gas and electricity. Will she be entitled to a share in the house?

There is no doubt that she has made an essential contribution to the family finances but has she, through these 'indirect contributions', acquired a share in the home? Does a contribution have to be financial; can credit be given for a non-owning woman's work in caring for the family, e.g. washing, cooking and cleaning?

The starting point is *Pettitt* v *Pettitt* [1969] 2 All ER 385, HL and *Gissing* v *Gissing* [1970] 2 All ER 780, HL. In the latter case the parties had married in 1935. She had worked throughout the marriage and had found a job for him where she worked when he became unemployed. In 1951 the matrimonial home was purchased in his name and with his money. She paid some £220 for furnishings and for laying a lawn. She also paid some household expenses.

The parties subsequently separated and, on divorce, the ownership of the home was in issue. (This was before the Matrimonial Causes Act 1973 which, as you have seen in **Chapter 6**, gives the court its wide jurisdiction to adjust property rights.)

SAQ 74

How would you decide the case on these facts?

The House of Lords decided that she was not entitled to any share in the property. She had made no contribution to the purchase price and so was not entitled to any beneficial interest. The court made it very clear that any claim must be based on accepted principles of property law.

These accepted principles require consideration of the intention of the parties at the time the property was acquired. If we are talking about the non-owner paying money towards the acquisition of the property, it must be clear that the payment was made to acquire a share and that it was not, say, a loan, which was the case in *Richards* v *Dove* [1974] 1 All ER 888.

The court must look to the intention of the parties at the time of acquisition, but the court is not prepared to 'manufacture' an agreement on the basis that the agreement would be an appropriate one in the circumstances. According to Lord Diplock in *Gissing* v *Gissing*, 'the court cannot devise agreements which the parties never made. The court cannot ascribe intentions which in fact the parties never had'.

How important, then, is agreement? It may be crucial. If you look at how a non-owner can acquire a share in property, it is all based on intention. As you saw earlier, a formal declaration of trust may be made: this is intention-based. A presumption may arise because money has been paid towards the purchase price: this is 'direct' contribution. However, can you go further and say that 'indirect' contributions, if intention-based, can give rise to a beneficial interest?

ACTIVITY 88

Read the extract from Lord Diplock's speech in *Gissing* v *Gissing* in *Cases and Materials* (7.4.3).

Having read the section of Lord Diplock's speech, consider how the trust may arise.

If you take the first sentence of the passage it would seem that a trust could be imposed simply because it was fair, and that to impose a trust would be 'just' between the parties. If, however, you look at the second sentence, you will see that the trust involves an element of agreement between the parties, the kind of agreement which, if acted on, will give rise to an interest – this must cover both direct and indirect contributions.

Lord Denning was particularly active in the sphere of the matrimonial home. He took the view in *Falconer* v *Falconer* [1970] 3 All ER 499 that indirect contributions would give rise to a beneficial interest in the home. He said: 'It may be indirect as where both go out to work and one pays the housekeeping and the other the mortgage instalments . . . so long as there is a substantial financial contribution towards the family expenses it raises the inference of a trust'.

Did you notice that Lord Denning seemed to be satisfied that a trust would arise where there was 'a substantial financial contribution'? It did not seem necessary that this should be based on agreement to share, or the payer acting to his or her detriment on the basis of an agreement. It seems hard to reconcile this with *Gissing* v *Gissing*.

We will leave the thorny issue of indirect contributions for the moment to consider the likely parties in any dispute. You will have noticed that the cases we have looked at so far concerned married couples. Married couples can now rely on the various pieces of matrimonial legislation to settle property questions: pure trusts law is only partly an issue for them where, perhaps, no matrimonial proceedings are envisaged. It is for cohabitees that this branch of law is particularly relevant. Should cohabitees be treated as strangers by the courts or as if they are married? Does this make any difference? The short answer is, yes it does. A cohabiting couple are, as we said earlier, involved in an emotional relationship rather than a business one. If the nature of this relationship is accepted it is, perhaps, easier to explain financial conduct and conversations which, arguably, could be construed as showing agreement; you probably will not find the detailed or, indeed, written agreement that would be likely between strangers. If courts could take notice of the husband-and-wife relationship, the same should be available to unmarried partners. In *Cooke* v *Head* [1972] 2 All ER 38 it was held that just as a trust is imposed in the case of husband and wife who acquire property by their joint efforts for their joint benefit, the same principle will be applied to a man and woman setting up home together.

If a cohabiting couple are to be regarded as no different from a married couple then we may need, perhaps, to consider whether anyone who lives with the property owner may qualify. If you get married, it takes 15 to 20 minutes in the Register Office, or however long the religious ceremony takes, and you have the relevant certificate to prove your status. How long must you live with your partner to be regarded as married? Is time a relevant feature? In cases in the 1970s the courts seemed to take the view that it was only legitimate to put a cohabiting couple on the same footing as a married couple if the parties would have married had they been free to do so. As more and more couples were taking the decision not to marry as a matter of choice rather than necessity, this kind of ruling became less appropriate. In *Bernard* v *Josephs* [1982] 3 All ER 162 the Court of Appeal recognised that the nature of the relationship was important when considering what inferences to draw from the way the parties conducted their financial affairs. What is vital is commitment. The court felt that it was only legitimate to treat an unmarried couple on the same footing as if they were married if they had the same degree of commitment as would parties to a marriage. It is difficult to see just how the degree of commitment could be established. Perhaps it would involve a consideration of the reason why the parties chose not to marry.

Therefore, cohabiting couples may be treated as if they were married, but we are still left with the thorny problem of indirect contributions. As we saw, Lord Denning was willing to infer a trust where there was a substantial contribution. It has always been the case that where a party acts to his or her detriment in reliance on an agreement or 'common intention' to share, the court will not permit the owner of the property to renege on the agreement relying on lack of formality. But what if there is no agreement? Lord Denning was willing to impose a 'new model' constructive trust in such a case to effect a just result. In some cases it is not at all clear whether a resulting trust or a constructive trust was imposed, although the language used in recent cases is that of constructive trust.

In *Cooke* v *Head* the parties acquired land to build a bungalow. The land was conveyed into the man's name. He paid the deposit and she made contributions to the mortgage payments. She did, however, contribute physical work – helping to demolish old buildings, wielding a sledgehammer and working a cement mixer and, according to the court, 'did quite an unusual amount of work for a woman'. Here the court took her work into account and held that she was entitled to a one-third share in the property.

The cases caused some difficulty in deciding just what type of trust arose. Presumably the non-owner was not in the least concerned about the technical nature of the trust, only about whether it existed. It does, however, matter to us as we need to know when and how a beneficial interest arises.

ACTIVITY 89

Read the extract from *Hussey* v *Palmer* [1972] 3 All ER 744 in *Cases and Materials* (7.4.3).

What conclusion did each judge come to?

Your answer should have been that Cairns LJ thought it was a loan; Phillimore LJ thought that she was entitled to a beneficial interest under a constructive trust and agreed with Lord Denning MR who stated:

> . . . it is a trust imposed by law whenever justice and good conscience require it. It is a liberal process, founded on large principles of equity, to be applied in cases where the defendant cannot conscientiously keep the property for himself alone but ought to allow another to have the property or a share in it.

This statement of Lord Denning's is extremely wide and has been much criticised. Just when will 'justice and good conscience' demand a share in the property for the non-owner? It does not help us with the thorny issue of indirect contributions. Subsequent courts have held that in order to acquire a beneficial interest, a non-owner cannot merely rely on 'justice and good conscience' but on agreement between owner and non-owner. The idea is that the parties should have a 'common intention' to share the property. Is a common intention to share enough? If I say to you, 'I wish you to have a share in my home', is this enough to prevent me from relying on the absence of writing under s. 53(1)(b), Law of Property Act 1925 when you come knocking on my door to demand your share? 'Justice and good conscience' may suggest that I should keep my promise but it is hardly fair on me if you have done nothing to warrant my giving you a share. There must be something more if I am to be treated fairly, something which makes it equitable, in the legal sense, for me to deny you a share. That something more is that you must have acted on my promise to your detriment.

In *Eves* v *Eves* [1975] 3 All ER 768 the property was acquired in the man's name. He freely admitted that he told his partner that the property could not be conveyed into joint names as she was under 21. This was true at the time of the statement, but not at the time of conveyance. He also admitted that this was an excuse. The house was dilapidated and, although she made no financial contribution, she did a great deal of work, 'much more than many wives would do', to restore the house and gardens. The relationship ended disastrously and she claimed a share. She was awarded a quarter share by the majority in the Court of Appeal on the basis of an agreement, inferred from their discussions on ownership, which she relied on in contributing her work. Lord Denning held that it was a 'new model' constructive trust.

Here, we have agreement plus detrimental reliance. What if there is agreement but no detrimental reliance?

In *Midland Bank* v *Dobson* [1986] 1 FLR 171 the parties intended to share their home beneficially. The wife's claim failed as a resulting trust because she had made no financial contribution; and also failed as a constructive trust because the Court of Appeal held that, although there was agreement, she had done nothing which would amount to acting to her detriment in reliance on the agreement.

Therefore, agreement is necessary, express or inferred, plus detrimental reliance. What will amount to detrimental reliance? It must be something over and above what might reasonably be expected of a non-owner living in the property, even if the 'contribution' is financial. In *Burns* v *Burns* [1984] 1 All ER 244 the parties started living together in 1961. The woman gave up work when their first child was expected and changed her name to 'Burns'. Shortly before their second child was born in 1963, the home was purchased in Mr Burns's name. Until 1975 Mrs Burns made no financial contribution as she stayed at home caring for the children. When she did resume employment her earnings were used for fixtures and fittings for the home and a washing machine.

The Court of Appeal was unable to hold that she had a beneficial interest; there was no express trust, no express agreement, and no real or substantial contribution which could be related to the acquisition of the home. For Mrs Burns, living with Mr Burns for 19 years, caring for the home and children, could not be used to infer a common intention to share the home beneficially.

ACTIVITY 90

Read the extract from *Grant* v *Edwards* **[1986] 2 All ER 426** in *Cases and Materials* (7.4.3)

Why was Mrs Grant entitled to a beneficial interest?

Did you answer that Mrs Grant was separated from her husband? Mr Edwards bought the home which was not conveyed into their joint names, as he told her that he did not want her to have an interest which would prejudice her in pending financial matrimonial proceedings against her husband. He paid the deposit and mortgage whilst she made substantial contributions to the general household expenses. The Court of Appeal held that she was entitled to a share. The 'excuse' for missing her name off the deeds raised a clear inference of common interest to share. So, what of her detrimental reliance? The court said that conduct relied on as detrimental reliance 'must be conduct on which the woman could not reasonably have been expected to embark unless she was to have an interest in the home' (Nourse LJ). So, it must be something that could be explained only by reference to a person, e.g. Mrs Grant, acting on the basis of having a beneficial interest. According to Browne-Wilkinson VC, 'setting up home together, having a baby and making payments to general housekeeping expenses . . . may all be referable to the mutual love and affection of the parties and not specifically referable to the claimant's belief that she has an interest in the house'. Therefore, what did Mrs Grant do which was over and above paying her way and could be regarded as over the odds only to be explained on the basis of their acquisition of a beneficial interest? The court regarded her contribution as being in excess of what would be regarded as normal and that, had she not made these contributions, Mr Edwards would not have been able to pay the mortgage.

SAQ 75

What was Mrs Grant's share?

Did you realise that when the house was damaged by fire, surplus insurance monies were put into a joint bank account? This, felt the court, indicated an intention to share equally.

Have you noticed that all these decisions were in the Court of Appeal? Also the language is moving from 'purchase money resulting trust' to 'common intention constructive trust'. What was necessary to resolve the difficulties encountered, particularly with indirect contributions, was a decision from the House of Lords which came with *Lloyds Bank* v *Rosset* [1990] 1 All ER 1111.

ACTIVITY 91

Read the extract from *Lloyds Bank* v *Rosset* in *Cases and Materials* (7.4.3) .

Consider the facts. Mrs Rosset was, understandably, desperate to stay in her home. The only way she could do so was to show that she had a beneficial interest which would, had she been in occupation before the bank's charge took effect, have been an overriding interest under s. 70(1)(g) of the Land Registration Act 1925, which you may remember from your study of land law and our discussion of matrimonial home rights.

SAQ 76

Reconsider the extracts from Lord Bridge's speech and make a list of when the non-owner may be entitled beneficially.

Did your answer look like the following?

(a) Look for evidence of agreement. The parties must have discussed ownership, although any agreement does not have to be precise, or even perfectly remembered. Where there is evidence of agreement then all that need be shown is detrimental reliance. This will occur with both direct and indirect contributions.

(b) Where there is no agreement, can conduct be used to infer a common intention to share? Yes, in the case of direct contributions (initially or by way of mortgage repayments).

(c) Where there is no evidence of agreement and where the only contribution is indirect, then there will be no trust.

Lord Bridge felt that it was legitimate to infer agreement only on the basis of direct contributions saying, '. . . as I read the authorities it is extremely doubtful whether anything less will do'.

Now let us consider Mrs Rosset's contribution. There was no evidence of express agreement. Her contribution involved decoration, chivvying builders who were renovating the property and purchasing decorating materials. Remember what was said about detrimental reliance in *Grant* v *Edwards*. Could her work be over and above what could be expected of a woman getting a home ready for her family? In Lord Bridge's terms she would have been hard-pressed to show detrimental reliance even if there had been express agreement. He said:

On any view the monetary value of Mrs Rosset's work expressed as a contribution to a property acquired at a cost exceeding £70,000 must have been so trifling as to be almost *de minimis*. I should myself have had considerable doubt whether Mrs Rosset's contribution to the work of renovation was sufficient to support a claim to a constructive trust in the absence of writing to satisfy the requirements of section 51 of the Law of Property Act 1925, even if her husband's intention to make a gift to her of half or any other share in the equity of the property had been clearly established or if he had clearly represented to her that was what he intended.

Her contributions were indirect, and, in truth, minimal. As there was no agreement there certainly could be no inference of common intention.

Do you feel that Mrs Rosset was hard done by legally? Perhaps not. Consider, however, a case where, say, a great deal of work or money had been contributed but there was no evidence of agreement – the non-owner would have gone away empty-handed. Suppose there had been no evidence of the parties' discussions in *Eves* v *Eves* and *Grant* v *Edwards*; these women would not, if Lord Bridge is correct, have been entitled to any interest in the homes to which they had contributed so much. Hopefully if such a case were to come before the courts Lord Bridge's doubts might not prove insurmountable.

Consider the following examples. Does Jill have an interest in the property?

(a) Jack purchases 10, Acacia Avenue. Jill contributes £10,000 to the purchase price.

(b) Jack and Jill buy 10, Acacia Avenue which is conveyed to them as beneficial joint owners. Jack pays £60,000 and Jill pays £10,000.

(c) Jack and Jill decide to buy 10, Acacia Avenue. They agree that it is 'their' home and Jill spends time and money making the property fit to live in. She also pays all the household expenses whilst Jack pays the mortgage.

Did you answer the following?

(a) Jill's contribution is direct so agreement can be inferred (*Lloyds Bank* v *Rosset*).

(b) Jill will be entitled to half the value of the property as she is a beneficial joint tenant (*Goodman* v *Gallant* [1986] Fam 106).

(c) There is evidence of agreement; Jill has acted to her detriment so she will have a beneficial interest (*Lloyds Bank* v *Rosset*; *Grant* v *Edwards*).

Can a non-owner acquire a share by improving property? If married then s. 37, Matrimonial Proceedings and Property Act 1970 says 'yes' unless there is contrary agreement. Lord Denning MR felt that s. 37 was declaratory of the existing law, and the existing law could be applied to cohabitees (*Davis* v *Vale* [1971] 2 All ER 1021). Therefore, as long as the improvement is substantial it may give rise to an interest or an enlarged interest on the basis of common intent.

You have established that a non-owner has a beneficial interest. The last step is to discover just how extensive that interest is. If the contribution is monetary and direct then the share will be proportionate. So far so good, but what if the contribution is, say, payment of household expenses, or wielding a sledgehammer to demolish and rebuild? If there is no express agreement as to the size of the share then the court will try to work out the value of the contribution on a broadly fair basis. 'Equality is equity' is to be applied only if all else fails.

To give you an illustration of the 'quantification' of beneficial interests, the case of *Midland Bank plc* v *Cooke and Another* [1995] 2 FLR 215 will be of assistance.

Read *Midland Bank* v *Cooke* in *Cases and Materials* (7.4.3). Can the court's decision be reconciled with *Lloyds Bank plc* v *Rosset* as easily as Waite LJ seems to make out?

You may feel that the waters have been clouded still further by this decision, but surely equity requires the 'whole course of dealing' to be considered – precisely what the court did in *Midland Bank* v *Cooke*.

For further information on a practical approach to resulting trusts/constructive trusts, read the article by Lawson-Cruttenden and Odutola [1995] Fam Law 560 in *Cases and Materials* (7.4.3).

7.7   Evaluating Shares in Equity

In all the above, the desired outcome for the non-owning spouse or partner will be the granting of ownership rights. As we have seen, this will result in a right to receive any proceeds from the value, or equity, in the property. However, it is one thing to state that ownership rights exist, but to what extent or value will that share be? If the non-owning party has contributed to the property in terms of money (and after *Lloyds Bank plc* v *Rosset* it is likely that this is the only means of evidencing a contribution), then the starting point will be the proportion of that contribution. This presumption may be rebutted by any declaration to the contrary, i.e. that the parties have agreed the property will be shared equally. This was the situation in *Savill* v *Goodall* [1993] 1 FLR 755 explained by Cretney (*Principles of Family Law*, 6th edn, 1997) thus:

> the Court of Appeal held that the trial judge had been wrong to assume that the shares of the parties could only be ascertained by reference to their contributions in all the circumstances. The court must first ask itself whether there has been an agreement, arrangement or understanding between the parties and if so the beneficial interests would be governed by what they had decided. No further inquiry was appropriate. On the facts, the parties had acquired the property with the intention that it be their joint property; and if 'an ordinary, sensible couple, without more, declare an intention to own their home jointly, they can only be taken to intend that they should own it equally'.

7.8 Proprietary Estoppel

In many ways, the doctrine of proprietary estoppel is similar to the concepts within resulting trusts that you have just studied. The doctrine operates by preventing a person asserting their legal rights (in this case the legal right of ownership) if it would be deemed to be unjust to do so. In some situations the courts will use proprietary estoppel to transfer ownership rights, but in others, a more contractual approach is taken, and tenancies granted instead.

The courts will consider criteria very similar to those in resulting trusts, namely has a party to a relationship acted to their detriment, either by incurring expenditure or by some other act, in the belief that they own, or will gain an interest in the property, with that belief being encouraged by the true owner?

ACTIVITY 94

To understand how this doctrine can operate, read and make notes on the cases of *Pascoe* **v** *Turner* **[1979] 1 WLR 431 and** *Coombes* **v** *Smith* **[1986] 1 WLR 808. You may also find the case of** *Matharu* **v** *Matharu* **[1994] 2 FLR 597 of interest. All these cases are in** *Cases and Materials* **(7.5).**

The position may be complicated with payments to the mortgage loan if there is no express agreement or understanding as to how the property will be owned. As you have seen, indirect contributions by way of payment of bills, may not be sufficient to increase the shares of ownership. This may be particularly so with reference to cohabitees, where the court may see payments of this kind (or even contributions to the mortgage) as being nothing more than payments in lieu of rent. The issue reverts to, what was the intention?

7.9 Summary

Having completed this chapter, you should be clearer on the way in which the law assists married couples with regard to financial matters, where the wide powers of the court under the divorce provisions are not applicable. The traditional approach of land law and equity is relevant to property disputes, since matrimonial law does not cover this area to any great extent. The land law rules are also applicable to cohabitees, and this is the same regardless of whether they are living together, or their relationship has broken down. You may wish to reflect on the question of whether this is fair or not. Should the law treat non-married couples the same? The starting point for this analysis must be, why do people cohabit rather than marry? You may be asked questions like that in an examination, but the following End of Chapter Assessment Question is perhaps more typical.

7.10 End of Chapter Assessment Question

Simon and Janice have lived together for seven years. They bought their current house in 1991; each having sold previously owned properties. As Janice was still going through her divorce, the new house was conveyed into Simon's sole name. The relationship between Simon and Janice has now broken down, albeit they are still living in the same property.

The house is worth £120,000 with an endowment mortgage of £50,000. Janice contributed £40,000 towards the purchase price, with Simon contributing £30,000. Janice, despite only working part-time, has paid half the endowment fees.

Explain how the courts will assess her claim to be entitled to a half share in the property.

See *Cases and Materials* (7.7) for an outline answer.

CHAPTER EIGHT

DOMESTIC VIOLENCE

8.1   Objectives

By the end of this chapter you should be able to:

■ appreciate the historical background to domestic violence laws;

■ explain the multifaceted aspect of domestic violence legislation prior to the FLA 1996;

■ discuss reasons for change and evaluate the effects; and

■ understand and apply the law to hypothetical situations.

8.2   Introduction

Given the links between domestic violence remedies in civil law and rights to occupy property, it is appropriate for you to look at this area of law now. In addition, this chapter will be a little lighter, and act as a breather between property and the maintenance of children in **Chapter 9**. The topic of domestic violence is to be studied less on a 'law now and FLA 1996 later' basis, since the provisions of the FLA 1996 came into force in October 1997. You will be required to understand the previous legislation, since this will no doubt act as interpretative guidance for the courts. In addition, you must also be in a position to explain why the law has been changed.

8.3   Definitions and the Historical Background

To appreciate fully the reasons why laws to protect individuals against domestic violence have developed in the manner that they have, a historical perspective is needed. But first, try this task.

Write down your definition of domestic violence.

If you can, ask some friends what they think, and see if you reach consensus.

Is domestic violence, within your definition, permissible?

Within your definition you have probably referred to some form of physical violence, the assaulting of one person by another within the domestic sphere. Violence may be quite minor, such as a basic assault, or more severe or even include murder. You may feel that violence, whatever the extent, is permissible if carried out 'behind closed doors'. When speaking on the issue of reducing the age of consent for homosexual intercourse, Edwina Currie MP said:

> The state should be kept out of our personal lives . . . everybody is entitled to his or her privacy. What my neighbours get up to in private is their business, not mine. It is not for the state to interfere. (*The Telegraph*, 22 February 1994.)

Despite the difference in focus, i.e. homosexual intercourse, not domestic violence, isn't the principle the same?

8.3.1 THE WIFE AS CHATTEL

Even if you do not agree that domestic violence is permissible in society, the fact that violence has been condoned within marriage is a historical fact. Wives and children were for a long time deemed to be the chattels of the husband – his property to do with as he wished. If that included beating, no one would complain. Indeed, despite recent commentary to discredit the belief, 'by the common law a husband was allowed to beat his wife so long as he did it with a stick no bigger that his thumb' (per Lord Denning in *Davis* v *Johnson* [1979] AC 264 at page 270). The notion of change had begun to infiltrate social thinking by 1775; again to quote Lord Denning in *Davis* v *Johnson* at page 271:

> He was able, Blackstone says, to give his wife 'moderate correction'. But Blackstone goes on to tell us that by this time this power of correction began to be doubted: 'Yet the lower rank of people, who were always fond of the old common law, still claim and exert their ancient privilege' (Blackstone's *Commentaries*, vol. 1, 8th edn, 1775).

8.3.2 BATTERED WIVES AS A MATTER OF CONCERN

Society has now moved on from the concept of a wife as a possession: husband and wife are now seen as equals. In addition, the use of violence within the home, or domestic life, is seen to be wrong, or uncivilised. Steps to protect victims were not taken until the mid 1970s following a Select Committee report on the issue in 1975. Legislation was enacted in 1976 with jurisdiction in the county courts and High Court, and in 1978 provisions to give jurisdiction to the magistrates were enacted. You will be considering those shortly. The passing of civil legislation did not end the incidence of violence which did, and still does, continue. The influence of a patriarchal society, with its roots in the 'wife as chattel' theory, can be seen in the offence of rape. It was not until 1991 that 'marital rape' was recognised by the House of Lords as being a criminal offence. The legal validity for the proposition that rape within marriage did not exist was that when a woman consents to marriage she irrevocably consents to consortium with her husband. In the case of *R v R* [1991] 3 WLR 767 the House of Lords upheld a husband's conviction for raping his wife. As Lord Keith stated, 'marriage is in modern times regarded as a partnership of equals, and no longer one in which the wife must be the subservient chattel of the husband . . .'. Parliament took until 1994 and the Criminal Justice and Public Order Act to incorporate this ruling into statute.

As you can see, domestic violence is not a matter that has given rise to concern until quite recently. In addition the law has responded to different issues in different ways. Legislation has been enacted as and when problems were perceived to exist. The consequence was 'a hotchpotch of enactments of limited scope passed to meet specific situations or to strengthen the powers of specified courts' (per Lord Scarman in *Richards v Richards* [1983] 2 All ER 807). It is this hotchpotch that you will consider first, before turning to the amendments, and potential clarity, of the Family Law Act 1996.

8.3.3   JUST BATTERED WIVES?

Write down who you would assume to be the victim in domestic violence cases. Ask some of your friends and neighbours what their perception is. If this is an issue you have not really considered, it may be worth discussing further in a study group (if you belong to one). You may also find it useful (although certainly not required) to read *Women and Crime* **by Frances Heidensohn, published by Macmillan.**

The common perception will be that it is wives (or girlfriends) who will be the victims of domestic violence. This fits in with the stereotypes for the genders, that the male will be aggressive, stronger, and more prone to uncontrollable outbursts than the female. Whilst this is often the case, the fact is that women can be violent too. In some cases the violence will manifest itself differently, but it is true to say that the way in which the law, and indeed society, deals with violence by women against men is different. The legislation on domestic violence is available to both genders, but would a lawyer or judge query why a man didn't defend himself against such violence? Would the question of manliness be raised, not necessarily explicitly but implicitly? Would the female aggressor be treated, or castigated in the same way as a male aggressor? In criminal law, analysis of sentencing shows that women are more likely to receive lighter sentences, or to be treated as 'mad not bad', where violence is concerned. However, for the purposes of this chapter, the victim shall be referred to as female.

8.4   Options, other than Domestic Violence Legislation

The legislation you will study, including the FLA 1996, operates within the arena of civil law.

What other options may be available?

Clearly the other area of relevance is the criminal law. Domestic violence will normally include the commission of an offence in criminal law, and one that will be punishable in the criminal courts. The crime may range from simple assault, to the more serious crime of rape or murder.

If you were advising a client, would you suggest that criminal law options should be the first choice?

Despite the clear criminality involved with domestic violence, in many situations the civil law will be preferred. For many years it was a general principle of the police to refrain from intervention with cases of domestic violence – perhaps this was due to the historical background you read about earlier. Albeit that this 'principle' has now changed, prosecutions are still not always pursued. Until the Police and Criminal Evidence Act 1984 made a spouse a competent and compellable witness, evidence was difficult to adduce. It has been suggested by Cretney and Davies that many prosecutions still fail because the complainant fails to give evidence or withdraws the complaint, and because the prosecuting agency does not compel attendance (A. Cretney and G. Davies, 'Prosecuting ''Domestic'' Assault' [1996] Crim LR 162).

Write a list of other reasons why the criminal law may not be seen as providing an appropriate remedy.

In addition to the evidential problems, the criminal law is a slow process. The victim of violence may wish to see the perpetrator punished, which is the aim of the criminal law, but often their aim will be to gain protection. The ability to keep a person accused of domestic violence in custody until trial is limited. If an accused is released on bail, there is always the potential for more violence to occur since the involvement of the police may exacerbate the situation. Also, the charge brought may be quite minor, with an equally minor sentence upon conviction that in reality will do little to help the victim. For these sorts of reasons, the civil law is generally the preferred route to take.

8.5   Civil Remedies Generally

Civil law can be invoked to obtain a range of orders that attempt to provide a more suitable remedy for the victim. The range of orders available have been reduced under the FLA 1996, but will, in theory, still result in the same type of remedy. Whilst statute will often be the first port of call, there is a general power of the court to grant injunctions ancillary to existing legal rights. This inherent jurisdiction may be useful to obtain protection against violence where domestic violence statutes do not provide a remedy.

Read the headnote and extracts of the case *Khorasandjian* v *Bush* [1993] QB 727 in *Cases and Materials* (8.1). Write down the reasons why an injunction could be granted.

In this case, the individuals could not come within the then existing domestic violence legislation, and hence the plaintiff had to prove the existence of some other legal right. This was the tort of nuisance. As the defendant had acted contrary to the right to be free from nuisance, the court could also grant an injunction to prevent the nuisance continuing.

The relevance of the inherent jurisdiction will diminish now the FLA 1996, Part IV is in force, since the limitation of possible applicants is considerably changed as you will see later.

8.5.1   THE DOMESTIC VIOLENCE AND MATRIMONIAL PROCEEDINGS ACT 1976

This was the first of the domestic violence Acts to be brought into being, and will be referred to as the DVMPA 1976.

Read ss. 1 and 2, DVMPA 1976 in *Cases and Materials* (8.1.1). What types of order can the court make?

Under this Act, the county court has the power to make injunctive orders to protect spouses (and cohabiting couples) against domestic violence. The orders are termed non-molestation injunctions and ouster injunctions. (You will normally see them referred to not as injunctions but as orders, however, they are injunctive).

8.5.1.1   Non-molestation orders

Non-molestation orders are more common than ouster injunctions since they are the less drastic of the two.

How would you describe molestation?

The DVMPA 1976 itself does not define the term, leaving it to the judiciary to establish whether or not acts constitute molestation. This permits a certain amount of creativity, and certainly flexibility, which is an asset in this area. Your answer to **SAQ 80** should have included acts which fall short of actual violence, as violence *per se* is not needed to obtain this injunction. For example, in the case of *Horner* v *Horner* [1982] 2 All ER 495 the husband was prevented from harassing the wife after he had intercepted her on her way to the station, given her upsetting notes, and hung 'scurrilous' posters outside her place of work.

Whilst violence is not needed to obtain the order itself, it will be necessary to show that violence, by way of actual bodily harm, has occurred, to enable the court to attach a power of arrest to the order (s. 2(1)).

How might this be proven?

Invariably to prove that violence has occurred, photographs showing the injuries, or medical reports will be needed, or witnesses who saw the incident. If the police have been involved it may also be appropriate to refer to this.

If a power of arrest is attached to the order, the injunction will be copied to the local police station, to ensure that officers there know that an arrest can be carried out. Anyone arrested under such a provision will need to be brought before the court within 24 hours (subject to some exceptions).

Will the court always grant an injunction?

If the court does not believe the evidence, naturally it would be an abuse of process to issue an injunction. However, even in cases where molestation or violence is proved, the court may accept an undertaking by the respondent not to act in that way again. The problem with the granting of undertakings under the DVMPA 1976 is that whilst the breach of an undertaking may be treated as the breach of a court order, frequently the enforcement proceedings merely result in the making of the injunction. Certainly no power of arrest can be attached at the undertaking stage.

8.5.1.2   Ouster orders

These are orders by which the court can order one party to the relationship to leave the matrimonial home, regardless of their rights of ownership, and even regulate the distance within which the party is allowed to come near to the home.

Do the courts make these orders willingly?

The effect of the order is such that the courts have indicated a general unwillingness to make them unless it is clear that the situation requires it. The order is a Draconian one and should be regarded as such. To illustrate this, see the case of *Summers v Summers* [1986] 1 FLR 343 extracted in *Cases and Materials* (**8.1.1.1**).

What are the criteria used by the courts to make ousters?

The sections of the DVMPA 1976 you have looked at do not actually make any reference to the criteria to be applied. You would therefore assume that it should be within the courts' discretion, as in the case of non-molestation. However, the House of Lords in *Richards* v *Richards* [1983] 2 All ER 807 decided otherwise.

Read the extracts from *Richards* v *Richards* in *Cases and Materials* (8.1.1.1). What criteria do the courts have to consider before making the order?

(Note: the Matrimonial Homes Act 1967, s. 1 is re-enacted in the Matrimonial Homes Act 1983, s. 1.)

The House of Lords believed that as an ouster is in effect achieving the same as a regulatory order under the Matrimonial Homes Act (MHA) 1983, the applications should preferably be made under that statute. In the event that an application is made under the DVMPA 1976 (likely to arise since the notice periods are lower), the same MHA 1983 criteria should apply.

Do you agree with this?

Whilst it may be deemed beneficial to have some form of structure or foundation upon which to make a judicial decision, it could be argued that if Parliament had wished there to be criteria to help decide the issue, it would have included them, or at least clearly stated in the subsequent MHA 1983 that the criteria were relevant to DVMPA 1976 applications. In addition, as Hayes and Williams comment:

> [W]hilst this ruling imposed some order on the chaos which had been emerging, arguably it created as many problems as it resolved. In particular, no heed appears to have been given to whether it is proper always to treat an unmarried wife with no property rights in the 'matrimonial home' in the same way as a spouse with a statutory right of occupation' (*Family Law: Principles, Policy and Practice*, London: Butterworths, 1995).

8.5.1.3   Duration of orders

How long should an injunction under the DVMPA 1976 last?

This will depend both on the nature of the order sought, and also the status of the parties, i.e. whether they are married or not. Whilst the DVMPA 1976 (and also the MHA 1983) does not give any guidance on the matter, the courts treat the orders in a short-term category, intended to give the couple breathing space. One could suggest that the courts give sufficient time to allow the couple to commence divorce proceedings or, if unmarried, to separate and sort out any other arrangements. The presumption that these orders are 'first aid but not intensive care' has been emphasised in the *Practice Note* [1978] 2 All ER 1056, which you will find in *Cases and Materials* **(8.1.1.2)**.

8.5.1.4   Nature of application

Must an application for a DVMPA 1976 injunction be on notice?

If an application for protection against violence were only available on notice, it is suggested that this would possibly expose the victim to an increased risk of further injury. Hence, whilst it is possible to apply on notice, in many situations it will not be practicable. This is more so in cases of non-molestation than ouster where the courts balance the need for protection against the Draconian nature of the order.

The courts' attitude to this is illustrated in the extracts from *G v G (Ouster: Ex Parte Application)* [1990] 1 FLR 395; see *Cases and Materials* **(8.1.1.2)**.

If ex parte orders are made, they will invariably be of a very short duration to protect the applicant until a full hearing with both parties can take place.

8.5.2   THE DOMESTIC PROCEEDINGS AND MAGISTRATES' COURTS ACT 1978

The inclusion of powers of protection in the 1978 Act was to achieve a quick and easily accessible forum for those who could not afford to take proceedings in the county court under the DVMPA 1976. The orders available in the magistrates' courts reflect those under the DVMPA 1976, but are less flexible and subject to more restrictive application criteria.

Read ss. 16 and 18, DPMCA 1978 in *Cases and Materials* (8.1.2). As with the DVMPA 1976, identify the types of orders, and also write down the qualifying criteria.

The DPMCA 1978 also has two types of orders, the personal protection order, and the exclusion order.

8.5.2.1 The applicants

Whilst the DVMPA 1976 is available to both spouses and cohabitants, the DPMCA 1978 is only available to married couples, thereby automatically restricting the protection available to those who are not married. The orders can be used to protect children of the family.

8.5.2.2 The personal protection order

Under the DVMPA 1976, a non-molestation order could be obtained subject to the discretion of the court and, as you have seen, without the need to satisfy specific criteria. This is not the same under the DPMCA 1978, as you will know having read s. 16. The criteria you should have listed in the earlier activity for obtaining a personal protection order are:

■ the respondent has used violence against the person of the applicant; or

■ the respondent has threatened to use violence against the person of the applicant; and

■ it is necessary to protect the applicant.

If all the above criteria are met an order may be made.

Would the facts of *Horner* v *Horner* (see 8.5.1.1) fit into this category?

The matters for the consideration of the magistrates are totally based on violence or the threat of violence. The hanging out of scurrilous posters would not fall within this set of criteria.

8.5.2.3   The exclusion order

This order achieves a similar end to that of the ouster. Under the DPMCA 1978 there are criteria established, in s. 16(3). You should have noted that they require:

■   the respondent has used violence against the applicant; or

■   the respondent has threatened violence against the applicant, and has used violence against another; or

■   the respondent has contravened a personal protection order and has threatened violence; and

■   the applicant is in danger of physical injury if the order is not made.

If these are proven the court can regulate the occupation of the home, but you will note that the magistrates can only deal with the home itself, they have no powers to exclude from the vicinity of the home, as does the DVMPA 1976.

How do the criteria in the DPMCA 1978 for exclusion orders compare with those imposed by the House of Lords in DVMPA 1976 applications?

Despite the tendency of the courts in DVMPA 1976 ouster applications to focus on conduct and anti-social behaviour, you may agree that the *Richards*, MHA 1983-style criteria do have a more holistic approach. They require the court to consider a range of circumstances. The DPMCA 1978, by contrast, purely focuses on violence. Also, there are some idiosyncrasies in the DPMCA 1978; in s. 16(3)(b), for example, evidence of violence to some other person is one of the criteria.

When does that violence have to have taken place?

If you go back to the section, you will find no guidance at all, because the Act does not require there to be proximity between the threats and the previous violence. Therefore an applicant could refer to the respondent's violence when 16-years-old at the local football match – it still fits the criteria.

8.5.2.4   Enforcing the orders

How can these orders be enforced?

This falls under s. 18, powers of arrest for breach of the orders. The section requires the court to be satisfied that the respondent has physically injured the applicant and that it is likely to happen again. This is almost exactly the same as the DVMPA 1976, except that that Act speaks in terms of actual bodily harm. The effects of granting a power of arrest are no different.

8.5.2.5   Nature of proceedings

Do the magistrates have the power to grant orders on an ex parte basis?

Although the procedure is not referred to as ex parte, the magistrates can act in situations of urgency and without the respondent being present. In the magistrates' court the order will be called an expedited order. In addition, if the matter is urgent, s. 16(5) permits the court to act, even though it may not be empanelled correctly. Any expedited orders made will not take effect until they have been served on the respondent (at the earliest) or may take effect at a later date. This latter timing is unlikely: if the matter is urgent and needs to be expedited, there will be little reason to delay the commencement of the order. Unlike the DVMPA 1976, the DPMCA 1978 states how long an expedited order may last, i.e. a maximum of 28 days or the date when proceedings on notice are commenced (s. 16(8)). This does not in reality create any substantial benefits over the DVMPA 1976, where ex parte orders normally last until the matter is heard on notice.

Draw up a list of advantages and disadvantages of the two statutes above.

Despite the relative expense involved in taking proceedings in the county court, the DVMPA 1976 jurisdiction is more frequently used than that of the magistrates. Certainly the DVMPA 1976 has a greater degree of flexibility in its approach to orders, but in some respects it is just as restrictive, e.g. powers of arrest are limited, the courts do not like ousting a person from their home, and the orders are only short-term. Another factor which may dissuade practitioners from advising clients to use the magistrates is the availability of legal aid. It may be perceived to be easier to get legal aid for the county court than for the magistrates' court, where matters are deemed to be simple and not always warranting legal assistance. Finally, the issue of unpredictability has been suggested by Hayes and Williams as being a factor acting against using the magistrates' court. Practitioners will often know a local judge and his/her attitudes better than the members of a local bench whose identity will be unknown until the date of the hearing.

8.6   The Family Law Act 1996

This Act, in Part IV, sets out a new coherent scheme for making occupation orders and non-molestation orders, and in so doing will repeal the DVMPA 1976 and DPMCA 1978 provisions set out above. This part of the Act was added in at a late stage, after the Family Homes and Domestic Violence Bill was defeated in the Lords and withdrawn (notably after a media campaign against giving cohabitants the same rights as spouses). The intention is to remove the complexity of the previous legislation, and to introduce a consistent range of criteria under which applications are to be assessed.

8.6.1   NON-MOLESTATION ORDERS

Read s. 42, FLA 1996 in *Cases and Materials* (8.2.1) noting what the order seeks to achieve, who can apply and when the order can be made.

8.6.1.1 The order

In establishing what a non-molestation order is, the FLA 1996 does not go any further than the DVMPA 1976, and indeed what is included in 'molestation' is not specifically defined. Hence, molestation will, in all probability, be treated exactly as it always has been. The precedent cases under the DVMPA 1976 will therefore remain good law. As with DVMPA 1976 practice, the non-molestation order under the FLA 1996 will be expressed either generally (i.e. the respondent shall not harass, molest or otherwise interfere with), or may refer to individual acts (s. 42(6)).

8.6.1.2 The applicant

Under the terms of s. 42(1)(a) and (b), the applicant must be an 'associated person' or a 'relevant child'.

Write down who you think will be classed as an 'associated person', and a 'relevant child'.

Unlike the range of applicants under the DVMPA 1976 and DPMCA 1978, the FLA 1996 has sought to be far less restrictive, and also to recognise that domestic violence does not just occur between spouses and cohabitants. Section 62 sets out the individuals who will be classed as 'associated' and also 'relevant children'.

Read s. 62 in *Cases and Materials* (8.2.1.1), and list all those who will be included.

As you can see, although the section refers to the traditional spouses and heterosexual cohabitants, it also includes former spouses and cohabitants. Same sex couples will be covered too under the 'live or have lived in the same household, otherwise than due to being an employee, tenant, lodger or boarder' provision.

Why will people be excluded if in any of the above four categories?

The reason for this distinction is explained by Bond, Bridge et al thus:

> the Law Commission (Law Com No. 207, May 1992) was of the view that it was inappropriate for the new jurisdiction to be enlisted to resolve disputes between tenant and landlord or those in similar relationships or to deal with sexual harassment at work. It was thought that the remedies provided under property or employment law were more suitable. (*Blackstone's Guide to the Family Law Act 1996*, London: Blackstone Press, 1996.)

Do you agree with this view?

Whilst some of this reasoning may be acceptable, it is hard to understand why ex-spouses who no longer live together should be able to apply to gain protection, and yet a resident landlord who has evicted a violent tenant cannot do the same if that tenant continues to harass or molest him/her.

You should note the restrictions imposed in s. 42(4), FLA 1996 in relation to applications by those associated persons who are associated due to an agreement to marry.

8.6.1.3 When can the order be made?

A non-molestation order can be made, even if it has not been formally applied for, if the court feels the order would be of benefit to a party in any ongoing family proceedings (s. 42(2)(b)). Applicants may wish to apply within the context of existing family proceedings or may wish to make a freestanding application.

The court may make a non-molestation order having had regard to 'all the circumstances including the need to secure the health, safety and well-being . . . of the applicant . . . and any relevant child' (s. 42(5)).

Is this better than the previous discretionary test in the DVMPA 1976, or the violence test in the DPMCA 1978?

In deciding whether or not to make an order, the court still retains its discretion, but must base its decision on the factors mentioned. The previous approach, with its emphasis on the violence or conduct of the respondent, was such that 'the response of the court would be dictated by the nature of the defendant's behaviour, rather than the effect upon the applicant or children concerned' (Law Commission No. 207, para. 3.6, as quoted in Bond, Bridge et al, *Blackstone's Guide to the Family Law Act 1996*).

8.6.1.4 Duration of the order

As you will recall, the DVMPA 1976 and DPMCA 1978 did not refer to specific periods for which the orders were to last. The practice was only to make orders for a short period of time, to allow other steps to be taken, such as issuing divorce proceedings. The FLA 1996 does not change this discretionary aspect of the order, but does clearly state in s. 42(7) that the order can be made 'until further order'. Hence implying the possibility of an almost indefinite order.

8.6.2 OCCUPATION ORDERS

These have replaced the ouster and exclusion orders, and are dealt with in ss. 33 to 38, FLA 1996 (excluding s. 34). The FLA 1996 is theoretically making the legislation simpler; however, if you look at these sections you may question this fact. The full text of these sections will be found in *Cases and Materials* (8.2.2). The basic principles for all applications are similar, what differs is the extent of the criteria to be applied and the available duration of the order. In these sections you will encounter references to other parts of the FLA 1996 which have not been extracted. Do not worry about this. What you are after are the basic principles.

8.6.2.1 Section 33

Read s. 33 in *Cases and Materials* (8.2.2) and write down who will be able to use it, the order that can be made, the criteria and the duration.

This section applies to those applicants who have some form of interest in the property as established in s. 33(1). It will cover spouses who have rights to occupy by virtue of status, joint owners, whether married or not, or individuals who are joint tenants. Additionally the applicant must have occupied, or have intended to occupy the property with the respondent as their home.

The nature of the order that the applicant can seek is a regulatory one, and may do any of the following:

■ enforce the applicant's right to remain in the property;

■ permit the applicant to enter the premises, and remain there;

■ regulate the parties' occupation;

■ prevent the respondent exercising any rights to occupy the property or regulating any matrimonial homes rights the respondent may have;

■ require the respondent to vacate the property;

■ prevent the respondent from entering a defined area within which the property is located.

In effect this does little to extend the existing law.

When being asked to make an order, the court is provided with a statutory list of criteria in subsection (6). These factors are:

■ the housing needs and resources of the parties and any relevant children;

■ the financial resources of the parties;

■ the effect of the order or decision not to make an order on the health, safety or well-being of the parties or any relevant child; and

■ conduct of the parties to each other and otherwise.

Does this add to the test from *Richards* v *Richards*?

The FLA 1996 has tweaked the criteria around, and the inclusion of the effect of the order must surely be beneficial. It will be interesting to see the extent to which the Draconian nature of occupation orders will affect the courts' power to make orders. This is especially so given the duty included in s. 33(7), where the court 'shall make an order' if the applicant or a relevant child would suffer significant harm if the order were not made. This duty to make an order if harm would otherwise be suffered is not absolute. The section introduces a 'balance of harm test' whereby the harm caused to the applicant by not making the order must exceed that harm caused to the respondent by making the order. How the courts will interpret this test, and the factors that will tip the balance, remain to be seen.

The possible period for the order to last is established in subsection (10) as being that period defined by the court in the order, or the occurrence of any event indicated in the order, or until further order – meaning indefinitely unless and until the court revokes it.

8.6.2.2 Sections 35 and 36

Read ss. 35 and 36 in *Cases and Materials* (8.2.2) and make notes on the same issues as you did for s. 33.

Section 35 covers ex-spouses where one of the couple has a right to occupy the home, whilst the other does not. An example where this might arise is where the husband is the sole owner and the wife had matrimonial home rights. On divorce, she would lose these rights due to the change in her status. In this situation the ex-wife would be able to make an application under s. 35 only in respect of the former matrimonial home or a property which was intended to be a matrimonial home.

If an order is sought, it may be to ensure that the applicant remain in the property if already there, or to be permitted to return to the property. It may also regulate the respondent's occupation and ability to enter into the area in which the home is located.

When deciding these cases the courts will again have regard to the circumstances, including the factors in s. 33(6). In addition to the factors for applicants under s. 33 the court must look at the length of time since the parties separated and also the time since the dissolution of the marriage and whether any other proceedings are ongoing (i.e. ancillary claims in divorce).

The balance of harm test applies to this section.

Is it right to give an ex-wife rights in the former matrimonial home?

Naturally this would depend on how long ago the marriage was ended, and it is not envisaged that the courts will be ousting an owner 10, 15 or 20 years after the other spouse left. However, once the divorce is made, if the parties are not living together, under the existing law, there is little that can be done to obtain occupation of the ex-matrimonial home. If the wife is claiming the home as part of the post divorce financial settlement, but has nowhere else to go in the meantime, it might be perfectly justifiable to 'oust' the husband (if he can maintain himself elsewhere) until the outcome of the proceedings.

Any order made under this section will have a limited lifespan – initially the order can last for up to six months. It may be extended on one or more occasions for similar periods.

Section 36 applies to cohabitants who are not co-owners/tenants, or former cohabitants who are not co-owners/tenants. The order that can be sought is one potentially to remove the cohabitant/former cohabitant with property rights, or to regulate his/her use of the property. It will be granted only after the court has considered all the circumstances of the case including the matters specified in s. 36(6) (which are very similar to s. 35). When the courts are considering the 'nature of the relationship' under s. 36(6)(e), they must 'have regard to the fact that [the couple] have not given each other the commitment involved in marriage' (s. 41(2)).

If the courts are faced with an application to remove a partner due to his/her violence, should s. 41(2) make any substantive difference?

As part of a package of considerations, you may agree that so far as occupation of a home is concerned, where otherwise the applicant has no rights at all, the fact that the couple are unmarried may be relevant. Many of you will not see the significance of the commitment as having any role to play. The reasons why a couple do not marry may have nothing to do with the level of commitment they feel to one another. Arguably by including this provision, the law is prejudging cohabitation and declaring it 'second-best' and certainly not indicative to any long-term intentions. It may be suggested that this provision was included to ensure the passage of the Bill through Parliament after its earlier defeat as the Family Homes and Domestic Violence Bill.

The duration of s. 36 orders is also more limiting than other occupation orders. The initial order may last for six months, with the scope to extend it once only for another maximum period of six months.

SAQ 100

If a cohabitant is seeking rights of ownership via a constructive trust, will this be achieved in a 12-month period? Will the applicant necessarily have alternative accommodation after her occupation order has ended and before her property action is concluded?

Given the current state of the civil jurisdiction, and the lengthy details encountered, it may be that s. 36 merely operates as a stop gap which will fall short of what is practically needed.

8.6.3   NATURE OF PROCEEDINGS

As with the preceding DVMPA 1976 and DPMCA 1978, it will be possible to obtain the FLA 1996 occupation order or non-molestation order on an ex parte basis. Consistent with the rest of the FLA 1996, the courts' powers to do so will be set out in the Act itself, including the factors which will support the making of the order without notice.

ACTIVITY 107

Read s. 45, FLA 1996 in *Cases and Materials* (8.2.3) and list the factors to be taken into account. Do you think these will be workable?

The issues the court must have regard to before making an order on an ex parte basis are founded on common sense, and probably reflect the factors that the judiciary already consider before making ex parte orders. By including s. 45 the FLA 1996 merely reaffirms the requirement of urgency that should be part of the making of orders in the absence of the respondent.

8.6.4   UNDERTAKINGS

As you saw earlier, in many situations the court will accept an undertaking from the respondent rather than impose an order. The giving of an undertaking does not have the same 'wrong-doer' stigma as being subject to an order, hence the popularity of them. The ability to accept undertakings will continue under the FLA 1996, and again statutory provision is made for this.

Read s. 46, FLA 1996 in *Cases and Materials* (8.2.4). Do you see the limitations imposed on the accepting of undertakings?

As well as limiting the situations in which the court can accept an undertaking to those where the court would not wish to attach a power of arrest to the order, the section also states that the undertaking is enforceable as if an order of the court. Whilst this does not change the previous situation, the fact that this is clearly stated may make a difference. Some respondents to domestic violence actions see an undertaking as an easy way out, and as it is not incorporated into an order, as something that could be broken easily. In practice, enforcement of undertakings is not highly successful, the best normally being achievable being the making of an order. Possibly this will now change.

8.6.5   ENFORCEMENT

The breach of an order will carry certain penalties, the prospect of committal for breach being the normal one. As under the previous statutory provisions, the court may also attach a power of arrest to any order made, including ex parte orders. The details of the courts' powers are set out in s. 47.

Read s. 47, FLA 1996 in *Cases and Materials* (8.2.5). Does the power of arrest differ from before?

The basis upon which a power of arrest may be attached is not that different, is it? The respondent must have used or threatened violence to the person of the applicant or a relevant child. What is missing is wording along the lines of 'and it appears that he is likely to do so again'.

Do you think that the wording in the FLA 1996 'unless satisfied that in all the circumstances of the case the applicant or child will be adequately protected without such a power of arrest' implies the same protection as the previous legislation?

You could argue that the FLA 1996 is a little more flexible. Adequate protection may not just mean protection from violence, it could refer to molestation short of violence, which is not apparent in the DVMPA 1976 and DPMCA 1978.

Another slight change in emphasis exists in the FLA 1996 in that it states that the court 'shall attach a power of arrest' to the order, unless it believes the applicant will be suitably protected. The previous legislation was not so mandatory, stating that the court 'may attach' the power of arrest.

Powers of arrest may be granted in ex parte situations. Here the only difference is that the court must believe that there is a risk of significant harm on an immediate basis. The need for significant harm is to reflect the harsh nature of attaching the power of arrest in a situation where only one party's side of the story has been heard.

8.7   Stalking

In 1997 after much publicity, the Protection From Harassment Act 1997 was passed which creates a new, criminally enforceable offence of stalking. In addition, the Act introduces civil remedies, which will include injunctive relief, as well as the prospect of a victim seeking damages. Whilst this Act may not be primarily focused on the domestic violence victim, the clear links with harassment and molestation may be another means to obtain protection. The victim will not have to be 'associated' in the sense of the FLA 1996; this is a clear benefit. However, although the victim may obtain civil law redress, the criminal law provisions will arguably suffer from the same problems outlined at the start of this chapter, notably the delay and the nature of the punishment that will ensue.

To understand the scope of the legislation, read the extracts from the Act in *Cases and Materials* (8.3), and also the extract from an article by T. Lawson-Cruttenden, which predates the Act. Note his criticisms and see if you agree with them?

8.8   Summary

Domestic violence is an issue within family law that has, over the last two decades, become more prominent. The realisation that violence does occur in the home environment has led to a variety of statutes being passed to deal with specific problems as they were seen to arise. The resulting plethora of legislation led to claims of undue complexity and overlapping jurisdictions. The FLA 1996 has tried to overcome this by introducing a coherent set of rules and orders that will be available to a wider range of applicants in a variety of courts. You should now understand the scheme under the FLA 1996, but be able to approach this using the previous legislation to assist in interpretation.

8.9 End of Chapter Assessment Question

Four years ago Ingrid began to cohabit with Max, in his three bedroomed house. Ingrid has no rights of ownership.

Max has always been temperamental with frequent bouts of depression. In the last 18 months these have become far more common, and Max has started to exhibit violent tendencies. Ingrid, in the last two months, has visited the local hospital's accident and emergency department twice with broken ribs, bruising, and a dislocated shoulder after being attacked by Max.

Max is always apologetic when he realises what he has done and always swears never to do anything like that again.

Advise Ingrid:

(a) what rights she has to obtain protection under the law in force before October 1997;

(b) whether those rights will change under the Family Law Act 1996.

See *Cases and Materials* (8.5) for an outline answer.

CHAPTER NINE

CHILD SUPPORT

9.1 Objectives

By the end of this chapter you should be able to:

■ explain the scope of the Child Support Acts;

■ describe who is subject to the Acts and the situations in which the CSA 1991 and CSA 1995 take precedence;

■ discuss the CSA 1991 and CSA 1995 formula and apply it to hypothetical facts;

■ evaluate the claims that the CSA 1991 and CSA 1995 are arbitrary and unfair;

■ compare the CSA 1991 and CSA 1995 with the jurisdiction of other statutes.

9.2 Introduction

The legislation governing child support and maintenance has undergone a major change in the last seven years, with the implementation of the Child Support Acts (CSA) 1991 and 1995. These Acts mark a more interventionist role for the state, and emphasise the responsibility of parents to care for children, if only on a financial footing. The impact of the two Acts has been widespread, but the CSA 1991 and CSA 1995 do not have total domination of child support: other statutes still have a supplementary role to play. You will, therefore, in this chapter concentrate on the CSA 1991 and CSA 1995 but will also look at the interplay between the various provisions in other legislation. This will lead in to your study on children and the law relating to child care.

9.3 What Sort of Children?

This may seem to be a strange heading, but do not forget that in this section we are talking about all children and not just those children whose parents are separating, or going through a divorce. The obligation to support a child is not dependent upon the status of the parent as married but purely upon the status of being a parent.

SAQ 102

Does this mean that only birth parents are liable to maintain children?

Whilst some of the statutory provisions reflect only the birth parents' liability to support, the blood relationship is not necessary to create obligations. If you think about the reality of family life, many children will be cared for and supported within stepfamilies, or possibly with other family members. From a moral perspective these carers will also have obligations towards the child. Therefore, for each of the statutory provisions that you study, you will have to ensure that you are clear on the status of the child, or family that is caught by the provisions. For example, as you will see, the CSA 1991 and CSA 1995 place a statutory obligation upon birth parents to support their children, whether those parents be married, separated, have never lived together or possibly even unknown.

ACTIVITY 111

As you go through this chapter make sure that you draw up a table or diagram, on a separate sheet of paper, to highlight the differences between the legislative provisions, focussing on such issues as status etc.

9.4 The Child Support Act 1991

No doubt some of you will have experienced the impact of the CSA 1991 at first hand, or at least know someone who has had to deal with the Child Support Agency. The CSA 1991 (and note that the Act will be referred to as the CSA 1991 – any references to the Child Support Agency will be to the Agency) came into force in 1993. The long-term aim is to remove child support from the hands of the courts and to make the assessment, collection and payment of support an administrative process. Arguably the implementation was designed to reinforce the notion of family values and to promote the responsibility of parents towards their children. Cynically, but correctly, the CSA 1991 was also introduced to cut back the amount of welfare benefits that were being paid out to single parents.

The changes that have been made by the CSA 1991 are:

■ to introduce an Agency with responsibility for assessing child maintenance and enforcing payment of the same;

■ to achieve consistency in maintenance payments by applying a strict assessment formula to all cases;

■ to remove the ability of other agencies – i.e. the courts – to make child support assessments.

9.4.1 THE CHILD SUPPORT AGENCY

The Agency is a national agency which 'belongs' to the Department of Social Security. It is divided into regional centres (six in all), each centre taking responsibility for the assessment of child support of individuals within its area.

Staff dealing with the collation of information and assessment of child maintenance are known as child support officers. This collation of information, assessment of levels of support and enforcement of payment is the main function of the Agency. The Agency has been the subject of much criticism for its inaccuracies in calculating assessments, and its overall inefficiency in contacting absent parents to enforce maintenance payments. Despite its earlier problems on this front, it would appear that some of these difficulties have been resolved, or at least, the nature of the service has improved.

In *Cases and Materials* (9.1.1), you will find extracts from the Agency's target performance tables as published by the Child Poverty Action Group to illustrate the improvement that has been achieved by the Agency.

9.4.2 TO WHOM DOES THE ACT APPLY?

The CSA 1991 places a duty on 'each parent of a qualifying child' to be 'responsible for maintaining him' (s. 1(1)). To meet this duty the 'absent parent shall be taken to have met his responsibility to maintain any qualifying child . . . by making periodical payments . . . of such amount, and at such intervals, as may be determined in accordance with the provisions of [the] Act' (s. 1(2)). These two extracts highlight new terminology, which is applicable to the CSA 1991, and refers to those subject to the CSA 1991, namely a 'qualifying child' and 'absent parent'. In addition, the CSA 1991 refers to a 'person with care' just to complete the set.

Write down your definitions of these three terms.

Then compare your definition with those set out in s. 3, CSA 1991 which you will find in *Cases and Materials* (9.1.2).

Does this really help? The definitions provided seem a little circular. What is meant by a child? Who is a parent? As you will learn in **Chapter 10**, there are differing meanings that can be applied to these words. The CSA 1991 further defines a child in s. 55. 'Parent' and 'person with care' are referred to in the interpretation section, s. 54, but these further interpretations again are not very helpful.

Look at these definitions in *Cases and Materials* (9.1.2). Are they any closer to your own?

9.4.2.1 Qualifying child

The meaning of 'qualifying child' is not problematic, in the sense of a 'child' but the decision as to their being qualifying relates to the parents.

A parent will be a legal parent, that is a biological parent or a parent by adoption. If the child has been conceived by medical reproductive techniques, then special rules will apply. You will learn later about parental responsibility under the Children Act 1989 and how this can be gained by obtaining certain orders under that Act. For CSA 1991 purposes, a person with parental responsibility will not automatically be classified as a 'legal parent': the crucial factor is the blood link or the status of adoptive parent.

9.4.2.2 Absent parent

For a parent to be 'absent' they must not live in the same household as the child and the child must live with a person with care. This would in many cases be the father of the child, for example where a married couple have separated (whether or not they divorce) where the child remains with the mother and the father lives elsewhere. If the child in this situation were living with the paternal grandparents, then both mother and father would be deemed to be 'absent parents'.

9.4.2.3 Person with care

A person with care will normally be a parent, but this need not be so as you just saw in the example above. To be classed as a person with care, the child must have their home with that person, and must be provided with day-to-day care by them.

In many cases, this day-to-day care may not be consistently provided by the same person. You may have a separated couple where the mother cares for the child during weekdays, and the father has contact at weekends, when the child lives with him and he provides day-to-day care. The CSA 1991 will acknowledge such shared care situations and the assessment of maintenance payable can be rejigged to reflect the extent of care provided by the minority carer. So, in our example of the father caring for the child at weekends, he will in a year provide almost one-third of the child's care. As an absent parent he would be required to pay child support, but a full assessment would be inappropriate given the extent to which he provides care. The assessment would need to be amended to reflect the father's caring role.

9.4.2.4 Habitual residence

The jurisdiction of the CSA 1991 is only wide enough to cover those habitually resident in the United Kingdom (s. 44(1)). All the relevant individuals, namely the absent parent, person with care and qualifying child must be resident. If one or more is not so resident, the CSA 1991 cannot be used to seek support.

9.4.2.5   Denial of parentage

As the responsibility to make maintenance payments falls on biological parents there is clearly no requirement for the parents to be a married couple – unmarried parents cannot escape liability. (As you will learn later an unmarried father may have no other rights or obligations towards his child other than to pay maintenance.) In some situations an unmarried father will wish to dispute paternity. The fact that paternity is denied should not be treated as a routine stage in the process, and assumptions should not be made about paternity on a basis of 'men always deny it'. If paternity is disputed, the assessment procedure should be brought to a halt to enable the paternity issue to be concluded – this means that no maintenance will be required. If, however, the father only denies paternity after an assessment has been made, payments will continue as normal, but may be refunded if paternity is disproved. Hence if paternity is to be disputed, it should be disputed at the earliest stage possible.

The procedure to be adopted in these cases is for the child support officers to interview both the absent parent and the person with care (who will normally be the other parent). Reduced price DNA testing will also be available, although it cannot be forced onto either party. Failure to undergo testing can be used as an adverse inference in deciding the issue. If testing is undertaken, and paternity disproved, any fees incurred by the alleged father will be returned.

9.4.3   WHEN WILL THE CSA 1991 BE USED?

This is an area that can be confusing to a student; however, by identifying the key rules, the simplicity of the system can be grasped. In theory at least, *all* payments of child support are to be dealt with under the CSA 1991 and through the Agency. To accomplish this, all existing child maintenance agreements and orders were to be taken on by the Agency by the end of the 1990s in addition to the Agency dealing with all new cases of child maintenance. In 1995 there was a partial U-turn, and now there has been an indefinite deferral of taking on applications where agreements already exist and where there are no welfare benefits payments. In addition to this change regarding full implementation, there are still some ways to avoid having to use the Agency.

ACTIVITY114

Read ss. 4 and 6, CSA 1991 in *Cases and Materials* (9.1.3) and try to establish when the CSA 1991 will take effect.

How did you get on? The CSA 1991 does not seem to pride itself on the simplicity of its language, however, you should have identified that there are situations where an application to the Agency *must* be made and situations where an application *may* be made.

9.4.3.1   Must be used

Let us look first at the mandatory section, i.e. s. 6. Under the provisions of this section, a parent with care must allow the Agency to make an assessment for child support under the CSA 1991 when that parent is receiving any of the following state welfare benefits:

- income support;

- family credit;

- other prescribed benefits (being income related job seekers allowance and disability working allowance).

What is the position if the child is not being cared for by a parent, but where the carer is in receipt of benefit?

In this situation, the person with care is not obliged to make an application, and may utilise s. 4 instead.

Can the parent with care refuse to authorise the application?

You should have been able to provide some form of answer to this from s. 6(2). Under this subsection authorisation to make an assessment is not required if by so doing 'there would be a risk of [the parent], or of any child living with her, suffering harm or undue distress as a result'. The meaning of harm or undue distress is not defined in the Act, and hence will depend on the interpretation of the child support officers or any tribunal dealing with complaints against the Agency. The child support officers when making decisions on undue harm or influence are assisted by guidance published by the Department of Social Security which refers to the dictionary definitions of harm and distress. However, you should note that this guidance is not legally binding. Situations that may be seen as falling within the exemption include:

- where the child was conceived as a result of rape or sexual abuse;

- the absent parent has sexually assaulted a child living in the household of the parent with care.

What will happen if the child support officer believes that there are no grounds for the exemption applying?

If this situation arises, then s. 46 will apply. You may have suggested that some form of financial penalty would apply, and this is exactly what happens.

Read s. 46, CSA 1991 in *Cases and Materials* (9.1.3.1) and note the process if the parent with care does not co-operate.

Failure to comply will not automatically reduce the benefits payable: initially the child support officer must serve written notification on the parent to elicit the reasons why they are not co-operating. Only if the response (if any) does not provide reasonable grounds will a 'reduced benefit direction' be made. The reduction in benefit will last for three years (it may be for a lesser period although the situations when this will happen are limited). After the expiry of those three years there is the possibility that the parent with care will be subject to another reduced benefit direction if they continue to fail to co-operate (Child Support (Maintenance Assessment Procedure) Regulations 1992 and Child Support (Miscellaneous Amendments) Regulations 1996).

The amount of the reduction in benefit is not inconsiderable: it amounts to 40 per cent of the income support allowances. The Child Poverty Action Group put this at a reduction of £19.66 per week in 1997/98. When the total amount of benefit for a single adult is set at £49.15 (before any additional premiums) this reduction is, it is suggested, harsh, or at least a strong motivator to co-operate.

Read s. 2, CSA 1991 in *Cases and Materials* (9.1.3.1). Will this make a difference to the making of a reduced benefit direction?

Whilst the welfare of the child is normally relevant to legislation dealing with children's issues, with respect to the CSA 1991 it is only applicable as a consideration when the exercise of discretion is in question. The imposition of a reduced benefit direction is arguably a discretionary matter, the section states that the child support officer 'may . . . give a reduced benefit direction'. Additionally, the question of whether the failure to co-operate is reasonable is also subject to discretion, which will necessitate the consideration of the child's welfare.

Would it make any difference if the parent with care had obtained a court order for child maintenance before the implementation of the CSA 1991?

In some cases the existence of a pre-CSA 1991 agreement or court order will prevent the Agency from acting. However, if the parent with care is claiming benefits, this is not so, and the CSA 1991 must be used, even if there is a pre-existing order. Any maintenance assessment by the Agency will overrule the previous order, and this will not be capable of resurrection if the parent with care ceases their benefit claim.

9.4.3.2 May be used

If the individual with care of the qualifying child is not a parent, regardless of whether they are on welfare benefits, there is no compulsion to use the Agency. The same is true of parents with care who are not claiming welfare benefits. Section 4 is applicable here giving the person with care the ability to seek an assessment.

From your earlier reading you will have noted that there are limitations on the use that can be made of s. 4. First, it cannot be used where a maintenance assessment is already in force under s. 6 (s. 4(9)). Secondly, s. 4 cannot be used if there is a pre-April 1993 maintenance agreement or court order in force (not necessarily pre-1993), or the parent with care is on benefit as specified for s. 6 purposes (s. 4(10)).

If the Agency is being used voluntarily there may be a fee payable for the administration of the application.

Can you think of any reasons why an application may be made voluntarily?

Voluntary applications may be made due to the perception that more maintenance will be obtained from the absent parent. Equally, if there are concerns as to the reliability of payments, the fact that a formal assessment has been made may result in a more consistent payment regime. For unmarried parents, the CSA 1991 is one of only two Acts under which child support can be gained – it may be that the CSA 1991 has a higher profile and so is resorted to more often.

Read s. 8 (1), (2) and (3), CSA 1991 in *Cases and Materials* (9.1.3.2). What will the effect of this be?

Section 8 establishes a prohibition on court involvement where the CSA 1991 is applicable and a child support officer could make an assessment. This does not mean that the assessment has been made: the Agency can decline to assess an application. If a case could fall within the Agency's remit, no application can be made to the court for an order.

What would an applicant do if no assessment were made?

The inability of the court to make child support orders may be one reason for voluntarily using the Agency. As all claims for support involving a biological child are caught by the CSA 1991 and are capable of being assessed under this Act, there are few situations where the court can now play a role. If the Agency refuses to assess (even though it could), the applicant may be able to argue that the case falls out of the Agency's remit and could be decided by the courts. This would be very tenuous. More likely the applicant would have to seek further review by the Agency.

9.4.4   AVOIDING THE CSA 1991

For those parents with care who are claiming benefit, it is not possible to avoid the CSA 1991 and the Agency. Those persons and parents with care who would fall within s. 4 do have an alternative to consider.

Read s. 8(5), CSA 1991 in *Cases and Materials* (9.1.4). In what situations does this give the court the power to act?

This subsection permits the courts to make consent orders where the person or parent with care would be a voluntary s. 4 applicant. The parties must have a written agreement, which may be negotiated after April 1993. As you can see from the wording of the subsection itself, the fact that the written agreement may not otherwise be legally enforceable is immaterial. The agreement has to be more than an expression of willingness to make payments, so if for example, the father has said he would be willing to pay £40 per week for the child, this would not amount to an agreement unless the mother has agreed to it. If this agreement were to become incorporated into a consent order, the court would have to replicate the agreement in 'all material respects' (s. 8(5)(b)). The fact of incorporating the written agreement into a consent order will make it legally enforceable. If this consent order needs to be changed in the future, it is unlikely that the court would have power to vary the order as s. 8(3) would prohibit it. However, there would appear to be no prohibition on the parties negotiating a new agreement to be embodied in a new consent order.

If the court order predates the implementation of the CSA 1991, the court retains its powers to vary or revoke the order since access will be denied to the CSA 1991 (s. 4(10), added by CSA 1995, s. 18(1)). It is unlikely that the court will revoke an order simply to enable an application to be made to the CSA 1991 and in reality there is now little difference between the orders made. Even though the courts will be making orders under legislation other than the CSA 1991, they frequently adopt a CSA 1991 formula based calculation when assessing the application. You will be considering the courts' jurisdiction later, and the criteria to be applied under the relevant Acts.

9.5 The Formula

The formula upon which child support is calculated is very un-user friendly (if such a term exists!). One of the major criticisms of the CSA 1991 and the formula is that it is rigid and non-discretionary, and does not adequately reflect the reality of many parents' situations. Calculations are made on the basis of the income and financial status of the parents, any second partners, numbers of birth children etc. This reliance on financial details for making the assessment makes it essential that both parents with care and absent parents complete the forms fully. Failure to do so by the absent parent will result in an interim assessment. Invariably this will be higher than the final assessment that is made. The fact that the interim assessment operates as a penalty is designed to encourage co-operation. Any overpayments made due to an interim assessment may be recouped. This will generally be by way of adjustment to the amount of ongoing maintenance.

The formula consists of five distinct elements which you will look at now. You should note that you will only be considering the stages in a very peripheral way because the details of the scheme are complex and many practitioners use one of the computer software programmes that are available. At this point in your studies, it is important that you appreciate the overall scheme of the CSA 1991 formula, without having a really in-depth knowledge. Also you should find that most family law courses at undergraduate level will not expect you to carry out detailed calculations. The CSA 1991 itself sets out the formula in sch. 1 in algebraic form – unless you are a mathematician, do not bother trying to get to grips with it from there. Once you have looked at the five stages, you will then move to the departure grounds, these being potential reasons for reducing the child support assessment.

9.5.1 STAGE ONE; THE MAINTENANCE REQUIREMENT

Read the extract from sch. 1, CSA 1991 (*Cases and Materials* (9.2.1)) which explains what the maintenance requirement is.

The figures that are used to calculate the minimum cost of maintaining a child are those relevant to income support payments. The maintenance requirement can be established by adding up the varying income support premiums, namely:

■ the income support allowance for the child itself;

■ the income support family premium;

■ the income support allowance for the carer, if the carer is the parent and this is based on a single person allowance even if the parent with care is in a second relationship.

Once this has been totalled, the amount of child benefit received will be deducted from the figure.

Do you think it is right to include a 'carers allowance' in the calculation?

The 'parent with care' element is, or has been contentious with many absent parents seeing this as maintenance by the back door for an ex-spouse. The personal allowance included in the maintenance requirement is not spousal maintenance, it is part of the child support. The CSA 1991 works on the basis that supporting a child includes providing care for that child. As a child gets older, the amount of care that will be required will decrease because the child is able to do things for his/her self. As the independence increases, so the personal allowance for the parent with care will decrease. The decrease does not occur when the parents believe the child is independent: it is an arbitrary process based on the assumption that children between 11 and 14 need 25 per cent less care, and children between 14 and 16 need 50 per cent less care.

If a parent with care is seeking child support for more than one child, will there be a parent with care allowance for each child?

Whilst it would be logical to say yes, since each individual child will need care, the CSA 1991 will only apply one carer's allowance even though more than one child exists. The reduction in allowance to reflect the increasing independence of a child relates to the youngest child for whom support is claimed.

9.5.2 STAGE TWO: EXEMPT INCOME

The next stage is to assess the parent's exempt income – this is 'income a parent can keep for his/her own essential expenses before any child maintenance is expected. The expenses are based on income support rates but also include housing costs.' (Knight and Cox, *Child Support Handbook 1997/98*, London: CPAG, 1997, p. 168.)

9.5.2.1 The basics

As with the maintenance requirement, the exempt income is calculated by adding up the relevant income support allowances for the absent parent and then taking housing costs into account. If the absent parent has a biological or adopted child living with them, there will be an inclusion of the income support allowance for that child. The situation is slightly more complex if the child living with the assessed parent is the product of a second relationship, since it is not always the case that full income support allowances will be included for exempt income purposes.

Housing costs will only be taken into account if they are 'eligible costs': the list of eligible costs will, however, cover most parents (see *Cases and Materials* (9.2.2.1) for the list of eligible costs). Even if the costs are the liability of a new partner (heterosexual), they may be included within exempt income. If it is believed that the partner can contribute to the housing costs, a departure direction can be sought (see later).

SAQ 111

What if the absent parent decides to reduce his liability for child support by purchasing a large house with an excessive mortgage?

If housing costs are believed to be excessive then an application for departure can be sought.

9.5.2.2 Property settlements pre-1993

As you are probably aware, prior to the implementation of the CSA 1991 many couples on divorce settled the whole of the ancillary matters on a clean break principle. This may have resulted in a large capital transfer in return for no ongoing maintenance payments for the ex-spouse or children. After the implementation of the CSA 1991, these settlements could in effect be overturned, since the CSA 1991 overrides any previous agreement where the parent with care is receiving benefits. Attempts to oust the CSA 1991's jurisdiction, or to reopen the ancillary case out of time have been unsuccessful.

ACTIVITY 120

Read the case of *Crozier* v *Crozier* [1994] 2 WLR 444 in *Cases and Materials* (9.2.2.2) to get an idea of the courts' attitude on this question.

As the judgment makes clear, spouses (and courts) are required to bring maintenance between them to an end as soon as possible (the clean break provisions). However, where a child is concerned, there is no power to achieve a clean break. The fact that parents may have made an agreement along those lines does not form a binding agreement with the state.

As a result of the perceived injustice to the transferor, the Child Support and Income Support (Amendment) Regulations 1995 have altered the calculation for exempt income to allow for pre-1993 capital transfers. However, any pre-1993 transfer which was intended solely to reduce maintenance payments for the spouse alone will not count for the purposes of this allowance. The maximum exempt income allowance available will be £60 per week.

9.5.2.3 Travel to work costs

Further allowances can be included in the exempt income if a parent has higher than normal travel to work costs due to travelling long distances. This allowance would not help a travelling salesperson who would be getting expenses towards travel costs. The distance travelled must be in excess of 150 miles per week based on a straight-line basis (i.e. as the crow flies).

Is this fair? What if the parent lives on one side of a large estuary with no bridges or tunnels – what can he/she do?

The fact that the exempt income allowance is so inflexible is recognised, in that a parent may apply for a departure direction in order that real distance rather than straight-line distances can be used to assess travel to work costs.

9.5.3   STAGE THREE: ASSESSABLE INCOME

Once the maintenance requirement and the exempt income levels are known, the next stage is to establish the amount of income a parent has available from which to pay child support. The Child Support Action Group defines assessable income as 'the parent's net income minus exempt income' (*Child Support Handbook*, p. 189). Net income comprises earnings, expenses and allowances paid in connection with employment, less the payments made for income tax and national insurance purposes (note: a full list of what constitutes income can be found in the Child Support (Maintenance Assessments and Special Cases) Regulations 1992). Payments made into pension schemes cannot be deducted in full to calculate net income, only 50 per cent of the payment will be allowable.

Can a parent claim to have no income?

This may be claimed, and validly so. However, if a parent allegedly has no income the child support officer may query whether or not the parent has deprived himself/herself of that income to avoid or reduce any CSA 1991 assessment.

Read the extracts from *Phillips* v *Peace* [1996] 2 FLR 230 in *Cases and Materials* (9.2.3).

Should this have been a case where the parent is treated as having notional income? As you see from this case, the court may have residual powers to make a different type of order. You will be learning about this 'residual power' later in the chapter.

Once net income has been calculated, the amount of the parent's exempt income will be deducted and the resulting figure is the 'assessable income'.

What if there is no assessable income?

It may be the case that a parent's exempt income is greater than net income. If this is so, then they may still be required to pay child support. However, this will be set at the minimum level of £5. Some parents would not even be required to pay this minimum amount if they are classed as exempt due to incapacity, because of their status as a prisoner or because they are the carer of a child.

9.5.4   STAGE FOUR: HOW MUCH WILL BE PAYABLE?

Do you think all the assessable income will be available to pay child support?

Given the fact that income support levels are used to establish the basic living expenses for exempt income purposes, the amount of assessable income is potentially high. Many people, even if not high wage earners, would find living on benefit levels to be difficult. The general rule on how much assessable income is available to meet child support payments is 50 per cent.

Therefore once the assessable income has been calculated it can be divided in half. There will then be, in effect, a comparison between the amount calculated in Stage 1, i.e. the maintenance requirement, and that in Stage 4. If half the assessable income is less than the maintenance requirement, the lesser amount is payable. If half the assessable income is greater than the maintenance requirement, again, the lesser amount is payable.

Look at the example given in *Cases and Materials* (9.2.4) to make sure you understand this before moving on to the next part of the text.

If an absent parent is a high earner, 50 per cent of the assessable income may easily meet the maintenance requirement.

Can the Agency reassess to increase the level of child support payable?

In this situation an additional element of maintenance can be required. The amount of the additional element is based on percentages of 15, 20 or 25 depending on the number of children involved and the amount of additional assessable income. The figures and calculation process is complex. All you need to know is that more can be sought if an absent parent is wealthy, but that this additional element will still be based on a mathematical approach.

9.5.5 STAGE FIVE: PROTECTED INCOME

This is a final stage to ensure that the absent parent's income does not fall below a set level – the calculations acting as yet another check and balance technique. It also acts potentially further to confuse anyone trying to work out how child support is assessed. Again, there is a basic rule that an absent parent cannot be made to pay more than 30 per cent of their net income in child support payments and to this extent income will be protected.

Once the Agency has established the amount of maintenance payable in stage 4, it must then work out that figure as a percentage of the amount in stage 3 for net income. If the maintenance payable in stage 4 exceeds 30 per cent of net income, the maintenance to be paid will be reduced. Again, to see how this works turn to the example in *Cases and Materials* (9.2.5).

In addition to the 30 per cent cap rule, protected income can also reflect the fact that the absent parent may be in a new family situation. So far the process has not taken second families into account. This additional protected income calculation is designed to ensure that the total income for the second family will not be reduced below income support levels due to the payment of child support. Again as you can see, the process is endeavouring to act as a check and balance, albeit only at subsistence levels. An example calculation is *not* included in *Cases and Materials* in an attempt to keep the calculations simple!

The above foray into the CSA 1991 formula may well have left you a little bewildered. Stop and reflect upon the process and try to reduce it into its component parts. You may find it useful to draw up a diagram or flow chart, on a separate sheet of paper, to highlight the various steps involved.

9.6   Departure from the Formula

As you will probably agree, the formula does not really allow for discretion or recognise the individual nuances that will arise in a child support case. Stage 5, protected income, tries to ameliorate some of the harshness inherent in the formula, but cannot go very far in doing so. Hence the CSA 1995 (and accompanying statutory instruments) have introduced a procedure whereby a departure from the formula can be sought.

Read the article by Susan Deas, 'Discretion, but not as we know it – departures from the CSA formula' [1996] Fam Law 759, and the extracts from sch. 2, CSA 1995 (inserting sch. 4B into CSA 1991), in *Cases and Materials* **(9.3).**

Write down the categories into which applications for departure will fall and the types of situations where applications will be considered.

There are three main areas within which applications for departure will fall:

■   special expenses;

■   pre-1993 capital transfers or property transfers;

■   additional cases where there is over generous provision or excessive out-goings.

The situations where an application may be sought are itemised in the Schedule, and some are matters which may have already been considered in relation to exempt income. However, the cost of caring for stepchildren, the disability of the parent or contact costs (for example) are matters which are not otherwise brought into the calculations.

The disregard referred to in Susan Deas's article is currently set at £15 and is applicable to those cases concerning travel to work, contact costs, debts and pre-1993 financial commitments.

Will this make much difference?

The fact that a certain level of disregard is applied is not unusual in many situations (e.g. insurance), but is not common in family law. The effect that the departure rules had in relation to levels of support are summarised thus by Knights and Cox:

> The system of departure application and decisions was tried out in some areas for six months . . . Only 10-15 per cent of departure applications were successful. Special expenses departures reduced maintenance by an average of £10. Where an absent parent's new partner was expected to contribute to housing costs, maintenance increased by an average of £15. (*Child Support Handbook 1997/98*, p. 310)

When do you think the relationship must have been formed for the costs of a stepchild or a child of the family to be taken into account under the departure directions?

If the logical approach were to be taken, you should have said it didn't matter. The CSA 1991 and accompanying regulations are not logical as you know. Under the regulations the child in question must have been part of the applicant's family since before 5 April 1993 (the applicant here being the absent parent). If the departure directions were to introduce discretion into the system, this is a strange view of discretion as Deas indicates. The argument that since the CSA 1991 has been introduced, all stepchildren or children within second families will be provided with maintenance by the biological absent parent does not carry much force. Maintenance may be forthcoming from a biological parent, but may be at a low level, or the parent may be outside the jurisdiction, or the parent may simply have disappeared, or the Agency may have decided not to take the case on. No doubt you can probably add to this list of reasons.

For any departure direction to be given, there needs to be an application. This can be from either the absent parent (likely to be in relation to special expenses) or by the parent with care (likely to be in relation to over generous treatment).

9.7   When is the CSA 1991 not Applicable?

As you have seen, the CSA 1991 focuses on parents and children with a biological link and bases the assessment on (almost) pure mathematical calculations.

9.7.1   CSA 1991 NOT AVAILABLE

There are situations when the CSA 1991 will not be applicable or where other legislation can be utilised in addition to the CSA 1991.

ACTIVITY 125

Read the extracts from s. 8, CSA 1991 in *Cases and Materials* (9.4.1) and note down the situations in which the Agency either has no jurisdiction, or if it does, where the court also has jurisdiction.

The CSA 1991 itself identifies the following cases where courts can be requested to make an order for child support even if a CSA 1991 assessment can be made:

■ where the parent has already been assessed under the normal process and has been required to pay an additional element out of assessable income, i.e. the parent is wealthy (s. 8(6));

■ where the child is undergoing education or training and the maintenance order is required to meet all or some of the costs involved (s. 8(7));

■ where the child is disabled and the order is needed to meet the additional costs involved with the disability (s. 8(8)).

SAQ 119

Can you think of any other situations where the court may be involved, other than those specified above and covered by s. 8(5)? (*NB:* s. 8(5) was covered earlier in the chapter.)

There are a few more situations that you could have mentioned where the court will be the only option available to seek maintenance:

■ where the habitual residence criteria are not met;

■ where the child does not fall within the definition of a qualifying child – he/she may be a stepchild for example, or may be in excess of the age range for the CSA 1991; and

■ where the parent with care is not seeking a periodical payment but a lump sum or
property transfer to the child.

9.7.2   OTHER LEGISLATION

Whilst the CSA 1991 does not have the jurisdiction to deal with cases in the above
categories, before a court can make an order it must find the authority from statute.

Can you think of any Acts that would be used to get orders?

From your work in previous chapters you should have been able to come up with two
of the alternative sources, i.e. the MCA 1973 and the DPMCA 1978. A third exists, being
the Children Act 1989 (CA 1989).

9.7.2.1   Status

**Read the extracts from the MCA 1973 and DPMCA 1978 in *Cases and Materials* (9.4.2.1)
and write down the status of child to whom the Acts are applicable, the nature of the
orders that can be made and the criteria that will be applied.**

Under both these Acts the child must be a 'child of the family' in relation to the parties
to a marriage.

How would you define a child of the family?

The MCA 1973, s. 52(1), refers to a child of the family in relation to the parties of a marriage as:

(a)   a child of both of those parties; and

(b)   any other child, not being a child who is placed with those parties as foster parents by a local authority or voluntary organisation, who has been treated by both of those parties as a child of their family.

Treating a child as part of the family will involve a common-sense approach, e.g. has the child received the level of care, physical and emotional, that would be expected from parents etc.? (See for example *Carron* v *Carron* [1984] FLR 805 in **Cases and Materials (9.4.2.1)**). This would easily refer to a stepchild, but may, under (b), cover other children who do not fit the standard norms. You should note that the MCA 1973 does not define child of the family by reference to any legal orders that may be obtainable. The definition in the DPMCA 1978 is the same, as is the interpretation.

The final thing to note with reference to status is that an application can only be made under these Acts where the adults are married. Neither of these statutes applies to cohabiting couples and their children. Also you should note the situations when these orders are being made, i.e. either on divorce or where there has been a failure to provide reasonable maintenance. You should be familiar with this from your previous work.

9.7.2.2   Orders

The nature of the orders that can be obtained are the same as for spouses, i.e. periodical payments, lump sums and property transfers (the last not being available in the Family Proceedings Court).

Which of these orders is most likely to be granted?

As with spouses the most common order made for maintenance will be the unsecured periodical payments order. Lump sum and/or property transfers are in the minority of children's orders.

Why do you think this is?

In many cases, as with spouses, there will not be enough available capital to meet this type of order. However, there is a more fundamental objection to transfers of property or large financial sums, namely the fact that the award will probably extend beyond the minority of the child.

Read the extracts from *Kiely* v *Kiely* **[1988] 1 FLR 248** and *T* v *S (Financial Provision for Children)* **[1994] 2 FLR 883,** in *Cases and Materials* **(9.4.2.2), to illustrate this point.**

9.7.2.3 Criteria

When a court is considering making an order with respect to a child, it will have to have regard to the welfare of the child as being one of the first considerations, but not the paramount one. There also will be a requirement for the court to consider the list of factors in MCA 1973, s. 25(3) and DPMCA 1978, s. 3(3). These lists are almost exactly the same as for spouses, which have already been discussed.

One significant difference can be seen in MCA 1973, s. 25(4) and DPMCA 1978, s. 3(4), which will have relevance to non-biological children only. Under these provisions the court must assess the nature of responsibility taken on by the parent being asked to pay maintenance, how long that responsibility has lasted, whether it was undertaken knowing the child was not his/her own and whether any other person is liable to maintain the child.

Given the greater chances of serial monogamy in today's society, it is not hard to imagine a situation where a biological father is paying child support via the CSA 1991, and a stepfather is being asked to pay via the MCA 1973.

9.7.3 THE CHILDREN ACT 1989

Read s. 15 of, and the extracts from sch. 1 to the CA 1989 in *Cases and Materials* **(9.4.3).**

Write down the status of the child covered by these statutory provisions, the nature of the orders and the criteria to be taken into account.

9.7.3.1 Status

As you should be able to see, the CA 1989 is a broader ranging Act and covers a wider range of children and situations. Status is referred to more in the context of the applicant for the order than the child themselves. The child can be the product of unmarried or of married parents. The applicant can be a parent, a guardian or an individual with a residence order (these will be covered in later chapters), and the respondent will be one or both of the child's parents. A child, under para. 2, may themselves apply for an order when they have reached the age of 18.

Does this not go against the notion of *Kiely* in 9.7.2.2?

An order may only be made to extend beyond a child's eighteenth birthday in exceptional circumstances and where the child is to be undergoing training or further education. Parents' income is assessable for the purposes of LEA grants and fees already, so the CA 1989 is in effect, merely giving the child the means to enforce payment.

9.7.3.2 Orders

The range of orders available are as in the MCA 1973 and DPMCA 1978. The same difficulties exist under the CA 1989 where the settlement of property is concerned as mentioned in **9.7.2.2**. An added problem is that if a property settlement is made in favour of a child of unmarried parents, the parent will gain an advantage that otherwise would not be available

Look again at the case of *T* v *S* (*Financial Provision for Children*) [1994] 2 FLR 883 and also look at *A* v *A* (*A Minor: Financial Provision*) [1994] 1 FLR 657, in *Cases and Materials* (9.4.3.1).

Do you think that it is right that the mother should only be entitled to reside in the property whilst the child is under the mother's control? What does Ward J mean by allowing the mother to reside in the property for 'so long as A does not object'?

9.7.3.3 Criteria

Paragraph 4 of sch. 1, CA 1989, sets out the factors to be considered by the courts when deciding an application. Unlike the MCA 1973 and DPMCA 1978, if the CA 1989 is being used the child's welfare will be the courts' paramount consideration (s. 1(1), CA 1989). Note: you will learn more about the CA 1989 in **Chapter 10**.

SAQ 125

Do you think this will make a significant difference?

The fact that the wording of the Acts is different should reflect alternative approaches. Any such distinction is hard to establish in the law reports, therefore principles can be extrapolated between statutes, or so it would seem.

ACTIVITY 130

To consolidate this last set of statutes, draw up a table, on a separate sheet of paper, illustrating the scope of these three statutes. This will assist in any revision you have to undertake.

9.8 Summary

Child support is an issue that will, as time goes by, play a lesser role within the court system due to the implementation of the CSA 1991. Even though cases still exist which will remain within the courts' jurisdiction, the starting points in financial terms are now expressed in CSA 1991 maintenance requirements. There is of course more discretion to be exercised in the courts! The ability to understand how the CSA 1991 operates is useful, even though in practice you would probably use a computer programme, clients still need an explanation. Having completed your study of this area, you should be able to explain the CSA 1991 remit and methodology. You should also be able to discuss whether alternatives exist, and those situations where the CSA 1991 does not apply at all. To ensure that you have understood all this, try the following End of Chapter Assessment Questions.

9.9   End of Chapter Assessment Questions

1. In what situations can maintenance be obtained for children without recourse to the Child Support Agency?

2. Steve is 32-years-old and employed as a fireman. He is unmarried. Just over a year ago he split up from his girlfriend Toni and he has had no contact since. Yesterday he received a letter from the Child Support Agency together with a maintenance enquiry form asking for details of his income etc. with regard to Toni's child, William. Toni is claiming Steve is the father of William.

    Steve seeks your advice. He does not believe that he is the child's father and he wishes to know how the Agency will approach this denial. Also he wishes to know how the Agency will assess the claim if he is treated as being the father.

See *Cases and Materials* (9.6) for outline answers.

CHAPTER TEN

THE LAW RELATING TO CHILDREN

10.1   Objectives

By the end of this chapter you should be able to:

■   evaluate the claims that childhood is a socially constructed concept;

■   discuss the notion of children's rights;

■   discuss the historical background to child law, and the Children Act 1989;

■   explain the theoretical backdrop to the Children Act 1989;

■   list and define the fundamental principles of the Children Act 1989.

10.2   Introduction

You are now moving on to a major part of family law, and one which interlinks with the law of marriage and divorce. Childhood is seen as a time of vulnerability and one which requires protection. The law therefore seeks to protect, but preferably in a non-interventionist way. This may sound a little contradictory, but the philosophy of the law will become clear in the next few chapters. You will start by learning about the Children Act 1989, the main legislation concerning children, and the principles that the Act introduces. After you have mastered this, you will move on to orders that can be made in respect of children in both private and public law. This latter topic will be quite a long chapter, and will take careful studying. You will conclude by looking at the areas of wardship and adoption. However, the whole topic of children's law is not complex once you have mastered the basic concepts. To start then, you will be considering the concept of childhood, whether children have rights and some of the fundamental principles of the Children Act 1989.

10.3   What is Childhood?

How would you define childhood? Write down the things that childhood encapsulates.

The things you could have written down for this activity are potentially endless – much may depend on the type of childhood you yourself had.

For many, childhood reflects a period of inexperience, vulnerability, dependency, learning and inquisitiveness, lack of responsibility and innocence.

Has childhood always included these notions? Do you think childhood is changing?

Obviously, different people will have different reactions to this type of SAQ, and it might be useful to discuss this in a study group. However, have you ever thought seriously before about what makes childhood? The changing nature of childhood should be apparent or known to you, whether you are a parent or not. How many times do the media present the image of children who have lost their naïvety, or children who act like adults in the sense of doing adult things? Do you long for the days when childhood was a simple and innocent period in one's life? The fact that what is expected of children, and indeed what children themselves seek and desire, has changed, and that many of those changes are accepted by society as a whole, points to the idea of the concept of childhood as being 'socially constructed'. This idea gains strength when you reflect upon the attitude to and perception of children in the past.

As you may be aware, children were for many centuries seen as property of the parents over whom the parents had considerable rights. Children were not perceived as having needs in the sense that you would understand today; their youthful spirits needed to be controlled:

> . . . the early training of children was directly equated with the baiting of hawks or the breaking in of young horses or hunting dogs . . . all animals which were highly valued and cherished . . . and it was only natural that the same principle should be applied to the education of children. (Stone, L., *The Family, Sex and Marriage in England 1500-1800*, London: Weidenfeld and Nicolson, 1977)

This implies that childhood, as a conceptual ideal, was already in existence. It has been argued that childhood did not, in early history, exist.

ACTIVITY 132

Read the extracts in *Cases and Materials* (10.1) entitled '*Postman's argument*' which are extracted from the Open University course, Social Problems and Social Welfare. It is based upon the text by N. Postman, *The Disappearance of Childhood*, London: WH Allen, 1983.

Do you agree with his arguments?

The hypothesis put forward by Postman is interesting, albeit capable of criticism. As Postman is a Professor of Media Ecology, it could be suggested that he is biased. A more realistic explanation can be based on the Industrial Revolution and the philanthropic movement of the Victorian era. The change in working patterns in the Industrial Revolution resulted in less home-working for children as part of the family. Children, due to their cheapness, were however integrated into factory employment. This did not continue:

> reactions against such dreadful conditions did, fairly soon, begin to be mobilised . . . By the late eighteenth century magistrates began to restrict apprenticeships, and by 1842 a number of parliamentary Acts had been passed to regulate the employment of children and young persons in mills, factories and mines. From then on a series of laws were passed which gradually improved conditions. (Wendy Stainton Rogers, *Received into Care*, OU Press, 1988).

In addition to the influence of the philanthropic movement, the need for adult male employment necessitated a reduction in child labour, which naturally was cheaper and more expendable.

Hence, childhood, as a period of dependency and lack of responsibility, could be argued to have been created in the eighteenth and nineteenth centuries. As this is also the time when more widespread schooling was introduced, the hypothesis is strengthened.

How long do you think childhood lasted in this historical period?

The length of childhood probably had nothing to do with the theoretical age of majority. The class of the individual child would be crucially important. Childhood lasted much longer in the higher classes. Most children of the lower classes, even if they were lucky enough to obtain some sort of basic education, would be in employment in their very early teens (if not before).

How does this compare with today? Which view is preferable?

Today, legally, childhood lasts until a child is 18. At least, that is the age of majority. Most children remain in education until they are 18, with a large percentage taking their studies further. The law today also places more restrictions on what children can do, when, and at what age.

Write down (on a separate sheet of paper) the major life events for those under the age of 18. To give you an idea what is expected, the following are some of the things a 'minor' can do:

At 10 a minor can be convicted of a criminal offence, provided it can be proved that the child knew what they were doing was wrong.

At 14 a minor can be convicted of a criminal offence whether or not they know it was wrong.

At 16 a minor can marry with the consent of all those with parental responsibility, or the courts' authority.

At 17 a minor can drive a car.

Once you have completed your list, turn to the one in *Cases and Materials* (**10.1**).

This list is probably incomplete, but should highlight the range of different activities that are permitted at the various ages up to 21.

Does this indicate how a child (and also childhood) can be defined today?

There appear to be as many inconsistencies with the way that law treats children today, as in times gone past. Much will depend on a child's age and understanding, or the test of competency as defined in the case of *Gillick* v *West Norfolk and Wisbech Area Health Authority* [1986] AC 112.

It also emphasises that there can be no clear definition of what a child is, nor what can be expected of children in society. Finally, you should note that many of the activities that are within the scope of a child's grasp are different from those in the past, illustrating how changes in society's attitudes directly affect the legislative provisions. An example is the age of marriage, which as you may recall from **Chapter 2** used to be 12 years of age.

10.4   Children's Rights

To what extent do children have rights?

Children, being semi-autonomous individuals, are theoretical holders of rights. As you can see from **10.3**, at certain (normally specified) ages, children can 'do' specified things. There is also the perception of gaining rights as the child increases in age and maturity.

ACTIVITY 134

Read the summaries/extracts, in *Cases and Materials* (10.2), from *Gillick* and *Polovchak v Meese* 774 F 2d 731. To what extent do they support the notion of rights based on maturity?

Both these cases illustrate a consensus, and one that many parents would agree with. But would the facts of the *Polovchak* case be such to cause concern? Would you agree with a child's right to decide where to live in this situation? Would it be different if there were no other family in the country? Accepting these principles does not, however, prevent the argument being raised that these rights may be somewhat illusory, in the sense of having a lack of enforcement powers.

SAQ 131

If a 13-year-old wishes to buy a pet dog, having saved his Christmas money, and his parents say no, how can he enforce his rights?

In this situation, who could he claim against other than his parents? Is this the manner in which children should be encouraged to act? More to the point, if he wished to take the matter to court, could he act in person? As you should have noted from the '*At What Age*' list in *Cases and Materials* (10.1), a child can sue through their next friend, generally a parent. Applications by children are not permitted on a carte blanche basis. Some applications can be brought under the CA 1989, subject to leave, and additionally to the assessment of a child's competence to make the application.

The difficulty with this is the specific nature of the rights in question. As stated earlier, if those rights are not truly enforceable, can they be said to be rights at all? Perhaps therefore children's rights should be considered from a more fundamental perspective.

ACTIVITY 135

Read the extracts from the United Nations' Declaration of the Rights of the Child, 1959 in *Cases and Materials* (10.2).

Does this give a child more rights, or more effective rights?

The rights enshrined in this Declaration stem from the ideal of ensuring a child has a happy childhood. Is this achievable, given the nature of the principles set out?

The principles which are included in this Declaration do not create rights available to be enforced by the child per se. In this regard, returning to basic human rights does not assist at all.

SAQ 132

Do any of these principles promote the freedom of the child?

The answer to this is a clear 'no': as Mary John comments (OU Press 1988):

> the document mentions no rights to autonomy, self-determination, self-advocacy or to be listened to . . . It is vague about the details of the rights, responsibilities, guaranteed enforcement and about the personhood of the child. It is in effect a manifesto, a statement of moral rights and ideal responsibilities, a general claim against those who make society's rules. It does not outline legal or institutional rights.

Therefore, perhaps the regime which you considered earlier, is sufficient.

The Declaration has been superseded by the UN Convention on the Rights of the Child which was adopted in 1989. The UK signed the Convention in 1990, and ratified it in 1991. It came into force in 1992 although as an international convention it is not incorporated into English law. Whilst the Convention has over 50 articles, it can be categorised thus:

(i)   provision articles which recognise the rights of children to minimum standards of health, education, social security, physical care, family life, play recreation, culture and leisure;

(ii)   protection articles which identify the rights of children to be safe from discrimination, physical and sexual abuse, exploitation, substantive abuse, injustice and conflict;

(iii)   participation articles which concern civil and political rights. They acknowledge the rights of children to a name and identity, to be consulted and to be taken account of, to have access to information, freedom of speech and opinion, and to challenge decisions made on their behalf.

Ratification of the Convention is said to ensure that the needs and interests of children are given a high profile across government departments. Although the government signified its intention to comply with its provisions, the Convention is not enforceable in the same way that the European Convention on Human Rights is enforceable. Individual children cannot make applications alleging breaches of its articles and there are no direct sanctions that can be applied to ensure that the rights it contains are protected.

Read the extracts from the Convention in *Cases and Materials* (10.2). Does this alter the effect of the Declaration?

Whilst the language of the Convention is somewhat more legal, and authoritarian, in reality it does little more to create substantive and enforceable rights for individual children.

10.5   State Intervention

When looking at the 1959 Declaration and the Convention, you should have reflected upon who can be expected to provide the child with each of the rights so specified.

If you did not so reflect, go back and do so now.

The main 'providers' are the child's own parents or the state. Today, it is accepted that the state will play a role in child care matters.

Who or what is meant by the state?

In connection with the CA 1989, the state refers not just to the local authority social services department (this is probably the first institution you thought of), but also to the court. Under the CA 1989 principles, the intervention of the court is to be avoided unless it is necessary in the interests of the child. This 'hands off' principle is intended to realign the balance between the state and families. It could arguably be seen as regressive, returning to the state of affairs of previous centuries. In order to assess this suggestion, and to obtain a more rounded understanding of today's child protection, and family law for children, it is necessary to consider briefly the history of legislation.

10.5.1   THE POOR LAW AND PROPERTY

For many centuries children were seen as property belonging to their parents. You may recall the earlier quotation (see **10.3**) which spoke of children being trained like hawks or hunting dogs, both of which were classed as prize possessions, implying the same was true of children. For certain classes children were important for their earning capacity. Linked to the property model was the belief that parents had a responsibility to care or provide for their children. If a parent did not provide for their offspring little would be done. The Poor Laws, an early type of welfare benefit, whilst making provision for children who were destitute, did not differentiate between children or adult destitutes. The ability to seek 'poor relief' was seen to be the 'last resort', and where children were concerned the main obligation to provide came from the family. Where state relief was sought, and latterly this would have been via the workhouse, it was made to be so unpleasant and harsh that many were discouraged from seeking any relief at all, which meant that the poor tax was also kept to a minimum. The attitude was very much that the 'idle poor' should not be maintained by the state.

The philanthropic movement in the Victorian era, following on from a time of great exploitation of children in employment terms, saw the beginnings of larger scale state intervention. Primarily this was directed at regulating the employment of children, and not at the actual care of children within the family. Schooling also became more widespread albeit not a legal requirement. The Ragged Schools, voluntary schools for the education of destitute children, originated in about 1818, around the time Dr Thomas Barnardo established his first home for destitute boys. Initially, only children who lived rough were provided with care and accommodation. This concept developed into the 'removal of children' who needed 'saving' from the poor care provided by their parents. At this point in time what was being done was illegal, and contrary to the proprietary rights which a parent had over their children.

Legal sanctions for neglect and abuse of children at the hands of parents did not arise until much later.

SAQ 134

Does this sound familiar?

The idea of state welfare being restricted only to those who are deserving poor is very reminiscent of the attitude today. Most state benefits are reliant on availability to work, or good reason for lack of availability. The levels of benefit, despite some political comment, are set at a level designed to be subsistence level, but also so low as to make it less worthwhile being on benefits compared with being in employment.

10.5.2 LEGISLATION

With regard to prevention of cruelty to children, it would appear that the UK was behind in its thinking. Legal action had been taken in the USA, and societies founded to prevent cruelty, several years earlier. However, even the USA did not initially recognise child abuse as a problem. The first case involving cruelty was based on US legislation designed to prevent cruelty to animals (see further Cathy Cobley, *Child Abuse and the Law*, London: Cavendish Publishing, 1995). The first Society in the UK to work to protect children was formed in 1882. The National Society for the Prevention of Cruelty to Children was granted its Royal Charter in 1894, having been formed from a conglomeration of smaller societies. This was in fact later than the formation and granting of a Royal Charter to the Royal Society for the Prevention of Cruelty to Animals.

Does this surprise you?

The first statute to criminalise child cruelty was passed in 1889, namely the Prevention of Cruelty Act. As well as making neglect or cruelty an offence, the Act authorised removal of children from their parents where this was deemed necessary. More legislation followed, with the Children Act 1908 establishing a juvenile court to deal with the cases of delinquent juveniles, and those children who were suffering neglect and cruelty. This link between children who are delinquent, and children who need care continued throughout the twentieth century. It was predicated on the view that children who act in a criminal manner are 'deprived' in some way of the care and upbringing that they need. Juvenile delinquents were not so much wrongdoers as individuals to whom wrong had been done, in other words they were equally 'victims'.

10.5.3 OTHER MEANS OF INTERVENTION

It was not just the increasing use of statute to prevent cruelty that introduced state intervention into the family. The concerns over the health of the nation also led to more state involvement. In the time of the Boer War, i.e. the last 20 years of the nineteenth century, the physical health of the recruits was exceptionally poor and this was blamed on lack of adequate parenting. Mothers in particular were 'accused' of being ill educated in child raising, and this lack of knowledge was placing the national stock at risk.

As a result, middle class spinsters (invariably) took to 'visiting' the working class to teach them the art of child rearing and the benefits of cleanliness. From this level of intervention, the origins of both social work and health visiting can be seen. These interventions have continued, and been given legal footing by legislation.

10.5.4 UP TO THE CHILDREN ACT 1989

After the implementation of the 1908 Children Act no great changes occurred until the Children Act 1948. Prior to this Act the state of child care has been described thus:

The situation immediately prior to 1946 was chaotic, with numerous departments in central and local government and a plethora of charitable and voluntary organisations all responsible in some way for children deprived of a normal life. (Wendy Stainton Rogers, *Received into Care*, OU Press, 1988)

The Curtis Committee, set up in 1946, recommended the establishment of a centralised child care service. This was done via the 1948 Act, and children's departments were created. There was no real distinction between delinquents and children who simply needed care. Also, reasons for being in care were more diverse than today. The numbers of children in care were large, up to 64,000 children were in care in 1952, although it is suggested that a large proportion of these children were there due to homelessness when their parents could not afford to pay rents. Preventative work was not as apparent as it is today in reducing the numbers of children in care.

The next major piece of legislation was the Children and Young Persons Act 1969, which came after the so-called discovery of 'baby battering', although it is unlikely that legislative changes were founded upon this (re)discovery of child abuse. Under the 1969 Act, local authority social workers (the replacements to children's officers under the 1948 Act) were given considerable powers to act in cases of child abuse and protection. A child could be received into care either voluntarily (the child may or may not have been at risk), or compulsorily. Under the former, no court action was needed, and following a reception into voluntary care, the local authority could pass a parental rights order. This would give all parental rights over the child to the authority. Several criteria were included to obtain compulsory care, via the courts. These included:

■ the child's development being avoidably prevented or neglected, or the child being ill-treated;

■ the child being exposed to moral danger;

■ the child failing to receive full-time education;

■ the child being convicted of a criminal offence and being in need of care and control.

SAQ 136

Do you feel these grounds are all justified? Would you expect a court to remove your child if any of these grounds existed?

In addition to these criteria and orders, there also existed the place of safety order, which was perceived to be an emergency order. This order could be granted by a magistrate, and would enable the child to be removed for up to 28 days. The criterion relevant to the order was that it was suspected that the child was being ill-treated, or alternatively that any of the criteria upon which a compulsory care order could be made existed.

Can you think of any criticisms that could be levelled at this order?

When you have thought about the above SAQ, turn to *Cases and Materials* (10.3.1) and read the criticisms made by Cretney and Masson in *Principles of Family Law*, 5th edn, London: Sweet & Maxwell, 1990.

10.6   Why the Children Act – Why 1989?

The state of child care law had been criticised by the Short Committee which in turn led to the setting up of the DHSS Review of Child Care Law in 1984. Many of the recommendations of this review were incorporated into the White Paper, *The Law on Child Care and Family Services*, published in 1987 (Cm 62).

Can you think of some reasons why the law was changed in 1989?

The primary impetus for change was the criticism that was levelled at local authority social workers throughout the 1970s and 1980s concerning the way that the 1969 Act was being used. You have already read some of the concerns expressed about the use of the place of safety order, but similar concerns were raised about parental rights resolutions, and care orders themselves. With an increased awareness of family rights and responsibilities and the notion of 'family first' that can be seen in political rhetoric of the Conservative era, the 1969 Act appeared Draconian and harsh. The interpretation of the criteria, and the lack of participation of parents when children were perceived to be at risk was criticised. The Act focused on what *had happened* as opposed to what *might happen*. Hence, the work of social services departments was still being directed to reactive situations, the idea of preventative work was not seen as a priority.

What other events encouraged the changes?

Whether you can answer this will depend on your age and memory! During the time period in question, a series of cases hit the media headlines. Not only did these highlight the issue of child abuse for the general public, but they also raised questions as to social work practice, and legislative effectiveness.

Some of the cases you may recall are:

■ Maria Colwell 1974;

■ Jasmine Beckford 1984;

■ the inquiry into child abuse in Cleveland 1987, published in 1988;

■ the Rochdale 'satanic abuse' cases of 1990;

■ the Orkney ritual abuse cases of 1991.

If you do not recall any of these, look at the various press extracts in *Cases and Materials* (10.4).

What two lines of argument can you see?

The differing cases highlight two competing issues, first, the lack of competent intervention by social workers. The media coverage of the Beckford case, for example, refers to
the inexperience of social workers, and their general failure to act. This is a familiar claim
in many cases involving child abuse, i.e. that those who could have acted, didn't.

The second line of argument is the exact opposite, namely that of the state intervening
too much into the lives of families. The reaction to the Cleveland cases in particular was
from the perspective of outrage that local authorities had such Draconian powers over
children suspected to be at risk. Also of concern were the very limited rights and powers
that were left to individual parents once children were removed.

Throughout the rest of the time you spend on this course, look out for cases of child
abuse in the media. Do they portray social services or other agencies (i.e. health
authorities) in a positive light?

**Which of the two lines of argument, outlined in Activity 139, do you think were
favoured?**

You would have had a 50 per cent chance of getting this right if the question was so
simple! There are, of course, many situations when local authorities may not act, or may
be unable to – you will reflect upon these in later chapters. However, generally the
balance was in favour of the latter point of view, i.e. an excess of state intervention.
Consequently, the implementation of the CA 1989 was designed to:

> realign the balance between families and the State so as to protect families from
> unwarranted State intervention, to emphasise that local authorities have an important
> role in supporting families in difficulty and to indicate that there is a continuing role
> for parents when their children are looked after by a local authority. (Masson and
> Morris, *Children Act Manual*, London: Sweet & Maxwell, 1992)

**So far you have been looking at the public law issues. Do you think there were any
concerns about private law matters?**

The level of concern about private law issues was considerably less. One of the main
problems was the extent of legislation that existed in relation to children (both in public
and private matters). The CA 1989 repealed many other Acts, or at minimum amended

them. As well as a plethora of legislation, there was also a question mark over the extent of state involvement via the courts into private matters, principally in divorce. In the majority of divorce matters the court would be asked to make custody orders even if parents were in agreement. This was not perceived to be necessary. The timing of the Review of Child Care Law (1984) coincided with investigation into the state of family law by the Law Commission. The two reports were combined to produce '[T]he most comprehensive and far-reaching reform of child law which has come before Parliament in living memory. (Lord Mackay, Hansard, HL, vol. 502).

10.7   The Children Act 1989 – Key Principles

Unlike older statutes, the CA 1989 clearly identifies key principles which underpin the whole operation of the Act.

Read ss. 1 and 17(1), CA 1989 in *Cases and Materials* (10.5). On a separate sheet of paper write down the key principles that you can identify from your reading.

Your list should include the following:

■   the child's welfare is the paramount consideration (s. 1(1));

■   that delay is not generally in the interests of the child (s. 1(2));

■   courts should have regard to certain identified factors when deciding issues relating to children (s. 1(3) and cases when s. 1(3) applies are in s. 1(4));

■   that the court should only make an order when it considers it to be better for the child than making no order at all (s. 1(5));

■   that the court has discretion which order to make out of the range of orders available to it under the Act;

■   that local authorities have a responsibility to safeguard and promote the welfare of children in need;

■   the best place for children should be with their parents.

Some of these principles are not new, and some clearly interlink.

10.7.1   THE CHILD'S WELFARE AND THE WELFARE CHECKLIST

10.7.1.1   Welfare

You may have believed that the interests of the child would be paramount when any question was being decided in relation to their upbringing, so why state it explicitly? Do you remember the MCA 1973 concerning maintenance for children? Did this make the welfare of the child paramount? Not all statutes relating to children have the child's interests first and foremost: consequently it does need to be expressly stated.

What is meant by paramountcy?

Once you have considered this question, turn to *Cases and Materials* (**10.5.1.1**) and read the extracts from *J v C* [1970] AC 668. Note that this case concerned an earlier Act, the Guardianship of Minors Act 1971, which provided in s. 1 '. . . the court . . . shall regard the welfare of the minor as the first and paramount consideration'.

Does the fact that the Guardianship of Minors Act 1971 refers to the welfare being first and paramount mean the interpretation in *J v C* can be distinguished?

Although Masson and Morris state that 'Paramount does not mean first and paramount', the Lord Chancellor explained the wording thus: 'the welfare of the child should come before and above any other consideration in deciding whether to make an order' (Hansard, HL, vol. 502). It can be argued that the interpretation of Lord MacDermott's speech does mean the same as that of Lord Mackay. Lord MacDermott concluded that 'the course to be followed will be that which is most in the interests of the child's welfare' – surely the same as saying that the child's welfare comes first? This is an even stronger argument when having regard to the factors that the courts consider when establishing what is in the child's welfare. Section 1(3) sets out the welfare checklist, which contains factors comparable with Lord MacDermott's facts, relationships, risks and choices.

10.7.1.2   The welfare checklist

The purpose of this checklist is to establish what is the 'child's welfare' by focusing attention on the individual, and to ensure a greater consistency across courts and advisers when dealing with children's matters.

Is the checklist exhaustive?

The factors included within the checklist cover the major issues that will be relevant to individual cases, but they are not the only factors that can be taken on board by the court. The Act says, 'a court shall have regard in particular', i.e. the list is not limiting.

Is the court bound to consider all the factors?

This question is perhaps a little harder to answer, but as with **SAQ 144**, the court has discretion. Not all the factors listed in the checklist may be relevant to the particular case and so it is not necessary for the court to consider them.

Is the list in order of importance?

Although lists normally indicate a hierarchy, this is not the case here. As you can appreciate, the wishes and feelings of the child may be unascertainable, or they may be contrary to the courts' and professionals' view of the child's best interests. Whilst the opinions of the child are to be given greater weight, the court is alive to the possibility of undue influence of parents. To meet this possibility, the involvement and opinion of professionals, such as court welfare officers, will often be preferred.

10.7.1.3   Delay

The principle of avoiding delay as enshrined in s. 1(2) is not just aimed at achieving a more efficient court system. The length of time for many child care cases to be heard was, prior to the CA 1989, almost as easy to predict as the length of a piece of string! The Law Commission proposed the inclusion of this principle since the delay and uncertainty of litigation was deemed to cause damage to the welfare of the child. Children, it is believed, need to have some form of stability in their lives and the lack of stability inherent in long-standing court action is therefore prejudicial to the child. The manner in which the court attempts to reduce this delay is by setting a timetable for child cases. This is the same regardless of whether the matter is in public or private law.

How is this timetable enforced?

The timetable is not imposed without reference to the parties to the action, it is a negotiated arrangement. If a party is unable to meet their timetabled obligations, it is always open to them to return to the court for directions, to amend the timetable. Good and appropriate reasons should be given. Failure to comply with a timetabled direction, for example the filing of statements, may mean that the evidence included within that statement will be excluded from the trial. In practice, whilst this is an option, it may not be deemed in the welfare of the child to exclude relevant evidence. There have been no major complaints levied against failure to comply with timetables, and it would appear that timetabling has been a success. Indeed, in public law matters, albeit that the aim of twelve weeks for a care order application has not been met, in the family proceedings court the average hearing takes around five months (Children Act Advisory Committee (CAAC) Report 1993/4).

10.7.1.4   No order

The principle enshrined in s. 1(5) is often referred to as the 'no order' principle since it requires the court only to make the order when it is necessary to do so.

Which of the criticisms of the previous legal regime is this principle designed to address?

The main purpose of the no order principle is to address the complaint that the state intervenes too much in family matters. As you know, 'the state' refers not just to the local authority but to the court too. The impact of the principle has been clearly seen in relation to private law cases. According to the Judicial Statistics 1991 (the last dealing with pre-Children Act 1989 orders) 88,488 custody orders were made in that year. By 1994, three years into the operation of the CA 1989, the number of residence orders sought (residence orders having replaced custody orders) was down to 32,700. Of those applications, only 24,900 orders were made, the remainder of applications having been withdrawn or refused (CAAC Report 1993/4).

Does this reduction indicate that the courts are refusing orders?

Whilst there has been a reduction in the number of orders made (down to nearly a third), this is not simply by the courts applying s. 1(5) – the figures relate to applications. This reduction in applications indicates that the principle of no order, reinforcing lack of state intervention, is relevant to legal advisers, other agencies, and the parties themselves. If a potential applicant knows that they may not get their order, even if they satisfy all the criteria, they will think twice before expending money in the attempt. Also, in so far as private law is concerned, the fact that the change from custody orders to residence orders incorporated a change in the rights that were gained or lost, has meant there may be little to gain from an order anyway.

10.7.1.5   The range of orders

Implicit within s. 1(5) is the court's discretion to make any of the orders available under the Act when hearing an application. Indeed, in defined family proceedings the court has the power to make an order even if an application has not been made.

Read ss. 10(1), 9(1) and (2) and 8(3) and (4) in *Cases and Materials* (10.5.1.2). You should also re-read s. 1(3)(g) in *Cases and Materials* (10.5). You will be introduced to s. 8 orders in Chapter 11, but for now, be aware they are private law remedies.

The same sort of discretion operates in public law matters, with private law orders being made on a public law application.

10.7.1.6   Social services

In s. 17, CA 1989 you were introduced to the concept that local authorities have a duty to safeguard and promote the welfare of children in their area. The means by which this should be done, under s. 17, is by the provision of services.

How does the provision of services help meet the principle of reducing state intervention?

If the local authority is considering providing services, there is clearly some sort of state involvement. However, in the scale of involvement, this is not overly interventionist. It is more of a supportive role rather than an enforcement role. In this sense it is in keeping with the main theme of reducing state involvement. The ability to work with parents to meet their child's needs is also an advance on the situation that existed when the Cleveland cases arose. The reference to keeping children with their families in s. 17 continues this theme, and reinforces the ideal of families first.

Does this continued reference to children being best provided for in the family home remind you of anything?

This reluctance to intervene, and the emphasis on the responsibility of the parents and family, is reminiscent of the situation in the nineteenth century when child care law was in its infancy.

Are we regressing with our legislation, or are we supporting an enlightened outlook on child raising and family values?

You may wish to save your response to this and then return once you have completed the rest of the work on the CA 1989.

10.8   Summary

You have now completed your introduction to the Children Act 1989, and the reasons for its implementation. As you have learnt, state involvement in the family, to support and promote good child raising, has developed over a long period. Some of the advances in child care practices were not based on welfarist principles per se, but on other, normally economic, grounds. The changing nature of society has caused changes in the expectations of children with, as you may recall, the invention of childhood as a concept. Having 'created' childhood as a period of vulnerability and lack of responsibility, parents have been expected to take on those functions. The failure of parents, especially in the last few decades of the twentieth century, together with a perceived overzealous state, has led to the introduction of the CA 1989. This Act operates on the basis that a child's welfare is paramount, and that welfare can be assessed with reference to a checklist of factors. The intervention of the state is to be avoided if at all possible, and the simple fact of establishing the criteria needful for CA 1989 orders does not mean that the orders will automatically be granted.

10.9 End of Chapter Assessment Questions

At the end of this chapter, which is intended primarily to be an introductory chapter, you have two short questions to attempt. The first may be a suitable revision question once you have completed the whole of child care law in this text.

1. The Children Act 1989 is designed to support child rearing with families, and yet to provide the state, through the local authority, with improved powers to protect children.

    Can these principles co-exist?

2. The welfare checklist in s. 1(3), Children Act 1989 supports the concept of children's rights.

    Discuss.

See *Cases and Materials* (10.7) for outline answers.

CHAPTER ELEVEN

THE PRIVATE LAW RELATING TO CHILDREN

11.1 Objectives

By the end of this chapter you should be able to:

- explain the concept of parental responsibility;

- advise hypothetical clients on seeking parental responsibility;

- discuss the meaning of the orders available under s. 8, CA 1989; and

- answer problem questions in relation to private law matters.

11.2 Introduction

If you are a lover of substantive law, you will be considering much more legislation in this chapter than in the preceding one. You are now commencing your in-depth study of the CA 1989. Initially you will be concentrating on private law matters, being the range of orders that are normally called into play in situations of parental separation or divorce. The principles you learnt in **Chapter 10**, found within s. 1, will be highly relevant to these orders. You will also need to understand the meaning and importance of 'parental responsibility' – a crucial concept under the CA 1989.

11.3 The Concept of Parental Responsibility

11.3.1 A DEFINITION

The phrase 'parental responsibility' is one which you came across in **Chapter 10**. In the sense that it implies a parent's moral duty over their children, its meaning should be clear. However, a moral understanding of the term is not the same as a legal definition.

ACTIVITY 142

Imagine you are the legal draftsperson in charge of defining 'parental responsibility' for the CA 1989. Write down how you would define it.

Having done that, turn to *Cases and Materials* (**11.1.1**) and read the actual definition contained in s. 3(1), CA 1989.

Did your definition bear any resemblance to the one in the Act? If it did not, don't worry, since the interpretation of parental responsibility is not really a definition at all if you understand a definition to provide a meaning of the phrase. Indeed s. 3(1) has been described as a 'non-definition' (per Lord Meston, Hansard, HL, vol. 502). What s. 3(1) does, therefore, is to provide another set of things to be explained.

What type of legal relationship does s. 3(1) envisage existing between parents and children?

The phrase parental responsibility connotes a relationship of decision-making by the parent for the child, it implies dependency with a protective role for parents. In this regard, the CA 1989 in introducing parental responsibility is trying to emphasise the responsibility and duty that a parent owes to the child. The term 'rights' is included in s. 3(1); however this term is in the minority, and the majority of terms give rise to an implication of a mere *power* relationship, with the child as the subservient partner. This argument can be supported by the statement by Lord Fraser in *Gillick* [1985] 3 All ER 402 when discussing how parental responsibility and the various functions within it should be utilised:

> They [parental responsibilities] exist for the benefit of the child and they are justified only in so far as they enable the parent to perform his duties towards the child . . .

Given that the phrase 'parental responsibility' implies a mixture of rights based powers and responsibilities or duties towards a child, the question arises, what exactly are those powers and duties?

11.3.2 WHAT IS INCLUDED WITHIN PARENTAL RESPONSIBILITY?

On a separate sheet of paper write a list of all the things you think are included within parental responsibility. What are the consequences for a parent if they fail in their duties?

Many of the aspects of parental responsibility are based on common law; as you have seen, statute does not provide a composite list. Things you should have included within your list are:

- the duty to provide the child with care;

- linked to the above, the duty to protect the child;

- the duty to ensure the child is educated;

- the duty to ensure the child receives timely and appropriate medical attention (you could include this with the general care duty above);

- the right to name the child;

- the right to choose a religion for the child;

- the right to discipline the child;

- the right to act or bring proceedings on behalf of the child.

As you can see, these functions of being a parent have been split into duties and rights; some authors (e.g. Cretney) refer to all of them in a rights based context. However, given that failure to comply with some of these functions can lead to criminal or civil action against the parent, it is perhaps less appropriate to talk of rights in all situations.

Some of these functions are quite easy to understand, and need little by way of explanation.

Is this list exhaustive?

If it is accepted that childhood is socially constructed, then it should follow that the matters within parental responsibility will be capable of change as society's views on children alter. Clearly there will be some fluidity within the concept of parental responsibility. Even if you do not agree with the notion of social construction, parental responsibility will change as the child develops. This was accepted by the Law Commission in their report No. 172:

> . . . the list must change from time to time to meet differing needs and circumstances. As the *Gillick* case itself demonstrated, it must also vary with the age and maturity of the child and the circumstances of each individual case.

11.3.3   SOME INTERPRETATIONS

11.3.3.1   The duty to care and protect

The duty to care for a child encompasses a wide range of different activities. It focuses not just on the physical care of the child, but also on the emotional and social development that should be nurtured. The fact that emotional care is important can be seen from the welfare checklist which causes the court to have regard to the emotional needs of the child. Practically, caring for a child requires suitable accommodation to be provided, the child to be adequately fed and clothed, and to be raised in as loving and stable an environment as possible. For some parents this duty will be reduced to the duty to provide financial maintenance, which as you know is governed by the Child Support Acts 1991 and 1995.

SAQ 155

If you have not already thought about the consequences for failing in this duty, do so now.

The duty to provide care is fundamental to a child's upbringing, and the consequences for failure can be harsh. Both civil and criminal law sanctions can be imposed. Under the criminal code, if a parent neglects a child, they may be prosecuted for cruelty under the Children and Young Persons Act 1933 (see s. 1 in *Cases and Materials* (**11.1.2**)). This section is often used in child abuse cases, even if the harm to the child has been quite severe (including death) since it is evidentially easier to prove.

Naturally charges may be under other statutes, e.g. the Offences Against the Person Act 1861.

Under civil law procedures, by failing to care for a child, the parent risks the child being removed from their care under the provisions of the CA 1989. Whilst you will be looking at child abuse in more detail in **Chapter 12**, it is important to remember that not all cases of neglect involve true moral culpability. It is easy to blame a parent for neglecting a child, but issues of socialization, and especially cycles of deprivation may have a role to play. If you are unclear what is meant by a cycle of deprivation, turn to *Cases and Materials* (**11.1.2.1**) where you will find an example.

The ability to protect a child from harm is obviously part of care. If a parent does nothing to prevent a child from endangering themselves, and this is more than an isolated event, then that surely equates with neglect.

11.3.3.2   The duty to educate

Education is seen as part of the developmental process for a child to pass from the status of a child to that of an adult. Today we accept that children should receive education until they are at least 16 years old. The duty to ensure that a child receives an education is placed upon carers by virtue of the Education Act 1944 as amended, the relevant section (s. 36) being set out in *Cases and Materials* (**11.1.2.2**).

The normal place for education is in a school setting.

SAQ 156

Is a parent constrained by the Education Act 1944 to send a child to school to comply with their duty?

Despite school being the norm, it is still possible for a parent to educate a child outside the school setting. The legislation requires a child to receive an 'efficient full-time education suitable to his or her age, ability and aptitude, either by regular attendance at school or otherwise'. The ability to educate at home for example has always proved difficult given the question of suitability. As Neville Harris has stated, it is now 'well-nigh impossible since the introduction of the National Curriculum' (*Law and Education: Regulation, Consumerism and the Education System*, Sweet & Maxwell, 1993).

Failure to meet this duty again results in potential criminal and civil sanctions. Under the Education Act 1993, a parent can be prosecuted for their child's non-attendance at school. The penalty imposed upon parents, invariably, is quite small.

The civil sanctions are to be found in the CA 1989.

Read s. 36 and the extract from sch. 3, CA 1989 in *Cases and Materials* (11.1.2.2) and note down the nature of the civil order that can be made.

The education supervision order is a new order under the CA 1989, and links in to the repeal of truancy as a ground for a local authority obtaining care over a child. This is not to say that truancy, or non-school attendance, will mean a child can never be taken into care.

Read the extracts from *Re O (A Minor) (Care Order: Education: Procedure)* [1992] 2 FLR 7 in *Cases and Materials* (11.1.2.2).

From this case, it is clear that if the criteria for a care order can be made out, even if it is purely on the grounds of non-education, the order can be made.

Does this mean s. 36 is irrelevant?

Whilst government statistics (Written Answers, Hansard, 28 February 1995, cols. 524-528) indicate that few s. 36 orders are made, it is not due to the care order route being preferred. Instead, most authorities prefer to prosecute under the Education Act 1993.

11.3.3.3 Medical treatment

Although this aspect of parental responsibility falls within the care function, it warrants separate consideration. Generally, due to a child's perceived lack of capacity, a parent is responsible for ensuring that the requisite consents to medical treatment are given. Without consent, unless treatment is deemed to be necessary in an emergency, that treatment will be unlawful.

If a parent fails to ensure treatment is received, they may find themselves being prosecuted under the Offences Against the Person Act 1861, or the Children and Young Persons Act 1933. If a fatality occurs, they may face murder or manslaughter charges.

Read the press extracts in *Cases and Materials* (11.1.2.3) on the Nakhira Harris case in 1993. Do you agree that the parents were culpable, or were they just doing what they believed was right?

In contrast to this case, read the article from the *Daily Telegraph* by Sandra Barwick, where a court permitted treatment to be refused, even though the child would ultimately die (*Cases and Materials* (11.1.2.3)).

Can these be reconciled?

The ability of parents to consent on behalf of their children raises difficult issues at law. In the above cases, the child's long-term prognosis, taken with the parents' knowledge of medical matters, may account for the divergence of decision made. What is more problematic is the situation where you have an older child, who may wish to have their own say on medical treatment.

What do you think should be the approach in that sort of case?

In this area the law is quite complex. If you have studied medical law, you will already know the difficulties. In the *Gillick* case the ratio concerned the narrow issue of whether a girl under 16 years could be given contraceptive advice and treatment. The obiter dictum of the case referred to the wider issue of when a child would have sufficient rights to make medical decisions for him/her self.

Read the extracts from *Gillick* in *Cases and Materials* (10.2), which you looked at in Chapter 10.

What does the House of Lords suggest the law is, particularly in relation to the concept of parental responsibility?

There naturally are slightly differing interpretations that could be made of these extracts. However, the accepted implication has been that where a child has the required age and understanding to make a decision on treatment (in other words has capacity), then the child's right to decide overrides that of the parent. The parent's previous rights or duties on this matter will be terminated.

A cessation of parental responsibility or a parallel right?
Gillick (as per Lord Scarman) implies a complete cessation of parental responsibility for specified matters once a child has Gillick competence. This view has been 'watered down' in subsequent decisions on medical treatment, primarily by Lord Donaldson. In the cases of *Re R (A Minor) (Wardship: Medical Treatment)* [1992] 1 FLR 190 and *Re W (A Minor) (Refusal of Medical Treatment)* [1992] 3 WLR 758, the idea of parallel rights was introduced.

Read the extracts in *Cases and Materials* (11.1.2.3) from *Re R* and *Re W*, and try to extrapolate the principles.

Concentrating more on the issue of parental responsibility you should be able to identify the differences between Donaldson and Fraser and Scarman in *Gillick*. Lord Donaldson believes that regardless of whether a child has *Gillick* competency, the parental responsibility of the parent is still retained, but runs in conjunction with that of the child. Hence, rather than two parents being capable of making a legal decision, there are three individuals who can do so, the parents and the child. In so far as medical treatment is concerned, this is not a satisfactory principle: would doctors wish to treat a non-consenting 15-year-old? Ultimately, the medical profession is left to decide, but the cases do ensure the doctors freedom from suit!

SAQ 159

Given the perception that parental responsibility is an extinguishing right, do the cases above support this idea? Which perspective is the best?

11.3.3.4   Name and religion

In comparison to some of the parental responsibility issues, names and religion are normally less contentious. A parent is free to name their child in whatever manner they see fit, and a child's name can be changed by deed poll (although there are some conflicting procedural rules relating to this). However names, and surnames in particular, do become more of an issue following divorce.

ACTIVITY 149

Read s. 13(1) of the CA 1989 in *Cases and Materials* (11.1.2.4). How does this prevent changes of name, and in what circumstances?

The restriction in the change of name only applies where there is a residence order in effect (under s. 8). If the court has refused to make an order under the auspices of s. 1(5), there would seem to be no automatic restriction to a unilateral change in name. If an order is in force then, as the section states, the change may take place where:

■   written consent is given by all persons with parental responsibility; or

■   the court has granted leave for the change.

The former is unproblematic.

On what basis do the courts approach an application for a change of name?

If you can remember **Chapter 10**, this should be easy to answer. The approach is to establish what will be in the best interests of the child.

To see how the courts deal with such cases, read the extracts from *W v A* [1981] 1 All ER 100 and more recently, *Re B (Minors) (Change of Surname)* [1996] 1 FLR 791 in *Cases and Materials* (11.1.2.4).

11.3.3.5   Discipline

To what extent do you believe a parent should be able to discipline their own children?

The subject of discipline is one which raises heated debate particularly where physical discipline is concerned. Some people fall into the 'anti smacking' category, with others in the 'pro smacking' category.

Your answer to **SAQ 161** should indicate which view you favour.

Currently our legislation does not prohibit physical discipline by parents, but any sort of corporal punishment in schools is forbidden.

Can you as a parent permit your child-minder to smack your child?

Logically the answer should be yes, since the doctrine of loco parentis and delegation of parental responsibility exists. However, this is an issue which has given rise to judicial argument. The result of this is set out in *Cases and Materials* (**11.1.2.5**) in the case of *Sutton London Borough Council* v *Davis* [1995] 1 All ER 53.

Smacking is one thing, but what about other forms of discipline? Returning to the 'cycle of deprivation' example of using a belt to discipline, would you agree that this was acceptable as a means of discipline for 'answering back'? Would your view differ if the child had broken into a neighbour's car?

Whilst you may believe that neither act should warrant that form of punishment, it should have made you think of matching the punishment to the crime. Discipline is permitted to the extent that it is commensurate to the crime and the child in question.

If a parent goes beyond the acceptable levels of discipline the consequences would be the same as you have already considered in relation to lack of care, i.e. civil sanctions to remove or criminal action for assault.

11.4   Who has Parental Responsibility?

It is all very well knowing what parental responsibility is, but it is essential to appreciate who has this responsibility since without it enforceable and legally acceptable decisions cannot normally be made.

11.4.1   AUTOMATIC PARENTAL RESPONSIBILITY

Write down those individuals you believe will have parental responsibility.

Once you have done this, compare your list of people with s. 2(1) and (2) of the CA 1989 in *Cases and Materials* (11.2.1).

How did your list compare?

The effect of s. 2 is simple: the only persons who have parental responsibility automatically are:

■   the mother;

■   the father if he was married to the mother at the time of the child's birth.

If one or both of the parents validly believe that they are married, but the marriage is in fact void, they will still have parental responsibility as of right (by virtue of the Legitimacy Act 1976, s. 1).

What is the situation if the birth parents marry after the birth?

In this case, the Legitimacy Act 1976, s. 2 will come into play. Under this Act, if parents of a child marry subsequent to the birth of the child, and both birth parents were capable of marrying at the time of the birth, the child will be legitimated by the later marriage. To help make this clearer an example may assist.

Anna and Bill are both single. Anna conceives and gives birth to Christopher. When the baby is six months old, Anna and Bill marry. Christopher will be legitimated.

By contrast:

Anna is single and Bill is married, but separated from his wife. Anna conceives and gives birth to Christopher. Bill's divorce is made absolute one week after the birth. Anna and Bill marry when the baby is six months old. Christopher will not be legitimated since at the time of the birth Bill was incapable of marrying Anna as his divorce had not been finalised.

Once a child is legitimated under s. 2(1), both parents will have parental responsibility.

Who is excluded from automatic parental responsibility?

The one category of individual whom you may have included in your list is the unmarried father. However, as you can see from s. 2 of the CA 1989, they do not have parental responsibility as of right.

This will affect a great number of parents. As you should recall from **Chapter 1**, the number of births outside marriage is increasing, with approximately one-third of births being to unmarried women.

11.4.2   THE UNMARRIED FATHER

The idea of child raising outside marriage is not uncommon or unacceptable today. You probably know couples with children who are 'only cohabiting'. If a child is being cared for and raised by both its parents in a stable relationship, should the law deny that father responsibility over that child? Would your response differ if the child had been conceived following a rape? This distinction between the reasons for child birth outside marriage is one of the factors behind the current legislation. It was believed to be preferable to enable unmarried fathers who did wish to be involved with their children to apply to be given those rights, rather than the option of giving rights and the application being to take those rights away.

Read s. 4, CA 1989 in *Cases and Materials* **(11.2.2) and write down the ways in which an unmarried father can obtain parental responsibility.**

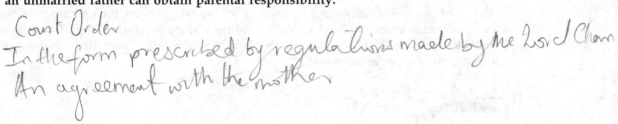

Court Order
In the form prescribed by regulations made by the Lord Chan
An agreement with the mother

Section 4 permits a more permanent parental responsibility to be granted. Under s. 2(9) the mother can delegate some of her parental responsibility. Section 2(9) reads:

> A person who has parental responsibility for a child may not surrender or transfer any part of that responsibility to another but may arrange for some or all of it to be met by one or more persons acting on his behalf.

There are two means by which parental responsibility can be granted to the father: first by means of a parental responsibility agreement and secondly, by means of a court order under s. 4.

11.4.2.1 Parental responsibility agreements

Section 4 requires mother and father to agree that the father is to have parental responsibility.

Do you think it will be sufficient for the mother to agree verbally to sharing parental responsibility?

Normally, oral agreements are just as enforceable as written ones. This general proposition can be rebutted, and this is the case here. Before a parental responsibility agreement can be effective it must be:

■ in the form prescribed by regulations made by the Lord Chancellor;

■ recorded in the prescribed manner (per s. 4(2)).

Under the regulations, to be valid the agreement needs to be in the required wording, and to be witnessed. It must also be filed at the Principal Registry of the Family Division of the High Court.

11.4.2.2   Parental responsibility orders

In the event that agreement cannot be reached between the parents, the unmarried father may apply to the court for a s. 4 order. Whilst the county courts and High Court have jurisdiction over private law matters, the family proceedings court (the magistrates' court) may be the preferred venue.

If an application is made, what factors will the court bear in mind?

As the matter will concern the upbringing of a child, the court will have to have regard to the welfare of the child, in the sense that the child's welfare is paramount. However, the welfare checklist is not a compulsory consideration since a parental responsibility order is made under s. 4. This section is not caught by the provisions in s. 1(4). The checklist may have a subsidiary role to play. Other factors are relevant to the decision whether or not a father should get parental responsibility.

Read the extracts from *Re H* [1993] 1 FLR 484 in *Cases and Materials* (11.2.2.1). Write down the other principles relevant to a s. 4 application.

As you will see, much of the judgment by Hollis J was referable to principles under the previous Family Law Reform Act 1987, but Hollis J accepted that these principles were applicable to s. 4 applications under the CA 1989.

The factors you should have listed were:

■   the degree of commitment which the father has shown towards the child;

■   the degree of attachment which exists between the father and the child;

■   the reason of the father for applying for the order.

Does it matter that the father will be in no position to do anything actively with his parental responsibility?

As the extract from *Re H* illustrates, the list of considerations is not intended to be exhaustive, and in some situations the considerations may not be entirely applicable. If, for example, the mother has persistently thwarted the father's attempts to see the child after birth, should the father be prevented from obtaining parental responsibility simply because the child is young and he has not had a chance to bond or develop a relationship?

11.4.3   PARENTAL RESPONSIBILITY FROM OTHER ORDERS

The birth parents are the most likely candidates for seeking parental responsibility, but parental responsibility can be obtained by others. In the following situation, on what basis can Grandma exercise parental responsibility?

Anna and Bill who both have parental responsibility, have left Christopher with Grandma whilst they go on a year's vacation. Since they are backpacking, they deemed it inappropriate to take a nine-month old child with them.

You should have thought of the delegation of parental responsibility that is permissible under s. 2(9). However, read s. 3(5) and s. 12(2) in *Cases and Materials* (**11.2.3**).

These provisions open up two more possibilities for Grandma. The former, s. 3(5), is designed primarily for temporary carers, and the carer can only do what is reasonable to safeguard the child. It would cover an emergency where parental responsibility has not been delegated. Note: if delegation does occur, it is preferable that it is in writing, then there can be less room for dispute.

Under s. 12(2) a more general parental responsibility can be granted, but only where a private law residence order is made.

You will learn more about residence orders shortly.

11.5   Joint or Individual Liability?

You now know that parental responsibility can be held by more than one person.

If parental responsibility is held jointly, do you think that both (or all) the individuals with parental responsibility must agree to the decision being made?

Is it practical to expect this?

If you have children, do you consult everyone with parental responsibility when you decide to give the children fishfingers for tea, or to allow them out until 10 p.m. in school holidays? Probably not as it isn't practical. It is even less practical if you are separated and your (ex) spouse lives some distance away.

The CA 1989 recognises that practical living prevents consultation in many situations. Hence s. 2(7) provides:

> Where more than one person has parental responsibility for a child, each of them may act alone and without the other (or others) in meeting that responsibility; but nothing in this Part shall be taken to affect the operation of any enactment which requires the consent of more than one person in a matter affecting the child.

Can you think of any such enactment?

If you recall, a child of 16 can only marry with the consent of all those with parental responsibility, or the agreement of the court: this is therefore such an enactment.

What if they cannot agree?

Inherent with a system of joint/individual responsibility is the potential for conflict. Section 8, CA 1989 provides a mechanism for dealing with such disputes.

11.6 Losing your Parental Responsibility

How do you think a person with parental responsibility can lose it?

Anyone with children (or parents for that matter) will know that parenthood is a lifelong commitment. Legally, most responsibility ends for children when they reach 18. This can exceptionally be extended – for example with regard to maintenance if a child enters higher education. Parental responsibility can be lost in a limited number of ways before a child reaches 18 but, to a degree, the ability to lose parental responsibility is dependent upon how you gained parental responsibility to start with.

If you are a parent with automatic parental responsibility the only ways it can be lost completely are:

■ by the child being adopted;

■ by death, either of the child or yourself.

Parental responsibility will survive divorce (the adage 'you can divorce your spouse but not your children' needs to be remembered), and it will also survive any orders made in respect of the child. If a care order, or wardship order is made, parental responsibility will not be lost, but a parent's ability to exercise that parental responsibility may be severely constrained.

If you are a parent (an unmarried father) who has gained parental responsibility by virtue of a court order (s. 4) or an agreement (s. 4), or any other person who has gained parental responsibility by virtue of court intervention (s. 8 residence orders), the parental responsibility obtained can be lost by:

■ the child being adopted;

■ death;

■ the court revoking or discharging the order that originally gave you parental responsibility.

In this case, the parental responsibility is less permanent, since what the court gives, the court can take away.

11.7   Private Law Orders

The holding of parental responsibility is important when it comes to seeking private law orders over a child. Not all individuals are able to seek orders automatically. Parents and persons with parental responsibility generally fall into the category of automatic application rights.

To see who has automatic rights to apply for s. 8 orders, and who needs leave, read s. 9(3) and (4) and s. 10(1) to (5) and (9), CA 1989 in *Cases and Materials* (11.3).

In case you are wondering who is deemed a 'parent' as mentioned in s. 10(4), the CA 1989 includes unmarried fathers within the definition of parent. Thus they have the right to apply automatically for s. 8 orders.

You should also note the prohibition in s. 9(2), which prevents certain of the s. 8 orders being made in favour of local authorities. This emphasises the notion that state involvement needs to be reduced, in effect by reducing the number of orders that are available to the local authority.

11.7.1   THE SECTION 8 ORDERS

Section 8 sets out four orders which can be sought in private law. Two of these orders are used on a far more frequent basis than the other two.

Read s. 8 in *Cases and Materials* (11.3.1). Write down the four orders that can be sought and identify the commonly used orders.

You should have written down the following orders:

■   residence order;

■   contact order;

■   specific issues order;

■ prohibited steps order.

The first two orders are the most commonly used.

11.7.2 THE RESIDENCE ORDER

Which of the previous legal orders does this replace?

It is highly likely that most of you will know the previous 'custody order' that gave very similar rights to the residence order of today. The residence order is designed to 'settle the arrangements to be made as to the person with whom a child is to live', which is arguably less stringent than a custody order which gave 'custody, care and control' to one parent over the other.

11.7.2.1 The question of parental responsibility

If married parents separate, and a residence order is made in favour of the mother, to what extent does this affect the father's parental responsibility?

Going back to **11.6**, you will see that the father's parental responsibility will not be removed. However, the fact that parents have separated will mean that it is harder for the non-caring parent to utilise their parental responsibility. Day-to-day care, which will be within the remit of the person with the residence order, and the exercise of parental responsibility to meet that care, will fall almost solely on the caring parent. More major decisions, perhaps where the child should receive its schooling, should remain as joint decisions. This cannot easily be enforced, because parental responsibility is an individual liability. However, the philosophy of the CA 1989 and indeed the FLA 1996, tries to encourage parents to work together in the best interests of the child, and that includes liaising on the future steps for that child.

11.7.2.2 Conditions

Within the new residence order, the phrase 'settling the arrangements' has been suggested to be 'a broad one and gives the court more scope for including conditions' (Masson and Morris, *Children Act Manual*, London: Sweet & Maxwell, 1992). Since the order does not now give all the rights and responsibilities to the carer (which a custody order arguably did), it may be necessary to lay down conditions. Authority for this power of the court is found in s. 11(7) which you can read in *Cases and Materials* **(11.3.2.1)**.

SAQ 174

What sort of conditions do you think may be included?

The range of possibilities is almost endless but for some idea see the extracts from *Re C* [1992] 2 FCR 341 and *Re KDT* [1994] 2 FCR 721 in *Cases and Materials* (**11.3.2.1**).

Other types of conditions you may have thought of include those relating to medical treatment, education, and religious upbringing.

Certain conditions will be placed automatically on residence orders. You have already come across one within s. 13 which prevents the changing of a child's name without consent of all with parental responsibility, or a court order. There are also restrictions as to removal of the child from the jurisdiction. Again these are in s. 13, and will be found in *Cases and Materials* (**11.1.2.4**).

Finally, no person with parental responsibility is able to exercise it if by so doing, they are acting in a manner which would be incompatible with an order made under the CA 1989 (such as a residence order). This prohibition is laid down in s. 2(8).

11.7.2.3   Split orders

ACTIVITY 156

Read s. 11(4), CA 1989 in *Cases and Materials* (11.3.2.2). What type of order does this permit?

The fact that parental responsibility is now not so closely bound up in orders relating to the person with whom a child lives allows a greater flexibility of ordering. It is now clearly enshrined in the CA 1989 that the possibility of a split residence order can be considered. Both holders of the order would have parental responsibility (which they probably would have anyway), but under a split order they will both have more ability to use it.

Do you think these orders will be commonly made? If not, why not?

Whilst these orders may be appropriate in some cases, they are not perceived as being the norm. The DoH Guidance states (at vol. 1, para. 2.28):

> it is not expected that it will become a common form of order, partly because most children will still need the stability of a single home and partly because in the cases where shared care is appropriate there is less likely to be a need for any order at al.

This highlights certain reasons for not making the orders. The notion of stability is important, since the courts must be assessing what is in the child's best interests. An order which would 'confuse' a child may not be in their interests. Also, the sharing of residence orders will normally be based upon the ability of the two carers to co-operate. If there are unresolved difficulties, or a lack of communication, it is unlikely the order will benefit the child. By contrast, if the parents/carers can co-operate, the court will look to the impact of s. 1(5): the 'no order' principle. If parents can agree and work together, will there be any benefit to the child in making an order at all?

For examples of cases on this issue, see *A v A (Minors) (Shared Residence Order)* [1994] 1 FLR 669 and *Re WB (Residence Orders)* [1995] 2 FLR 1023 in *Cases and Materials* (**11.3.2.2**).

11.7.2.4 Criteria for orders

What factors will the courts consider before making an order?

Section 8 itself does not lay down any criteria to be satisfied before the orders can be made. Hence the court is reliant on s. 1 principles of welfare. The welfare checklist will apply, but is only directly called into play where the making of the order is contested.

With the impact of s. 1(5), fewer residence orders are being made. Whilst this may be beneficial in the terms of reducing state involvement, it has potential implications with reference to child abduction and utilisation of the Hague Convention on Child Abduction. Detailed knowledge of this area is beyond the scope of this work and if more information is needed, reference should be made to texts such as Cretney and Masson, *Principles of Family Law*.

11.7.2.5 Duration of the orders

How long do you think a residence order will last?

There are a number of answers to **SAQ 177** – since residence orders have a range of potential cut-off points.

Read s. 9(6) and (7) in *Cases and Materials* (11.3.2.3) to establish one end point.

As you can see from this section, residence orders (and indeed all s. 8 orders) will normally end on the child's sixteenth birthday. This is at odds with the age of majority which is set at 18.

Can you think why this? Can you foresee any problems?

Exceptional circumstances may give rise to the extension of the order until the child is 18. However, exceptional circumstances are perceived to be only those cases where a child is suffering from physical disability or learning difficulties. If a child falls into these categories then they will be unable to make decisions for themselves. This link into *Gillick* competence is therefore one reason for setting the limit at 16.

Difficulties may arise, however, if for example a non-parent cares for a child under a residence order. Morally once the child reaches 16, continued care should be provided but there would be no *legal* obligation to do so. A 16-year-old may find themselves without a roof over their head. Local authority accommodation may be provided, but resource shortages may limit this. Also the young adult may find themselves caught in the crossfire of local authority departments passing responsibility from one department to another. Finally, at 16 a young person cannot legally enter into a tenancy agreement; this might possibly lead to homelessness.

As courts can impose conditions on orders, they may impose a time condition, which reduces the duration of the order.

The order may be discharged upon the application of the parents, child or party to the order. Note, however, that if the child seeks to discharge the order, they must obtain the courts' leave first.

Finally, if parents obtain a residence order, and then cohabit for a period of six months or more, the residence order will lapse automatically (s. 11(5)).

11.7.3   CONTACT ORDERS

This is also one of the commonly sought orders and tends to go hand in hand with a residence order. The contact order replaces the pre-CA 1989 access order. The change in terminology also reflects a change in emphasis in the law.

11.7.3.1   Rights?

Look at s. 8 again in *Cases and Materials* (11.3.1). From the wording of the contact order in s. 8, whose right is it to contact, and whose duty is it to see that contact takes place?

The actual definition of a contact order does not clearly refer to the right to have contact. However, a common supposition from the CA 1989 is that contact is the right of the person named in the order. Equally, from the wording, it is assumed that the duty to ensure that contact occurs is placed on the person with care of the child. Only the second assumption is correct.

If, therefore, it is not the right of the person named in the order to have contact, whose right is it?

If contact can be said to be a right, it is seen as being a right of the child. This principle was established well before the implementation of the CA 1989 in the case of *M v M (Child Access)* [1973] 2 All ER 81 which you will find in *Cases and Materials* (**11.3.1.1**). Cases decided since the CA 1989 continue with this principle; see, for example, *Re W (A Minor) (Contact)* [1994] 2 FLR 441 in *Cases and Materials* (**11.3.3.1**).

Cretney argues that the issue of contact as a right is 'side-stepped by addressing the order to the carer' and also comments, '[a] contact order is thus not a legal recognition of a right by a way of ensuring that one of the child's needs is met' (Cretney and Masson, *Principles of Family Law*, 6th edn, Butterworths, 1997). The child's needs will, in a majority of cases, require that some form of contact is given (see, for example, Wall J in *Re M (A Minor) (Contact: Conditions)* [1994] 1 FLR 272 extracted in *Cases and Materials* (**11.3.3.1**).

11.7.3.2   What is contact?

Regardless of who (if anyone) has a right to contact, what is meant by contact needs to be established.

Write down what you would include in a definition of 'contact'.

Contact falls into two categories: direct and indirect. The former should be considered the norm, and is traditionally viewed as such. Direct contact involves face-to-face meetings between the child and the person named in the order. In many situations this direct contact will involve overnight stays, or even longer term visits, especially in school holidays.

What is the difference between a contact order that allows the child to stay every weekend with its father with a residence order to the mother, and a shared residence order with the father's order specifying that he has residence for the weekends only?

In many cases where contact can be negotiated between parents amicably, the court should consider refusing the order on the basis of s. 1(5). However, contact is easier to deny and is also a source of much acrimony. If a contact order is to be made, then it may appear similar to shared residence orders. In reality there may be no difference, other than in the names of the orders. If, however, the father of the child is not married to the mother, the granting of a shared residence order would automatically give him parental responsibility (s. 12(1)).

In some cases direct contact, whilst seen to be in the best interests of the child, may not be appropriate if the child and adult were left alone. This may be because allegations of abuse have been made, or because the child does not really know the adult and may become upset, or because the caring parent is concerned and will not allow contact to happen unless supervised.

Just as direct contact may have conditions as to supervision, it may also have conditions as to time/duration/venue, all of which will be decided in the interests of the child.

Indirect contact, by contrast, does not include face-to-face meetings. The child may therefore be contacted by telephone or by letter. If this would be detrimental to the child's welfare, but it is seen as appropriate for the absent parent to have knowledge of the child, reports and photographs may be sent to them instead. Indirect contact, i.e. going against the principle as stated by Wall J in *Re M* (see **11.7.3.1**) should be considered either only where it is clear that the child would suffer as a result of contact, or as a means of establishing direct contact if none has existed before.

ACTIVITY 160

Can the courts impose conditions on the caring parent to facilitate indirect contact, i.e. if the child is very young and illiterate and needs to have letters read to them?

Reread the case extracts from *Re M (A Minor) (Contact: Conditions) (Cases and Materials (11.3.3.1))* and *Re O (Contact: Imposition of Conditions)* [1995] 2 FLR 124 in *Cases and Materials (11.3.3.2)*.

Which approach do you feel is better?

11.7.3.3 Enforcing contact

Imagine you are a parent with care. You have two young children and the court has granted a contact order allowing contact with their father for each Saturday afternoon. You refuse to allow contact to take place since you believe that the father will abduct the children. Can you do this?

What would the situation be if it were the father who was refusing to take up his contact. How could you enforce this?

Refusal of contact is a matter that has taken up considerable judicial time in recent years. Invariably it is the refusal of contact rather than the failure to take up contact that is at issue.

Refusal of contact
If a caring parent does not agree to the making of the contact order, then the immediate option is to appeal it. An application for discharge may be pursued, although a court order does not adequately displace the presumption that contact should occur. It is far better to seek an order for no contact which would at least clarify the situation.

If an appeal or application is unsuccessful, the immediate solution is often to ignore the order and stop contact.

If the parent with contact is still seeking to exercise the order, an application for enforcement may ensue. The range of options for the court in this case is wide. The court may:

■ agree with the hostile caring parent, and refuse contact;

■ amend the nature of contact, perhaps reducing the amount of direct contact time to make the order workable;

■ change direct contact to indirect contact (perhaps with conditions);

■ swap over the orders, so that the parent with contact becomes the parent with residence rights;

■ if all else fails, imprison the non-compliant parent.

The first option has been utilised in the case of *Re H (A Minor) (Parental Responsibility)* [1993] 1 FLR 484 (extracts in *Cases and Materials* (**11.3.3.3**), although this case may be confined to its facts. Many more cases prefer to try to obtain a workable option, even though this may mean changing direct contact to indirect. This may seem like 'giving in' or acting contrary to the original 'best interests of the child'. However, the assumption would appear to be that anything is better than nothing. If an alteration to the nature of contact is not effective, the court may be faced with no option but to commit for the breach of the order.

Is this in the best interests of the child?

For a long time, the imprisonment of the carer has been seen as an inappropriate resolution; it is certainly unlikely to be in the interests of the child. However, judicial opinion is changing, whether you agree with it or not, and failure to comply with a contact order is seen as something that will not be countenanced.

To understand the approach of the courts to this problem, read the article by T. Ingman in *Cases and Materials* (11.3.3.3) and the extracts from the case of *A v N (Committal: Refusal of Contact)* [1997] 1 FLR 533 which was decided after the article was published.

From this activity you should be clear how the courts will deal with the matter. Ward LJ's judgment is particularly robust, and also clear in import. The fact that the welfare of the child is not an issue for committal proceedings may be of surprise, but logical.

Failure to take up contact
Contrary to the legal armoury that has been built up in relation to failure to *allow* contact, there is nothing to rely on in relation to a failure to *take up* contact. From the wording of the order in s. 8, there is no clear implication of rights or duties as Cretney points out in *Principles of Family Law* (6th edn). But, by placing responsibility on the person with care, there is no means of enforcing contact by that individual. One means by which it could be done is to threaten to stop contact completely. However, this may not have the desired effect, especially since it has been suggested that most contact will end or tail off after only about two years. That families need fathers may not be disputed, but the vocal minorities highlight the case of fathers being denied contact, not mothers who cannot ensure that it continues.

11.7.3.4 Duration of orders and criteria to be applied

These are subject to the same rules and considerations as residence orders. You should recall the fact that the courts apply a positive presumption in favour of contact since it is nearly always seen as being in the best interests of the child.

11.7.4 SPECIFIC ISSUES AND PROHIBITED STEPS ORDERS

Go back to s. 8 in *Cases and Materials* (11.3.1) and reread the definitions of these orders. Write down what they set out to achieve.

The fact that both of these orders deal with questions of parental responsibility is certain, but the terminology of the orders is possibly confusing. Both orders seem to do the same thing: they are different sides of the same coin. The main function of the orders is to deal with any dispute between persons who hold parental responsibility. This possibility of conflict should be known to you from your work on parental responsibility earlier in this chapter. If resolution is not possible, the court can be asked to step in. The court will then make a decision based on its perception of the child's best interests.

To illustrate how the orders can be used to achieve the same ends, consider this example.

Anne and Bill cannot decide to which school Christopher should go. Anne would like to register him at the local state infants school which has reasonably good teacher/pupil ratios. Bill, however, would like him to go to a nearby private school where he could attend as a day boarder. Bill considers the presence of large numbers of children from the local travellers' campsite to be detrimental to a state education.

If the couple are incapable of deciding this issue, they could approach the courts.

Anne could seek a specific issues order to ensure that Christopher does go to the local state school. She could alternatively seek a prohibited steps order to prevent Bill sending him to the private school.

Whichever she applies for, if she is successful, she will achieve what she set out to do.

Should local authorities be able to use these orders?

As the orders refer to the use of parental responsibility, it may seem logical to prevent authorities from utilising these provisions.

Read s. 9(2) again and also s. 9(5) in *Cases and Materials* (11.3.5) and note down the restrictions.

From this reading you should have noted that the only restrictions on local authorities are to prevent them seeking residence or contact orders and not specific issues or prohibited steps orders. Section 9(5) limits the scope of the latter orders to prevent a potentially quicker order (in the sense of procedural quickness) being used to acquire rights that should be sought under a slower procedure.

If a local authority does try to use these orders, it must restrict itself to matters of parental responsibility.

Read the extracts from *Nottinghamshire County Council* v *P* [1993] 3 WLR 637 in *Cases and Materials* (11.3.5) which illustrates this principle.

You will be referring to this case in **Chapter 12** since it raises other issues concerning child protection.

11.8   Summary

You have now come to the end of a reasonably long chapter, and have covered a large amount of material. You will possibly find it useful to consolidate your learning by making shorter revision notes now. You will need to refer to the concept of parental responsibility, focusing on:

■ what it is;

■ who has it;

■ who can get it and how.

Your notes should also refer to the consequences of failing to comply with one's duties and responsibilities as a parent.

The private law orders available would then form the next part of your notes. Definitions of the four s. 8 orders would be needed, together with supplementary information on:

- who can apply;

- what the criteria are;

- how long the orders last;

- any potential problems with the orders.

If you do this you will have a suitable set of notes from which to learn. A final stage of learning for this chapter is the following End of Chapter Assessment Question.

11.9   End of Chapter Assessment Question

Hussein and Jayne married 10 years ago. They have two children, Robina, aged 5, and Joshua, aged 3. The marriage started to deteriorate shortly after Joshua was born, and now the couple have decided to separate. No divorce is planned yet, although Jayne would like to dissolve the marriage in the not too distant future. Jayne is planning to go to live with her parents, who live in Cumbria in a large farmhouse. She would therefore have plenty of space for herself and the children. Hussein is not pleased at this decision, since it would be very difficult for him to travel the 200 miles to see the children. He is also concerned about Jayne's inability to bring up the children in the Muslim faith.

Advise Hussein who wishes to prevent this move, and would prefer Joshua to remain with him so he can be raised in accordance with the Muslim faith.

What advice would you give Hussein if he wished to take the children to Iran to see their paternal grandparents and other relations?

See *Cases and Materials* (**11.5**) for an outline answer.

CHAPTER TWELVE

THE PUBLIC LAW RELATING TO CHILDREN

12.1   Objectives

By the end of this chapter you should be able to:

■ define and explain the meaning of child abuse;

■ produce a flow diagram indicating the stages of local authority intervention;

■ discuss the variety of legal orders that can be utilised by the authority;

■ evaluate the effectiveness of some of these orders;

■ apply the law to hypothetical scenarios and give relevant advice to clients.

12.2   Introduction

It is now time to move to what will be a lengthy chapter dealing with the variety of legislative provisions in public law relating to child care. The principal agency you will be concerned with is the local authority social services department, which, by virtue of the Local Government Act 1970, has responsibility to protect children within its area. The principles you have studied under the CA 1989, s. 1 will all be applicable to public law (some considerations being more relevant than others). You must always remember the principles of 'non-intervention' and 'working in partnership', since these are crucial to social work practice in this field.

Remember, this is a long chapter, and you should divide up your study time rather than attempt both parts of the chapter all at once. Suggested sections to study together are:

Part One: **12.3** to **12.6**   child abuse and investigation

        12.7 to **12.10**   short-term orders

Part Two: **12.11** to **12.17**   long-term orders

PART ONE

12.3 Child Abuse

As you will recall from **Chapter 10**, the 'discovery of child abuse' has always been linked to the passing of legislation. However, child abuse is a recent phenomenon. By this what is meant is that some actions which are today perceived as abusive or harmful to a child, have in the past been accepted as normal behaviour. In previous generations the use of corporal punishment, say by use of the belt or slipper, was perfectly acceptable. Today this attitude is questionable. The recognition of child abuse, as we understand it today, has been linked to the 'battered baby' syndrome which was 'discovered' in the 1960s by Dr Henry Kempe. Thereafter came the 'discovery' of other forms of abuse. Cathy Cobley traces this series of discoveries in *Child Abuse and the Law*, London: Cavendish Publishing, 1995.

Turn to *Cases and Materials* **(12.1) and read the extracts from this text. Do you find this history a tenable argument?**

The idea of 'discovering' child abuse seems far-fetched, but the series of events that Cobley refers to are clearly supported by other evidence, i.e. the differing public enquiries, the change in emphasis in legislation. Society has, over a period of time, become more willing to accept that these sorts of things do go on. This belief may have been held before, but the major change was the public voicing of concerns.

12.3.1 WHAT DO WE MEAN BY CHILD ABUSE?

Child abuse tends to be defined by category, albeit that fitting an alleged act of child abuse into a specific definition is often an arbitrary and artificial process.

Write down the categories of child abuse that you think exist. If you can, try to define what constitutes abuse within the category.

There are four categories used for defining child abuse. They are:

■ physical abuse;

■ neglect;

■ sexual abuse;

■ emotional abuse.

You should have been able to identify these from your reading from Cobley and earlier studying. If you did not identify the same categories, try to write a definition for these four.

When you have done this, compare your definitions with those set out in *Cases and Materials* (**12.1.1**). How did you do?

Naturally, there will be some limitations with these definitions.

Can you think of some of those limitations?

Looking at sexual abuse as a category, would you agree that allowing a child to watch a sexually explicit video is abusive? What about underage sexual activity – is that abusive? On what basis do you answer those questions? Are you answering on behalf of yourself and your own opinions, or on behalf of everyone? If you can, why not ask others for their views on what equals abuse.

Neither of these activities are adequately caught by the definition (*Cases and Materials* (**12.1.1**)) as it stands: allowing the child to watch a video may incorporate acts to which a child cannot consent, but is it engaging in sexual activity? If a child is sexually active with another child, again there may be the question of consent, but the definition refers to the actions of adults. You may question whether the circumstances militate against a finding of abusive behaviour. Two 13-year-olds who are behaving in a sexual way with one another (assuming of course it is heterosexual behaviour) would be perceived in an entirely different way from a 13-year-old engaging in the same activities with a 4-year-old.

This should have highlighted that one of the problems with these definitions is that they are potentially highly subjective. They may appear to be objectively assessed, but this is questionable as you can see from the variety of questions and scenarios posed above.

Consider now the indicators of abuse which you will find in *Cases and Materials* (12.1.1) (which you will see suggest that sexual abuse can be at the hands of other children). What other difficulty with the defining and recognition of abuse do these suggest?

Looking initially at physical abuse, two of the indicators given are multiple bruising and scratches, and injuries of different ages. If a child leads a reasonably active life, it is suggested that bruises and/or scratches at different times will be inevitable. (Do you recall how many times you fell off a bike whilst learning how to ride it, or fell out of a tree scrumping?) Therefore, simply having regard to the nature of the injuries cannot be sufficient, especially if only one set of injuries is presented. If the harm suffered is severe then the degree of concern may be higher. But how is that judged, and must more than one of the indicators need to be satisfied? In addition it is stated that there should be inadequate/no explanation, or a reasonable belief of harm being deliberately caused. Here again you return to a subjective element, and the ability to assess evidence. The link between injury and cause of harm may therefore be difficult to prove, if a reasonable explanation can be provided.

Hence another problem is the difficulty of proving that abuse is occurring (see the indicators for emotional abuse and decide if you could assess abuse from those factors alone).

12.3.2 THE EXTENT OF ABUSE

Why might it be difficult to assess the degree of child abuse that occurs in England and Wales?

There is no clear, definitive picture as to the extent of child abuse within England and Wales. Two reasons identified for this difficulty in finding 'figures' have been suggested by Cobley:

> First . . . there is no standardised definition of the subject matter. The term child abuse conceals the different meanings which may be attached to it, and these different meanings inevitably affect the results of any research conducted. Secondly, any figures on the prevalence of the problem must either be gleaned from cases reported to the authorities or be obtained from surveys, which must necessarily be retrospective in nature. (*Child Abuse and the Law*, 1995).

Cobley then goes on to review the evidence available to assess the extent of abuse.

The prime source of figures is often seen to be the numbers of children placed on the local authority's child protection register. This is a formal record of children perceived by the local authority to be suffering or at risk of suffering harm due to abuse within one or more of the four categories. The registers do not record the numbers of children who may be suffering abuse, but have not yet been discovered, or those who are not felt to warrant registration.

The figures for 1994 can be found in *Cases and Materials* (**12.1.2**), and you will note that these statistics produce both figures for each category, and a total figure. If you add up all the individual figures, you will exceed the total given. This accounts for the fact that some children are registered in more than one category. The figures have shown a decrease in registrations since 1991, when 45,300 cases were registered, or on the register. Cobley suggests that this decrease is possibly due to the removal of the registration category 'grave concern'. An alternative explanation is given thus:

> From an optimistic point of view, it can be argued that the decrease in registration reflects the success of the Children Act 1989 in encouraging professionals to work in partnership with parents and carers. (*Child Abuse and the Law*).

Two criticisms of this reasoning can be made: first, in many situations where a child would have normally been registered under 'grave concern', the removal of the category meant children were just registered under one of the remaining categories and secondly, there is no reason why a child should not be registered where social workers are acting in partnership with parents and carers, since registration is not a precursor or indicator of future legal action.

Surveys are often a good means of discovering the extent of abuse, and two are referred to by Cobley in connection with sexual abuse.

Read the extracts concerning the findings of these surveys in *Cases and Materials* (**12.1.2**) and note the areas of concern that are suggested with regard to the results.

Do you think child abuse is increasing? Do you agree that the existence of charities such as ChildLine make it easier for children to make accusations of abuse, or to threaten to do so? Has the whole issue of child abuse swung too far in favour of the children's rights movement?

No answers to this will be suggested. Think about these issues and if possible discuss them in a study group.

12.4 The Local Authority's Role in Child Protection

Despite a concentration on child abuse and child protection work, it is important to remember that not all cases where the local authority gets involved will involve abuse: the local authority's duties are much wider than that. However, as you should remember from your existing work, the fact is that crisis work has a higher priority than it should perhaps receive. This is due to budget constraints which reduce the ability to act in a preventative way.

12.4.1 THE BASIC DUTIES: s. 17, CA 1989

Write down what you think is the basic duty of all local authorities in relation to child protection.

Now read s. 17(1), CA 1989 in *Cases and Materials* (**12.2.1**).

The duty to support children and their families is, under this section, by way of the provision of services. By so doing, the aim is to meet the requirements of sch. 2, para 7. You will find this provision, together with other paragraphs from this schedule in *Cases and Materials* (**12.2.1**).

The provision of services, and attempting to keep children with their families is consistent with the fundamental principles of the CA 1989.

If services are to be provided, are they only provided to the child?

Whilst the child is the primary client of the local authority, services may be given to any member of the child's family if 'it is provided with a view to safeguarding or promoting the child's welfare' (s. 17(3)). You should have got a clue that certain others could be assisted from reading sch. 2, para. 9. The family of a child for the purposes of this duty are perhaps a little wider than the normal definition. Under s. 17(10), family includes 'any person with parental responsibility for the child and any other person with whom he has been living'. This latter aspect operates to widen the potential beneficiaries of services.

Which children will be provided with services?

Whilst you have been referred to this in **Chapter 10**, the definition of children to whom services can be provided is set out in s. 17(1) and (10). You will find this in *Cases and Materials* (**12.2.1**), together with sub-section (11) which adds further definition.

Must the local authority itself provide the services?

Anyone involved in local government will be aware of the process of 'contracting out' which has been utilised for many local government services. Social services have been no different, and many services will be made available via voluntary or private organisations. The social services department will pay for the provision of services, and has the authority to request payment from the child's family (s. 17(7), (8)). Before charges can be levied against the client and family, the local authority must assess the family's ability to pay. It is suggested that some services should not be charged for (i.e. if a service were provided to keep a child out of care) particularly if parents are in receipt of benefits (s. 29).

It is unlikely that local authorities would consider enabling parents/families to purchase required services direct, and support that purchase by the provision of finance. The CA 1989 does permit this, but only in exceptional circumstances (s. 17(6)).

12.4.2   OTHER SERVICES

Section 17(1) makes reference to 'other duties imposed' on local authorities by virtue of the CA 1989. Can you think what these might be?

These 'other duties' are found in the following sections:

- s. 18(1), (3): day care for some children aged under five and other children;

- s. 20(1): provision of accommodation for some 'children in need';

- ss. 22, 23 and 24(1): duties to children 'looked after' by the local authority;

- s. 24: duty to provide advice and assistance for certain children.

12.4.2.1   Day care for children aged under five and others

Read s. 18 in *Cases and Materials* (12.2.2.1) and note down who can gain access to the services and decide if this is a duty or a power.

The purpose of the section is to impose a duty on local authorities to provide day care for pre-school age children and supervised care and activities after school for school age children, if those children are 'in need' within the definition of s. 17. The local authority is empowered to extend these services to other children even if they are not in need. However, these services are not commonly provided.

Should they be commonly provided if this is a duty?

If this was an outright duty, local authorities would be open to legal action for failure to comply, given the general lack of such services. A careful consideration of the section shows that the duty is discretionary, i.e. the local authority need only provide services 'as are appropriate'. If the local authority reasonably decides that existing facilities are appropriate, or that no facilities are appropriate, it has met its statutory requirements.

12.4.2.2   Accommodation

The general duty is specified in s. 20(1).

Read s. 20(1) in *Cases and Materials* (12.2.2.2) and write down the three situations when accommodation must be provided.

The situations envisaged in subsection (1) relate to children in need and you should have noted the factors in s. 20(1)(a), (b) and (c). If a child is not classed as being in need under the terms of s. 17, the local authority may still provide accommodation if the situation is within s. 20(4).

Read s. 20(4) and write down how this power to provide accommodation is limited by subsections (7), (8), (9) and (11), which are all extracted in *Cases and Materials* (12.2.2.2).

Whilst the local authority may provide accommodation, if any person with parental responsibility (and this will normally be someone other than the person seeking the accommodation) objects to this *and* is able to provide or arrange suitable accommodation themselves, the local authority's powers are ended. Of course, there is the question of who decides on suitability! If the child concerned is the subject of a residence order under s. 8, CA 1989, the picture is a little different. Here, if it is the person(s) with whom the child is to live who requests accommodation, then no other person with parental responsibility can stop the local authority assisting.

Do you think the child should have any rights? If so, what?

Section 20 is unusual in that it gives a child a specific right with reference to accommodation. This right is, however, subject to the discretion of the local authority. Under s. 20(3), the local authority 'shall provide accommodation for any child in need . . . who has reached the age of 16 and whose welfare the authority consider is likely to be seriously prejudiced if they do not provide him with accommodation.'

It is clear that the 16-year-old faces some hurdles here, i.e. they must be a child in need and they must convince the local authority that their welfare will not just be at risk, but will be seriously prejudiced if accommodation is not provided.

Note the effect of subsection (11) on the ability of a person with parental responsibility to object to accommodation being provided or to remove the 16-year-old child from accommodation.

When the local authority is considering providing accommodation, regardless of the reason or provision for so doing, it should discuss the matter with the child and try to establish the child's wishes (s. 20(6) in *Cases and Materials* (**12.2.2.2**)).

Is this type of accommodation provided by way of compulsion?

Prior to the CA 1989, accommodation was provided either on a 'voluntary' basis or 'compulsory' basis. The distinction was that the former did not rely on any legal intervention before it could arise, whilst the latter was dependent upon an order placing the child into the local authority's care. Whilst the terminology of voluntary and compulsory care has gone, the idea of children being cared for by the local authority in the absence of a court order continues.

Under s. 20 children are provided with accommodation on a voluntary basis. Consequently, the local authority does not gain parental responsibility, except to the extent that it is delegated by the person placing the child with it. When a parent seeks to remove the child from s. 20 accommodation, there is nothing the local authority can do if it does not feel removal is appropriate, other than seek a court order (you will be considering these shortly).

If a child has been made subject to a legal order (for example a care order), then the local authority are obliged to provide accommodation. They cannot avoid responsibility by refusing to classify the child as in need. The local authority would in this situation have parental responsibility and parents, or others with parental responsibility, would not be in a position to remove the child at will.

If a child is being provided with accommodation, whether it be by virtue of a legal order or by agreement with the parents under s. 20, the child will be said to be 'looked after' by the local authority. This is a generic term, and simply knowing that a child is 'looked after' will not clarify the child's status. The terminology that is appropriate to distinguish looked after children is either that the child is 'in the local authority's care' – meaning subject to a legal order placing the child with the local authority, or 'accommodated', meaning that the child is being provided with accommodation under s. 20.

If a child has been looked after by the local authority at any time after they have reached the age of 16, but whilst still a child, for a minimum consecutive period of three months (this period includes time prior to the sixteenth birthday), the local authority is under a duty to provide advice, assistance and befriending. The purpose is to promote the child's welfare when they cease to be looked after (s. 24).

12.5   The Duty to Investigate

Before a local authority can take any action towards the provision of services, it needs to establish to which families or children to direct its attention. In some situations this is easier than others, for example the single mother requesting accommodation whilst she goes into hospital, or the disabled child who attends a specialist school. However, as you are aware, the majority of child care work is not spent with these types of families.

12.5.1   SECTION 47

In what ways will suspected cases of abuse become known to the social services?

A case will normally become apparent via some form lof referral to the local authority. Referrals may be from anyone, e.g. neighbours, friends, family, health visitor, GP, hospital casualty department, police or school.

SAQ 196

Should a doctor make referrals, or is this contrary to his/her duty of confidentiality?

For many professionals, the making of referrals of suspected child abuse may conflict with the ethical duty to maintain confidence. However, the public interest in disclosing abuse, and the emphasis that is placed on the welfare of the child means that this duty may be breached. The guidance to the CA 1989, *Working Together under the Children Act 1989*, HMSO, 1991, makes specific reference to the ethical perspective, and you will find the relevant paragraphs in *Cases and Materials* (**12.3.1**). The duty to co-operate and to share information across different professional agencies is confirmed in the CA 1989 itself.

ACTIVITY 172

Read s. 47(9), (10) and (11) in *Cases and Materials* (12.3.1) and note down the agencies to whom this duty to co-operate is addressed and the extent of this duty.

Once a referral is made, the local authority is under a duty to make enquiries about the child. This duty arises under s. 47, CA 1989.

ACTIVITY 173

Read s. 47(1) and (3) in *Cases and Materials* (12.3.1). When will this duty be triggered, and what is the purpose of the investigation?

From your reading you should have identified that there are three potential trigger criteria for the commencement of a s. 47 investigation:

- that the child is subject to an Emergency Protection Order (EPO);

- that the child is in police protection;

- that the local authority has reasonable cause to suspect that a child is suffering or is likely to suffer significant harm.

Do not worry if you do not know about EPOs or about significant harm, you will consider all these issues later.

The purpose of the investigation is set out in subsection (3) as being to establish whether certain steps should be taken; i.e.:

- whether the local authority should apply for any legal order under the CA 1989 for the purpose of safeguarding or protecting the child's welfare;

- where the child is subject to an EPO and not in local authority accommodation, whether the child should be provided with such accommodation;

- where a child is in police protection, whether an application should be made under s. 46(7) which permits an application to be made for an EPO.

All these areas are focused on the possible legal orders that could be obtained.

12.5.1.1 Police protection

Read s. 46(1) to (8) in *Cases and Materials* (12.3.1.1) noting its main purpose.

Under this section, the police are provided with short-term protective power where they believe a child is likely to suffer significant harm if no action is taken. The police may either remove a child to suitable (and safe) accommodation, or prevent removal from (safe) accommodation. The example of a hospital is given to illustrate the point.

The accommodation that is provided (if any) should normally be via the local authority.

Any removal of the child under s. 46 will be time limited, and if you had not picked up on the duration, re-read subsection (6).

Do the police need to seek a court order to remove under this section?

Despite the fact that the police may be removing a child from its parents, there is no necessity to seek court authorisation before acting, or indeed at any time. It is perhaps for this reason that the police do not gain parental responsibility over the child, and the only section which would permit any aspect of parental responsibility to be met by the police would be s. 3(5).

12.5.1.2 The focus and means of investigating

What do you think that the local authority should focus on initially?

If the spirit of the CA 1989 is to be complied with, then s. 47 should perhaps reflect the need of the local authority to provide services under s. 17 since these may be all that is required to protect the child and safeguard its well-being.

Is the duty to investigate absolute?

You should be familiar with this type of question, and the answer, by now. Whilst the section states that the local authority *shall* make enquiries, it then states 'such enquiries as they consider necessary to enable them to decide whether they should take any action'. The local authority may consider it unnecessary to make enquiries, and in so far as this is based on reasonable grounds, judicial review would be unsuccessful in challenging the decision.

Must the child be seen?

If enquiries are considered to be necessary, it is hard to see how the local authority can assess the child's risk of suffering harm without actually seeing the child. Section 47(4) requires the local authority to:

> take such steps as are reasonably practicable—
> (a) to obtain access to [the child]; or
> (b) to ensure that access to him is obtained, on their behalf, by a person authorised by them for the purpose, unless they are satisfied that they already have sufficient information with respect to him.

Again, the duty is qualified.

ACTIVITY175

Read s. 47(6) in *Cases and Materials* (12.3.1.2) and write down the consequences where access is sought and not obtained.

The actions to be taken by the local authority all involve legal action, unless the local authority believes the child's welfare can be protected without such action. Qualified duties strike again!

When legal action is not to be pursued, the local authority needs to decide whether or not to review the case (s. 47(7)). By including this provision, the local authority is at least directed to producing reasons why no later review is deemed necessary, and this should prevent cases being allowed to drift.

ACTIVITY176

Read the extracts in *Cases and Materials* (12.3.1.2) from the case of *D v D (County Court Jurisdiction: Injunctions)* [1993] 2 FLR 802, where the trial judge had imposed restrictions on the local authority to prevent its continued involvement and investigation of the family.

Summarise the views of the judges as to the level of interference by the local authority.

As the family was already involved in private law proceedings, do you think there should be a means to involve the local authority?

The attitude of the judiciary in *D v D* was to a degree surprising. The local authority had intervened, as it was required to do under s. 47 after the allegation of physical injury was made. The judges did not appear to disagree with this, but with the subsequent decisions. The local authority was of the belief that the child L might be at risk of suffering harm, and so decided to conduct an in-depth assessment. A s. 47 investigation, at least initially, will not be in depth due to time constraints. To carry out a full assessment, it is common practice to see all the relevant family members, including siblings, in order to get the whole picture of the family dynamics. The court, by contrast, appeared to believe that the child was not at risk of any harm, and even if he was, this was something that could be addressed via the private law proceedings. This belief, that the court can ensure risks of harm are addressed in private law, may be misconceived.

What the case illustrates is a tension between the powers of the court and the ability to control local authorities in carrying out their duties under the CA 1989. In this case, by deciding it could place a restriction on the parent co-operating with the s. 47 investigation, the court is in reality fudging the issue.

12.5.2 SECTION 37 INVESTIGATIONS

The private law in the CA 1989 has investigation procedures, although in the majority of cases parents will have agreed a solution. If this is not so, or the court is not totally happy with the parents' solution, it can utilise the Court Welfare Officer's services. The CWO can be requested to provide a report on the family to the court (under s. 7). The CWO will not normally have protracted contact with the family members. In some situations the court will request a s. 7 welfare report from the local authority. However, this is generally the exception since local authority budgets do not set aside funds for this purpose.

In some private law matters, the court may believe that the child is at risk of significant harm, and that the local authority needs to be involved. It might be a case where child protection is an issue, but one where the family is unknown to the local authority, or where no referrals have ever been made. In this type of situation, s. 37 can be invoked.

Read s. 37 in *Cases and Materials* (12.3.2). Write down the situations in which it will be used and the purpose of the investigation.

The trigger criterion for the section is where it appears to the court that it may be appropriate for a care or supervision order to be made in respect of a child.

Why do you think the court cannot simply make a care order?

In the review of the legislation it was believed that the giving of power to the court to commit a child to the care of the local authority, without necessarily having involved the local authority, or without the need to comply with specific criteria, was inappropriate. It also reflected an imbalance of power and responsibility between the courts and the local authority. See further the comments from the Law Commission in *Cases and Materials* (12.3.2).

Where a s. 37 investigation is carried out, the focus of the local authority should be to consider whether it needs to apply for a care order or supervision order, provide services or any other assistance or take any other action. As with s. 47, the extent to which intervention is needed, and the nature of that intervention must be carefully assessed. If a child's welfare can be safeguarded satisfactorily with a minimum level of intervention, this is the path that should be taken.

Return to s. 37. How long does the local authority have to complete its investigation? How does this compare with s. 47?

Under the terms of subsection (4) the local authority must report back to the court within eight weeks, unless the court directs otherwise. This may mean a shorter period rather than a longer period. By contrast, you should have discovered from your earlier reading that there is no set time limit for s. 47 investigations. Whilst it is naturally in the child's best interests to conclude matters quickly, there is no legal obligation to finish the investigation by a specified time.

If the court orders a s. 37 investigation, and the local authority decides to do nothing, and the court disagrees, can the court force the local authority to act?

The best way to answer this is to get you to read the extracts from *Nottinghamshire County Council v P* [1993] 3 WLR 637. Look at the extracts now in *Cases and Materials* (12.3.2).

As you have seen, the courts are in a difficult position if the local authority decides to do nothing: the courts cannot make it do anything. This was highlighted as being a major gap in the law, but as yet no moves have been made to change the situation. The gap arises simply because of the need to reduce the local authorities' powers and those of the courts to remove children from the care of their parents. Such Draconian state intervention should only be done in accordance with set criteria.

To see how s. 37 normally operates, read the extract from *Re H (A Minor) (Section 37 Direction)* [1993] 2 FLR 541 in *Cases and Materials* (12.3.2).

12.6   Child Protection Case Conferences

You may recall the mention of case conferences in the case of *D* v *D* earlier. The holding of case conferences are part and parcel of the child protection process, and *Working Together under the Children Act 1989*, gives details in Part 6 as to how and what should be done in a conference.

12.6.1   WHAT IS THE CONFERENCE THERE FOR?

The conference is intended to:

bring together the family and the professionals concerned with child protection and provides them with the opportunity to exchange information and plan together. The conference symbolises the inter-agency basis and the conference is the prime forum for sharing information and concerns, analysing risk and recommending responsibility for action. (*Working Together*, para. 6.1)

Who would you invite to a child protection case conference? Make a list of those you would feel ought to participate.

The invitees will reflect the inter-agency approach. Your list should look something like that set out in *Cases and Materials* (**12.4.1**), which is taken from *Working Together*.

Do you agree that the child and the parents should always be invited?

The decision to include the child in the attendees is not nor should be automatic. It will depend upon the age and understanding of the child. Indeed, in some cases, even if a child had reached a certain level of understanding it would be contrary to the child's interests to attend due to the potentially harmful conflict that may arise between the child and parents. Even if the child is invited, it is always open to exclude him/her from part of the conference, and this is true of the parents as well. Occasionally it may be the case that the presence of the family will inhibit the free exchange of information that is needed.

12.6.2 WHEN WILL A CONFERENCE BE NEEDED?

Conferences fall into two categories:

■ the initial child protection case conference;

■ the child protection review.

The former needs to be convened when a referral into suspected abuse has occurred, the latter acts as a means to ensure that cases do not drift.

The initial conference is clearly part of the child protection process, but should not be used to delay protective work.

Read para. 5.15.3 of *Working Together* in *Cases and Materials* **(12.4.2). Note the time frame indicated. Is this realistic?**

The ideal is to hold the first conference within 8 days of the referral, although 15 days is set as a maximum. In many cases this maximum is not even achieved. Despite this being contrary to the guidance document, there will be no comeback, since the guidance document does not have the force of law: it is guidance only. The delay is inevitable given the nature of the invitees. A conference will only work at an acceptable level if professionals can attend, and convening a conference at short notice does not promote good attendance rates.

Review conferences are subject to different time frames, since a decision has already been made, and the purpose of the review is different. Reviews will examine the existing level of risk to the child and ensure that the protection plan that has been put into effect is working.

12.6.3 WHAT DECISIONS CAN BE MADE?

What do you think?

If you work within the field of child care or child protection you may have attended a case conference. If you have been to several, you may have seen different approaches to the range of decisions that are made. In line with the guidance document, there is only one decision that can be made at the conference.

Read para. 5.15.4 from *Working Together* in *Cases and Materials* (12.4.3) to see what that decision is. Did it match with your thoughts?

One of the major difficulties with case conferences is that they are perceived to be the forum within which the decision to take legal action is made. This is one decision that is *not* within the conferences' remit. As you have seen, the function is to decide whether or not to register the child's name on the child protection register. If the child is already registered, the review conferences will assess whether it is safe to remove the child's name from the register. As part of this decision making process, or rather as an adjunct to it, the conference can formulate a child protection plan. This plan may set out the variety of different agencies involved and the extent to which they will act. The benefit of establishing this plan is that everyone will be there, and this may include the parents.

Whose decision is it to take legal proceedings?

The only decision makers will be the local authority (which is charged with this function), and in particular the social services department. The legal department of a local authority will not make the decision but merely act to advise the social workers.

12.7 Short-term Orders

By now you will be familiar with the notion that the local authority will intervene by means of legal action only where it is necessary.

The preferred route should always be to attempt the voluntary options. In some situations a voluntary route may not succeed. Indeed some families may actually co-operate better if subject to a court order. If legal action is needed, the local authority will approach each individual case on its facts and history. Whilst the CA 1989 gives both short- and long-term orders, there will be no guarantee as to how intervention will first arise. For study purposes you will look at short-term and emergency orders first before considering long-term intervention.

12.7.1   THE CHILD ASSESSMENT ORDER: s. 43

Turn to s. 43 in *Cases and Materials* (12.5.1). What is the purpose of this order?

The reason for introducing the child assessment order (CAO) has been suggested by Masson and Morris as being due to 'concern that the more rigorous requirements for an EPO could mean that it was impossible to get an EPO where there was fear for the child's safety but no hard evidence.' (*Children Act Manual*, London: Sweet & Maxwell, 1992) The CAO is a new order and not really preceded by anything similar. It could be argued that by allowing the assessment of a child, the order is akin to a fishing exercise, to enable the local authority to get evidence on which to base a future application. The use of the order to gather evidence is incontrovertible. However, that it is a 'fishing exercise' is a less valid suggestion, since the CAO can only be obtained after the criteria in s. 43 have been proved.

12.7.1.1   The criteria

A CAO can only be applied for by the local authority, or an 'authorised person'.

Who do you think is authorised?

The Secretary of State is responsible for authorising agents under the CA 1989 to carry out specified functions or duties. The only person so authorised at present is the National Society for the Prevention of Cruelty to Children.

Before the court can make the order it must be satisfied of three things.

Having read s. 43 in *Cases and Materials* (12.5.1), what do you think those three elements are?

You should have the following listed:

- the applicant has reasonable cause to suspect that the child is suffering or likely to suffer significant harm;

- an assessment is needed to establish whether the child is so suffering;

- the assessment is not likely to happen without the order.

All three elements need to be satisfied.

How do you think the local authority can prove the latter point in this list?

This may be proved from a variety of acts or omissions by the child's parents. For example, the local authority may be seeking to work voluntarily with the family and may have set up a series of appointments with various professionals to assess the child. The parents may refuse to assist, or fail to attend. Alternatively, the parents may simply refuse to allow access to the child. If access is refused, then Masson and Morris comment, 'refusal may provide grounds for an EPO under section 44(1)(b) or (c). That being the case, it is not clear when a child assessment order will be used. The provisions will provide the background against which professionals concerned with a child's care negotiate with the parents for access.' (*Children Act Manual*). The suggestion here is that a CAO is possibly a threatening device as opposed to a 'real' order. The fact that CAOs are hardly used would support that suggestion, which cannot really be in accordance with the principle of voluntariness. Is co-operation voluntary when supported with the threat of legal action?

In addition to proving the criteria set out in s. 43, any applicant must also satisfy the court that the making of the order will be better than making no order at all (s. 1(5)) and that the order is in the best interests of the child (s. 1(1)). There will be no need to go through the welfare checklist as s. 1(3) is not applicable, because s. 43 is within Part V of the CA 1989 and hence not directly referred to in s. 1(4). Practically, any applicant will do well to remember the checklist and ensure that statements make some reference to the issues within it, since the checklist is taken as indicating the factors by which the child's welfare can be assessed.

12.7.1.2 Consequences

A CAO is only available for a period of seven consecutive days. All the assessments and examinations which the local authority wishes to conduct must be completed within this period. The local authority cannot remove the child from the parental home, unless this has been authorised by the court itself. The local authority will not obtain parental responsibility for the child, so this remains with the parents. In some cases the court, if faced with an application for a CAO, may consider the case to be too serious for a mere investigative order. In such cases, under subsection (3), the court can treat the application as being for an EPO. This potentially reduces the effect of the CAO, since the court, consisting of lay magistrates in the majority of cases, will perhaps not wish to be seen placing a child in potential risk, regardless of the views of the local authority.

If a parent refuses to comply with a CAO, whilst it would be unlikely that any action to commit for breach of a court order would arise, the chances of a successful EPO or care order application are certainly higher.

12.7.1.3   Advantages

Do you perceive there to be any advantages in seeking CAOs? (It is appreciated that this is going to be hard to answer in the absence of knowledge of other orders!)

The advantages of the order, as identified by Jim Harding of the NSPCC, are:

(a)   parental responsibility is retained by parents;

(b)   the child may be seen by the family doctor in a familiar environment;

(c)   parents are more likely to co-operate with this type of order and the social work relationship with the family will not be damaged;

(d)   the child can be protected in serious but not emergency situations.

(Extracted from Masson and Morris, *Children Act Manual*.)

Think about these advantages for a moment. Do you agree with them?

Some criticisms of them have been raised by Masson and Morris, *Children Act Manual*, along the following lines:

(a)   the child may be removed by the court order which will order assessment where the parents do not wish the child to be assessed;

(b)   the child may not see a GP, since the assessments may be needed to be carried out by specialists;

(c)   the CAO is predicated on non- co-operation, and will be used where there is suspicion regarding the child's welfare. 'It will take great social work skill to establish a relationship with the family in such circumstances';

(d) 'This order does not protect the child, it permits assessment. Where protection is required and evidence exists, care proceedings should be started.' In addition, the need to give notice (seven clear days) to the parents of proceedings militates against a protectionist ideal. If you have to wait for the hearing, does the child even need to be protected?

Can you understand why the order is used infrequently?

If you wish to see the situations where the orders are likely to be used, refer to the extracts from the *Children Act 1989 Guidance and Regulations*, vol. 1, in *Cases and Materials* (12.5.1.1).

12.8 Emergency Protection Orders: s. 44

Whilst CAOs are under utilised, EPOs certainly are not. The EPO is a short-term order, with the main aim being to protect in an emergency situation.

12.8.1 CRITERIA AND APPLICANTS

Read s. 44(1) and (2) in *Cases and Materials* (12.6.1) carefully. Write down who can apply and in what situations.

Section 44(1) is often misunderstood or confused by students, primarily since they mix up the criteria and fail to appreciate how they operate.

The section sets out three different criteria upon which an application can be based, and dictates which type of applicant can use which of the criteria.

12.8.1.1 The any person criterion

Section 44(1)(a) is referred to as the any person criterion, since 'any person' may apply for an EPO under these grounds. There are certain elements to the criterion on which you need to be clear.

First, to be successful, there must be 'reasonable cause to believe that the child is likely to suffer significant harm'.

Who has to hold that belief?

The common sense reaction would be to say, the applicant. However, if you have read the section carefully, you will know that it is the court that must hold that belief. It is the applicant's function to convince the court that the child is at risk.

Secondly, the risk of harm must arise from the child remaining in his/her current accommodation, or being removed from it (s. 44(1)(a)(i) and (ii) respectively).

The burden of proof to be satisfied will be the civil standard.

Can the local authority utilise s. 44(1)(a)?

As the subsection allows an application by 'anyone', the local authority can most certainly use it to obtain an order, and frequently will do so. Others you may come across using it include hospitals, if they believe that removal of a child from hospital care will be detrimental to its welfare (this falls within s. 44(1)(a)(ii)), the police and family members.

If an EPO is gained under this provision by anyone other than the local authority, the court will notify the local authority of the making of the order. This will trigger the investigation of the case and the child by the local authority under the provisions of s. 47.

12.8.1.2   The local authority criterion

Section 44(1)(b) is specific to the local authority only. To gain an EPO under this part, the local authority needs to establish that:

■ it is carrying out a s. 47 investigation;

■ the enquiries are being frustrated by access being denied;

■ it believes that access is needed as a matter of urgency.

All three elements of the criterion must be satisfied.

SAQ 12

Is this easier to satisfy than the any person criterion?

Arguably the answer is yes. Under s. 44(1)(a), it is the court that has to be satisfied that the child is at risk of harm, but under s. 44(1)(b) only the local authority has to believe anything. You will see that there is no mention of significant harm in s. 44(1)(b); that is because it is implicit from the fact of the s. 47 investigation. But again, note the differences in wording. For s. 44(1)(a), the court must have reasonable cause to believe, whereas under s. 47, the local authority must only have reasonable cause to suspect. The differences are subtle, but it is suggested that suspicion implies a lower threshold than belief. The extent to which any court would question the evidence of the local authority for holding that suspicion is also a matter for conjecture.

The inability to gain access to the child is linked into the s. 47 investigation. You should recall that the local authority under s. 47(4) is under a duty to see the child (unless it has sufficient information) and if access is refused, s. 47 directs the local authority to consider legal action. The question you should be thinking is, 'what is meant by access?'. Naturally it will refer to physical access, but the local authority social worker may wish to see the child in the home setting, whilst parents only allow 'access' at the local authority's offices. The social worker may wish to gain access to examine for injuries, which may be prevented if parents refuse to allow examination, or the child to be undressed.

'Urgency' is another issue open to interpretation, but it clearly means something more than the social worker wanting to see the child on a set day. Urgency will be assessed in the light of the overall situation, and history of the case, the age of the child and also whether other venues for seeing the child can be arranged and agreed between the family and the local authority.

12.8.1.3 The authorised person criterion

The final criterion in s. 44 is available only to 'authorised persons', the NSPCC. The criteria to be satisfied under s. 44(1)(c) are a conglomeration of s. 44(1)(a) and (b). Note that there has to be some evidence of suspicion of harm but here it is the applicant that must have the suspicion, not the court. Then s. 44(1)(c) replicates s. 44(1)(b) in that there must be enquiries being carried out and refusal of access which is needed urgently.

SAQ 213

Why might the NSPCC be carrying out enquiries?

If you remember s. 47, the wording of the section requires the local authority, when any of the three trigger criteria are met, 'to make, or cause to be made' any necessary enquiries. Hence, the local authority may 'contract out' enquiries to the NSPCC.

When the court is considering the making of an order under s. 44, regardless of whom the applicant is, it must have regard to the basic CA 1989, s. 1 principles, i.e. that the child's welfare is paramount, that the court should not delay, that it should consider the need to make an order at all. The welfare checklist is not directly called into consideration since the proceedure for seeking EPOs, as with CAOs, is to be found in Part V of the Act.

12.8.2   CONSEQUENCES OF MAKING THE ORDER

Read the rest of the extracts from s. 44 and also s. 45 in *Cases and Materials* **(12.6.2). List the consequences that arise following the making of an order.**

12.8.2.1   Removal

Section 44(4) authorises the removal of the child by the applicant to alternative accommodation. If the child is already in suitable accommodation (i.e. a hospital) the subsection will permit the retention of the child in that place. This needs to be read in conjunction with s. 44(10). As you can see from this provision if the EPO is obtained, but when the child comes to be removed there is found to be no reason for removal, this should not be done. In addition, if the child is removed, and the source of that harm subsequently disappears, then the local authority must consider returning the child. To give you an example, consider the following.

Anne and Bill cohabit, and have one son, Christopher. Bill is known to be violent. After a routine health visitor checkup, a referral was made to Wollham Social Services. The social worker has paid two visits to the home, on neither visit did she get into the house. An EPO was obtained, and Christopher removed to foster care. Two days after the order was made Anne obtained an ouster injunction against Bill. In this situation, if Anne has not been seen to be causing harm to the child, then it may be deemed appropriate to return Christopher.

If Christopher is returned, and Bill is accepted back into the home (contrary to the ouster) what can the local authority do?

If the child is returned, this will not automatically result in the termination of the order. So, if the source of harm reappears, the child can be removed again, for the remainder of the EPOs duration and without the need to seek further approval from the court.

Has the local authority any power to order a suspected abuser out of the premises?

Nottinghamshire County Council v *P* [1993] 3 WLR 637 (*Cases and Materials* (**12.3.2**)) should spring to mind, since this was a case where the local authority had attempted to use a prohibited steps order to do just that. The court held that it was not an appropriate use of the section. Now the Family Law Act 1996, Part IV, is in force there is judicial power to include an exclusion order when making an EPO. The amendment in sch. 6, FLA 1996 is reproduced in *Cases and Materials* (**12.6.2.1**) and inserts s. 44A into the CA 1989. The court will still need to make the EPO, but if the exclusion order is made, then the child will be expected to remain in the family home. Undertakings to leave voluntarily may also be acceptable. You should note that the EPO must be made, presumably to enable the local authority to remove a child if the suspected abuser reneges on the undertaking or breaches the injunction.

Even without the FLA 1996, a suspected abuser may be encouraged to leave, since the CA 1989, sch. 2, para. 5 permits the local authority to assist by provision of accommodation or even money. This provision is also in *Cases and Materials* (**12.6.2.1**).

12.8.2.2 Contact

If a child has been removed from its family, there is an expectation that the child will be given reasonable contact with its parents/carers during the life of the EPO (s. 44(13)). It is hoped that the trauma to the child will be lessened by allowing contact. However, it may not be appropriate for contact in all cases, or certainly not unsupervised contact. The court may therefore be asked to restrict or prevent contact for the benefit of the child. The court has the power to grant such directions under s. 44(6).

12.8.2.3 Duration

The EPO, as its name indicates, is designed to meet emergency situations and is therefore only of a limited duration. This accords with the attempt to move away from the previous, and quite Draconian place of safety order. The EPO will last for *up to* eight days on the first application (s. 45(1)). The applicant must be ready to persuade the court to grant the maximum since this cannot always be guaranteed. During this period, the local authority (whether the applicant or not) will be assessing the child to establish whether further legal action is needed or if services can be provided.

Do you think that eight days is long enough to complete an assessment?

It is hard to imagine a full assessment being carried out in the currency of an EPO to enable a fully informed decision to proceed (or not) with other legal action. Indeed, as an application for a supervision order or care order needs to be on notice, the eight days is an unrealistic proposition. If necessary, an application can be made to extend the initial order, by *up to* seven days (s. 45(5)). Only one such extension is permissible.

If no other application is made, then at the end of the EPO the situation will, legally, revert to normal. Practically this may not be so, since the parents may agree to work voluntarily with the local authority.

12.8.2.4   Parental responsibility

During the existence of the EPO, the applicant will obtain limited parental responsibility for the child (s. 44(4)(c)). The gaining of parental responsibility will not extinguish that held by the parents. It will, however, restrict the other holders' ability to exercise it. As you should remember, the other holders will not be able to act in a manner to conflict with the order.

The extent to which decisions can be made by the applicant is strictly limited. Section 44(5) confirms this.

Should any liability accrue if this requirement were breached?

You might, logically, assume so. However in the case of *F* v *Wirral Metropolitan Borough Council* [1991] 2 WLR 1132, the contrary was held. You will find the headnote in *Cases and Materials* (12.6.2.2). You will note that this decision is based on the actions of the local authority under the legislation prior to the CA 1989.

12.8.2.5   Appealing the order

Can you appeal against the making of, or refusal to make an EPO?

Most orders of the court are appealable: the EPO is not. This is logical given the limited time duration for the order. If an order has been made, the child, a parent of the child, anyone with parental responsibility or the person with whom the child was living before the order was made, may apply for it to be discharged (which is not the same as an appeal) (s. 45(8) to (10)). The discharge option is not available for all EPOs, it depends on the procedure used to get the order. If the individual(s) seeking to discharge the order had been given notice of the hearing and was present at the hearing, or in relation to an extension, was present when the extra duration was ordered, then he/she cannot discharge the order. In any event no application can be brought to discharge until 72 hours have expired. If the local authority is successful in getting the order, it will always have a minimum of three days before the order can be ended.

The situation where *no* order is made highlights the fact that gaps do exist in this legislation. The only viable option is to reapply to the court. The case of *Re P (Emergency Protection Order)* [1996] 1 FLR 482 illustrates the difficulties surrounding this point; see *Cases and Materials* (**12.6.2.3**).

12.8.3   PROCEDURE

From the previous paragraphs you will know that an EPO can be obtained 'on notice'. That notice is, under the Family Proceedings Rules, sch. 2, set at one day.

Is this consistent with the notion of emergency?

You should you have answered this in the negative. Can it really be said that a child is being protected if parents/carers are given a day to do something worse, or disappear (if you take a very pessimistic view of human nature). Due to the inconsistency with 'emergency', very few EPOs are sought after giving notice. Normally, they will be applied for ex parte, with the result that most parents can seek to apply for discharge of the order.

SAQ 220

Which court will be involved?

For all public proceedings, the starting place is the magistrates' court, or the family proceedings court as it is called. Therefore if an order is to be sought ex parte, it can be obtained out of court hours from a single magistrate. Indeed, under the Family Proceedings Rules a single court clerk may be empowered to grant an out of hours EPO.

Make sure you have included both the CAO and the EPO within your jurisdiction diagram of the court hierarchy in **1.6**.

12.9   The Guardian ad Litem

In certain specified proceedings, as established in s. 41, CA 1989, which is in *Cases and Materials* (**12.7**), the court is required to appoint a guardian ad litem for the child, unless the court is satisfied that it is not necessary to do so. It may not be necessary if the proceedings are relatively simple or uncontested (primarily agreed discharges), or if the child is considered mature enough to participate on his/her own behalf. The guardian ad litem will be a qualified social worker, but must not have worked in that particular social services department to avoid claims of lack of impartiality.

The role of the guardian ad litem is to act on behalf of the child, and to safeguard the child's interests. In effect the guardian ad litem is an independent expert who is there to put forward his/her views as to the childs need's and welfare in a given situation. The guardian ad litem is entitled to appoint a solicitor for the child. Normally this does not cause any difficulty. However, the solicitors client is in fact the child. Problems can arise if for example, you have a mature child, who disagrees with the guardian ad litem's recommendations. In this case, the solicitor would have to accept instructions from the child not the guardian ad litem.

As guardians ad litem are independent and have legal right (s. 42) to gain access to all the social work files on a case to which they are appointed, their recommendations are given a great deal of weight in the proceedings.

12.10   Summary of Part One

You have now come to the end of a major part of child protection legislation. There is a lot of information here to learn and consolidate. This is not helped by the general lack of reported cases, which should not surprise you since they are mainly in the family proceedings court, and EPOs are not subject to appeal. This will change when you move on to the long-term orders under s. 31, CA 1989. To assess your understanding to date, attempt stages one to three, inclusive, of the case study below. If you feel that any orders may be needed (which is not to say that they are) complete the application form which you will find in *Cases and Materials* at the end of **Part One**.

CASE STUDY: FACTS

Mr and Mrs Porter have been married for 10 years. Mr P (35) is out of work, and has been for several years. Occasionally he does a little odd-jobbing, but this is very infrequent and all on the sly. Mrs P (29) is known to have a learning difficulty. She was assessed when a young adult to see if she had any form of mental illness when she went through a period of severe depression; no further medical intervention occurred. She still suffers from bouts of depression, but never as bad as when a teenager.

The couple have four children, Emma is the eldest at six-years-old. She is at primary school. Her siblings are Tom, who is four, and the twins, Winifred and Steven, who are only 10-months-old. Mrs P is pregnant again, having just conceived.

The family live in a council house in a part of town with a 'bad' reputation. There are known to be drug pushers in the area. Mr P is not suspected of being involved in drugs, small time fiddling of the dole is his thing. They have a car, which Mr P seems to devote much of his time to and it always appears in good condition. Both parents smoke heavily.

Emma is a small child for her age, and is very thin. She is also quiet, and she finds it hard to join in the class activities, to play or to talk to the teacher. She always enjoys physical contact, e.g. having her hand held, and this is normally one of the few times she can be made to smile. When Emma arrives at school, she is 'grubby' and normally smells of urine. Indeed some days the smell is so bad that she has to be washed and changed into 'school clothes'. If she returns home in these clothes they are never seen again. When she is bathed her skin is ingrained with dirt. Emma receives school meals, but she cannot eat with any cutlery and always prefers the mashed potato and gravy. It is almost as if she does not know what the other things on her plate are. These concerns have been referred to the head, and the school is now keeping an unofficial diary of events.

One day on the way to the school bus after school Emma soils her underpants. She is cleaned up and sent home (having had to keep the bus waiting). The next day the staff at school go through the usual wash and change routine. They are shocked to find that she is still wearing the same soiled underpants which clearly have not been washed. When bathing her they also see two very clear bite marks on her arm and slight bruising on her buttocks. The head witnessed these injuries, and both class teacher and head write down what was seen.

Stage One   What may happen now?

Two weeks later a case conference is called. At this case conference evidence is heard from Social Services, primarily about the parents. The details of Mrs P's learning difficulties are elaborated. It is noted that Mrs P is good with the care of her babies, but that once the children get to the age of about three, she loses interest in them. Mr P has not been observed carrying out any caring role.

Both parents attend for part of the case conference. Mr P's attitude to his wife is somewhat derogatory. He repeatedly states that Mrs P is unable to cope, and that he now leaves her to 'get on with making a mess of things'. He says how bad she is with the kids, and that she just won't learn.

The health visitor, who is the only person who has been inside the home on a regular basis, confirms that Mrs P cannot cope with the children. She goes through the four children's centile charts. All are well below average with Emma at about 3 per cent. Winifred is the best in relation to the charts, but again is small for her age. Developmentally, all seem below average, having not met the milestones expected.

The children's GP provides a written report suggesting that the bite marks were those of a child, and Emma's brother is suspected of having caused them. The bruising was several days old, and not caused at the same time as the bites.

In relation to the state of the home, it is reported that it is always cold, and it seems that there is only one open fire (without fireguard). There is no dining room table, which may account for Emma's poor eating habits. The floors are not carpeted, and there is a pervading odour of urine. The health visitor has not been upstairs.

Stage Two   What may happen now?

It is now three months later. Emma has continued to arrive at school in a similar condition, but as the weather has deteriorated with the winter, she has not arrived in winter clothing. On more than one occasion she has turned up in her summer frock (dirty). Today she has had to be bathed before school starts. She has got severe bruising to her back and buttocks, and the injuries to her back have come up in weal-like lines. She is noticeably quieter, and it seems as if she is trying to be brave and not cry. The teacher wonders if she knows how to cry. The head has also observed the bruising, and has asked the school nurse to attend to Emma. The class teacher stays with Emma.

Whilst Emma is being cuddled by her class teacher she starts to talk without any prompting. She says that Daddy got very angry last night because she was naughty. When asked what she had been doing to be naughty, she says she had asked for some more dinner, since her Daddy had left his, and she was hungry. It transpires that Mr P had hit her with his belt and then sent her to bed. When asked if she is still hungry Emma nods her head. Some food is brought to her, which she wolfs down, naturally eating with her fingers.

Stage 3   What may happen now?

See *Cases and Materials* at the end of **Part One** for an outline answer.

PART TWO

12.11   Long-term Orders

The two orders that you are concerned with here are supervision orders and care orders, both of which are dealt with in Part IV of the CA 1989. The section which establishes the primary criteria for seeking either of the orders is s. 31, although you need to turn to other sections to learn more about the consequences of the orders. In this part of the chapter you will study the criteria for, and consequences of making these orders, and also a little about the process of making an order in the sense of the courts' involvement.

12.12   The Criteria

Read s. 31(1) to (3), (5), (9) and (10) in *Cases and Materials* (12.8) and using a separate sheet of paper make notes on the requirements these provisions lay down.

These are some of the major conditions that govern the use made of care/supervision orders, with subsections (2) and (3) establishing the primary qualification criteria. As you go through the rest of this chapter add and amend your notes to **Activity 186** for revision purposes.

Before analysing the criteria in depth, which of the two orders do you think is the more Draconian?

Purely from your reading of s. 31(1) and without knowing any of the consequences of the orders, it can be suggested that the supervision order is the less onerous of the two. It merely places the child under the supervision of the local authority, whereas a care order will potentially remove the child from the care of its parents.

Do you think it is appropriate to have the same qualifying criteria for two distinct orders?

You may find this difficult to answer at this stage. Write down your initial thoughts, and then return to **SAQ 222** when you have learnt more about the orders.

12.12.1   SECTION 31(2)

Go back to your notes on this subsection; how many parts to the criteria did you identify?

This subsection has two distinct elements to it before the tests have been satisfied. These two elements are often called the 'threshold criteria' since they form the basic threshold to be reached before the courts' power to make an order kicks in.

The first stage of the test is to establish that the child 'is suffering or is likely to suffer significant harm'. The second stage is to establish the reason for that harm or risk of harm. It should be due to the 'care given to the child . . . not being what it would be reasonable to expect a parent to give' or 'the child being beyond parental control', both of which relate the harm suffered by the child to the ability of the parents to care or control. Of the second element only one aspect needs to be proved, i.e. that the child is not being given adequate care, or is beyond control.

12.12.2   SIGNIFICANT HARM

This is a phrase which has run throughout the orders available to the local authority, and their duty to investigate.

How does the reference to significant harm in s. 31 differ from that in s. 44?

The difference in the wording within the sections is subtle but crucial. The s. 44 reference is to reasonable belief that the child is suffering significant harm. In s. 47 it was only reasonable suspicion. However, in s. 31 the reference is to the fact that the child *is* suffering or *is likely* to suffer. This is a more definite statement: you have gone beyond the realms of belief to actual knowledge. This higher burden is clearly necessary since you are dealing with far more interventionist orders.

12.12.2.1   The meaning of significant harm

The definition in subsection (9) (and (10)) has been described by Masson and Morris (*Children Act Manual*) as 'constructed like a Russian doll'. You may or may not agree, but it is true that the definition is not easy to deconstruct.

Go back to your notes on s. 31 – what did you identify as being meant by 'harm'?

Harm is clearly defined in subsection (9) as being 'ill treatment or the impairment of health or development'. These terms are then further defined. The definitions place more emphasis than was evident in pre-CA 1989 legislation on the effects of emotional harm, and the impairment of a child's emotional development, or socialisation, can therefore lead to a possible application.

Having regard to the definition of ill-treatment, do you consider that physical ill-treatment is included?

Your immediate reaction is probably yes, it has to be included. However, if you look closely at the wording, you could argue that it is not. The definition states ill-treatment 'includes sexual abuse and forms of ill-treatment that are not physical'. On a point of construction, does the word 'include' just refer to the sexual abuse and non-physical treatment? Or should it be interpreted to mean that these forms of abuse are included, but not to the exclusion of other forms of ill-treatment?

The courts have consistently interpreted it in its wider meaning. Masson and Morris quote the Lord Chancellor's explanation of the term, namely that 'Ill-treatment is not a precise term and would include, for example, instances of verbal abuse or unfairness . . .' (*Children Act Manual*). Note that there is no mention of physical ill-treatment there.

Go back to your notes on s. 31 – do you agree with the definition of significant? Is this sufficient?

When looking at this provision, you should have noted that the means to establish whether harm is significant, given in subsection (10), only relates to harm turning on a child's health or development. There is no reference to ill-treatment. Also, comparing a child with another does not really *define* 'significant', it merely highlights the method used to prove harm is significant.

The Royal Commission on Child Care Law stated in relation to 'significant' that it meant 'substantial' and that 'minor shortcomings in the health and care provided or minor deficits in physical, psychological or social developments should not give rise to any compulsory intervention unless they are having, or are likely to have, serious and lasting effects on the child' (para. 5.15).

If the courts are required to compare one child with another, how should they pick that other child?

Whilst many judges with experience in family matters will have a good knowledge of child development, some will have only a limited knowledge of this subject. The decision on whether a child is suffering harm will thus be based upon the expert evidence that is put before the court. In relation to comparison under subsection (10), the Lord Chancellor indicated during the CA 1989's passage through Parliament that it referred to a child of similar physical attributes but that the background of the child should not be brought into account. Masson and Morris argue that 'this ignores the fact that social and environmental factors contribute very significantly to what can be achieved' (*Children Act Manual*). The Lord Chancellor's view is also contradicted by the *Children Act 1989 Guidance and Regulations* (vol. 1, Court Orders) HMSO, 1991, which states 'the meaning of similar in this context . . . may need to take account of environmental, social and cultural characteristics of the child.'

Could therefore the court compare the health and development of one sexually abused child with another sexually abused child and decide that no significant harm has occurred?

If all environmental and social factors had to be included, this would be a possible outcome. However, a balance will need to be struck to prevent contentious issues such as this arising.

To illustrate how the courts are interpreting the meaning of significant harm, turn to the various cases extracted in *Cases and Materials*.

First, you should look at *Re O (A Minor) (Care Order: Procedure)* [1992] 1 WLR 912, to be found in *Cases and Materials* (11.1.2.2). Next, you should look at *Cases and Materials* (12.8.1.1) and read *Humberside County Council* v *B* [1993] 1 FLR 257, *Birmingham City Council* v *D* and *Birmingham City Council* v *M* [1994] 2 FLR 502 and *Re M (Care Order: Parental Responsibility)* [1996] 2 FLR 84.

12.12.2.2   When will significant harm need to be proved?

By this what is meant is, at what point in time during the process of intervention must the court be able to say 'the child is suffering, or is likely to suffer significant harm'.

On the diagram below, which indicates a stereotypical care order application, mark the point when you think this issue has to be satisfied.

History of a Care Case

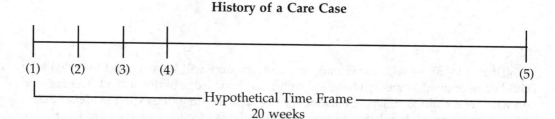

(1)   (2)   (3)   (4)   (5)

Hypothetical Time Frame
20 weeks

(1)   Local authority begins investigation under s. 47, CA 1989.

(2)   Local authority provides services under s. 17, CA 1989.

(3)   Crisis occurs, and EPO is obtained under s. 44(1)(a).

(4)   Application for care order made by local authority under s. 31.

Between points (4) and (5), there are numerous direction hearings and appearances to obtain interim care orders under s. 38, CA 1989.

(5)   Final hearing of care order application.

The court will naturally make the decision at the time of the final hearing since this is the time when all the criteria are considered to see if the order can be made. But did you think this was same point in time when the significant harm test must be satisfied?

ACTIVITY 188

Read the two extracts from the case of *Re M (A Minor) (Care Order: Threshold Conditions)* which are in *Cases and Materials* (12.8.1.2). You will note that the court concerned is not identified.

Which of these two propositions do you think are most appropriate? Do either of them meet with your assessment in SAQ 230 above?

Extract number one was taken from the Court of Appeal decision ([1994] 2 WLR 200) and, as you have seen, decided that 'significant harm' should be assessed at the date of the actual hearing. If this is the case, and a child has been removed from the source of harm, then arguably the child can no longer be said to be suffering. The second extract, which is from the House of Lords decision ([1994] 2 AC 424), chose the time at which the local authority took steps to protect the child. This makes far more sense as there has been no removal from the cause of harm.

SAQ 231

Go back to the line diagram. As the local authority is working within the clear non-interventionist framework of the CA 1989, it investigated and then it provided services. Only after these failed to achieve change was an EPO sought. Which of these events equals 'taking steps to protect'?

Whilst it is not totally clear, and you may of course argue in a different way, it is suggested that the investigation of the family by the local authority is certainly not within the remit of 'taking steps to protect'. The provision of services is somewhat more ambiguous, and may depend on the nature of services provided. Some may not include sufficient intervention to be truly protective. The application for the EPO is clearly 'taking steps to protect'.

12.12.3   PAST, PRESENT OR FUTURE HARM?

Return to s. 31(2)(a) in *Cases and Materials* (12.8). Of the three alternatives in the heading, i.e. past, present or future, which do the criteria for harm fall into?

The CA 1989 here is focusing on the present and the future risks to the child. It does not act retrospectively by asking what has happened to the child previously.

Does this mean that 'past harm' can never be used evidentially?

Masson and Morris answer this question thus: 'The fact that there has been harm in the past will not be sufficient unless it is likely that it will be repeated' (*Children Act Manual*).

The simple fact is that past harm, by itself, will never be enough to satisfy the threshold criteria: past harm must be accompanied by cogent evidence which indicates that the harm may happen in the future. When 'predicting' future harm there does not need to be certainty that it will happen, the criteria state 'is likely to'. It is often easier to satisfy this test where cumulative harm is concerned, i.e. neglect. If you are dealing with a one-off incident, it is much harder to show that it will happen again.

To illustrate how past harm may be evidence to prove future harm, and when it will not, consider the cases of *Re D* [1993] 2 FLR 423 and *Re H and others* [1996] 1 All ER 1.

Read the extracts from *Re D* and *Re H and others* in *Cases and Materials* (12.8.2) and note down the reasons why the approaches towards future harm were different.

In *Re D*, despite the previous harm being to another child (and not even a sibling), the court made the care order due to the high risk the father posed. Of particular importance were the nature of the injuries, the criminal conviction, the lack of acknowledgement by the father that he had caused harm, and also the lack of acknowledgement by the mother and wider family that the father posed a problem.

In *Re H and others*, there were several legal arguments involved, principally concerning the nature of the burden of proof in sexual abuse cases. However, the case illustrates situations where there is suspicion of future harm, but no evidence to support that contention. The allegation of sexual abuse had been dismissed in the criminal courts. By itself this would not prevent civil proceedings as the burden of proof is lower in civil cases. However, as the (disproved) allegation was the only fact that the local authority relied on in making the application, the court was unable to make the order. Simply put, the factual evidence suggesting future harm was absent.

To enable you to get a rounded view of the arguments on future harm, read the article by Rohan Auld, [1996] *Family Law* 488 which was based on *Re H and others*. You will find the article in *Cases and Materials* (12.8.2).

12.12.4   THE STANDARD OF CARE BY PARENTS

The second element of the threshold criteria concentrates on the cause of harm to the child. This may either be poor care or lack of control.

With regard to the care available to the child, what is the nature of the test?

Poor parenting has for some time been grounds for intervention, and the standards to be imposed have, in the past, reflected a very middle class attitude. Even today, it can be questioned whose values of what makes good parenting are being applied.

The standards to be required are not those of the perfect parent, this is reflected in the fact that minor problems are to be ignored when assessing harm. However, the test to be applied is clearly of an objective nature, i.e. not what is *this* parent capable of providing, but what is *a* parent capable of providing by way of care?

Read the extract from the *Children Act 1989 Guidance and Regulations* in *Cases and Materials* (12.8.3). Do you agree with this view?

Why is 'beyond parental control' included?

This existed as a means to obtain a care order under the preceding Children and Young Persons Act 1969, but today it will only be applicable where the child is suffering significant harm. It could be suggested that a child who is beyond control is not being provided with adequate care, and therefore this duplicates s. 31(2)(a). This may be the case, but it is also true to say that parents may be doing all they can for a child, and all that a reasonable parent would do, and still be left with a child beyond their control.

To see what type of behaviour may class as being beyond control, see the case extracts from *M v Birmingham City Council* [1994] 2 FLR 141 in *Cases and Materials* (12.8.3). Note that this case was decided after the Court of Appeal decision in *Re M* but before the House of Lords decision in *Re M*. Look at how Stuart-White J manages to avoid any type of precedent.

12.12.5   AGE

Although it is only a short subsection, you should not overlook the importance of s. 31(3), which prohibits the making of a care or supervision order once a child has reached the age of 17 years, or 16 if the child is married.

If a child is 17, but below 18, can you think of ways in which they may be protected?

You may need to come back to this question once you have studied Chapter 14.

12.12.6   WHY THE 'THRESHOLD' CRITERIA?

Can you think why the criteria are described in this way?

This should not be difficult as you have encountered the reasons before. The answer is simply that the proof that a child may be suffering significant harm, and that this is due to the parents, is only the first hurdle that needs to be overcome. Thereafter, the court is required to consider the welfare of the child, the welfare checklist (since the order is within Part IV), and the no order principle. Linked to the welfare checklist is the need to consider all other options or other orders that would be available under the CA 1989. Proving the threshold criteria may not result in the order sought.

12.13   The Process

As you have seen from the earlier line diagram, a care order application will take a considerable time to complete its passage through the courts. This time has, however, been somewhat reduced since the implementation of the CA 1989.

Proceedings for care or supervision orders do not, generally, begin without there having been any involvement with the family by social services. The gaining of an EPO or CAO is not a prerequisite to the application, neither is the provision of s. 17 services. In many local authorities if an EPO is obtained by way of crisis management, a care order application will invariably follow.

12.13.1   THE APPLICANT

Who is the applicant?

Only two possible applicants exist, the local authority or the NSPCC, as authorised person (s. 31(1)).

As you know, the court cannot make an order of its own motion (again s. 31(1)) and the court cannot make the local authority apply for an order (*Nottinghamshire County Council v P* [1993] 3 WLR 637; *Cases and Materials* (**12.3.2**)).

By introducing these restrictions, the amount of state involvement should be reduced.

12.13.2   WHERE TO APPLY AND WHEN

Again, you will know that the local authority must make the application to the family proceedings court. Whereas applications for EPOs and CAOs will remain in the family proceedings court in the majority of cases, care orders and supervision orders can be, and often are, transferred to other courts. If a case is perceived to be complex, i.e. if it will last over three days' duration, if it will involve expert evidence and cross examination, or if there are other family proceedings with which the application can be consolidated, it may move to the county court or the High Court. Only certain county courts are authorised to deal with care applications, and these courts are named as designated care centres. Any judge dealing with these issues will concentrate on family cases.

Applications must be made on notice which, according to the Children Act Rules, will be of three days but these are clear days' notice.

12.13.3   WHO WILL BE INVOLVED?

The parties to the proceedings will be the child, all persons with parental responsibility and of course the local authority. If there is a parent without parental responsibility (an unmarried father), that parent will be told that the proceedings are taking place. That unmarried father may then seek leave to be joined to the action. Once the application has been made, if it was not preceded by an EPO, the court will appoint a guardian ad litem for the child.

If you cannot recall the functions of the guardian ad litem, return to 12.9 and refresh your memory.

12.13.4   DIRECTIONS

The first hearing that will take place in court after the application has been filed, will merely set down the timetable for the running of the matter. The court, having consulted with the parties, will lay down the dates for the filing of statements, expert reports, the guardian ad litem's report and the final hearing. Several weeks may be taken up with this process of gathering and exchanging evidence. For the guardian ad litem it is crucial since he/she knows nothing or very little about the case on appointment.

The gap between applying and the final hearing is also important to the local authority which will probably still be in the process of investigating and formulating a future plan for the child.

12.13.5   CARE PLANS

Whilst the local authority will be required to produce statements to the court, it is also required (via case law not statute) to produce a 'care plan' for the child. The document will outline the future plans that the local authority has for the child, and will be an important element in the court's assessment of what will be in the best interests of the child. The local authority must address issues such as:

■   where the child will live;

- what the long term plans are, i.e. rehabilitation, fostering or adoption;

- what the level of contact will be between child and family.

A discussion of the child's needs will have to precede these conclusions and evidence provided if available. If the local authority is seeking a supervision order, it will still need to produce evidence of the reasons why this is the preferred option.

What happens if the court does not agree with the local authority's proposals?

Several alternatives could be suggested:

- the court refuses to make the order;

- the court adjourns the final hearing to allow reconsideration;

- the court makes the care order but with conditions attached;

- the court makes a private law order.

Whether any of these are suitable remedies depends upon the nature of the situation, the child's best interests, and the legality of the remedy.

Read the extracts from *Re J (Minors) (Care: Care Plan)* [1994] 1 FLR 253 and *Re T (A Minor) (Care Order: Conditions)* [1994] 2 FLR 423 in *Cases and Materials* (12.9.1) and identify the main principles.

You will see that *Re T* refers to s. 100, CA 1989. This will be considered in **Chapter 14** in connection with wardship. You may wish to come back to this case then.

12.13.6   WHAT HAPPENS TO THE CHILD WHILST PROCEEDINGS ARE ONGOING?

Whilst all this investigation and report writing is proceeding, the child will have to be cared for.

If the application is for a care order, will it be appropriate for the child to remain with its parents?

In some cases, the child may be left with its parents, but these are likely to be the minority of cases. If a child has been removed under an EPO it is very unlikely that a return will be planned until the s. 31 proceedings are concluded. Hence, the court can make interim care orders under the provisions of s. 38, CA 1989, a fact you may have picked up on when reading *Re J* in **12.13.5**.

Read s. 38 now in *Cases and Materials* (12.9.2) and highlight the situations in which the provision can be used by the court.

It is very important to be aware of the limited situations in which the court's powers to make interim care orders (ICOs) arise. A local authority cannot apply for an ICO, and so an ICO is not a protective option in that sense. The court can only make the ICO if it has an application for a care or supervision order before it, which is going to be adjourned, or the court in private law proceedings has made a s. 37 investigation direction.

In both cases, under s. 38(2), the court must have reasonable grounds for believing that the threshold criteria are satisfied.

Does this mean that the making of an ICO will guarantee that a full care order is made?

When an ICO is made, it is going to be without the benefit of all the relevant evidence. Hence, the burden to be satisfied re the threshold criteria is lower. The court is not looking for absolute proof that it will be satisfied, but the reasonable belief that it will – not the same at all. The making of a s. 38 order will not therefore mean that the full order will necessarily be made.

To fit in with the 'no delay' principles of the CA 1989 the ICOs are time limited. To prevent a child drifting into care and the court system, an ICO can initially be made for eight weeks maximum only. It may be necessary to renew this order, and any renewals can be for up to four weeks' duration. On each renewal the court must reasonably believe the threshold criteria to be met.

12.13.7 ASSESSMENTS

Under s. 38(6), the court can give directions as to assessments that are to be undertaken during the course of the ICO. The CA 1989 refers specifically to medical and psychiatric assessments.

Could the court order a residential assessment, i.e. one whereby the mother (and sometimes father) are observed and supervised in a residential setting (often called mother and baby units)?

An assessment of this sort is clearly focused on the capabilities of the parents, and yet the section indicates that the assessment must be of the child. This issue is one which has led to judicial comment in the case of *Re C (Interim Care Order: Residential Assessment)* [1997] 1 FLR 1 which was decided by the House of Lords.

SAQ 242

Read *Re C* the case in *Cases and Materials* (12.9.3) and note down the principles established by the court.

The opinions of the House of Lords could lead to some difficult decisions for local authorities, especially when financial effects are taken into account. Is it right to spend several thousands of pounds on assessing one child's parents, especially if the result can be predicted as being negative, and deprive several other children from receiving services or preventative work? The decision in *Re C* did not rule out the costs argument being successful, it has just made it harder to run.

12.14 The Final Hearing: What are the Options?

If the court is satisfied, at the final hearing, that the local authority has proved the threshold criteria at the time when steps to protect the child were taken, it may then make the order sought.

SAQ 243

What are the other issues/factors that the court must consider before making the order?

You should have thought of:

■ the welfare of the child;

■ the welfare checklist;

■ other options available under the CA 1989;

■ no order at all.

12.14.1 NO ORDER

If a court has found that the threshold criteria have been satisfied, can it ever be said to be in the child's interests for the child to return to the parents without the making of an order?

The concepts may seem contradictory. However, the court may believe that the parents will co-operate in a satisfactory manner to ensure the child's welfare is protected (in many cases of this sort the court will make a supervision order). In addition, there is a growing body of research which would suggest that the removal of a child from its home environment by virtue of a care order is more damaging to the long-term welfare than leaving the child where it is. Also, the very nature of the care system may result in longer term harm. Many children who have been through the care system have lower than average qualifications, little or no real employment prospects and a higher chance of being involved in crime

In *Cases and Materials* (12.10.1) you will find extracts from two research articles indicating that removal, in itself, can be harmful.

12.14.2 OTHER OPTIONS

Despite the action being commenced in the public law domain, the court can make a s. 8 residence order if it deems it appropriate. In developing its care plan, the local authority should have regard to the extended family of the child, and consider whether suitable carers can be found from this category of individuals. The fact that the local authority may support the placement of the child with the wider family does not necessarily mean that it will not wish to have a care order. In some cases though, the local authority will be perfectly amenable to the making of a s. 8 residence order. To illustrate this, consider this example:

Anne had a relationship with Bill and conceived a child. They split up before the birth of Christopher. Bill has so far played no role in the child's life. Anne presents at the casualty department of her local hospital with Christopher and non-accidental injuries are diagnosed. Anne is believed to have beaten Christopher and burnt him with cigarettes repeatedly. The local authority commences care proceedings. They give notice of the application to Bill, but as an unmarried father without parental responsibility he is not a party to the proceedings. Bill has now settled down, has a stable relationship and a reasonable job. He and his new girlfriend wish to care for Christopher. The local authority assess the couple and agrees that their care would be appropriate, as does the guardian ad litem. At the final hearing the local authority recommends the making of a s. 8 order.

If the court agreed with the local authority and the guardian ad litem on the outcome, a s. 8 order could be made, without Bill having even been party to the action. However, in the majority of cases where a s. 8 order is sought, the party so seeking it will apply for leave (if necessary) to be joined to the action. One problem with the making of s. 8 orders is the lack of control by the local authority. Hence the court may consider the need to impose conditions on the residence order, or combine it with a supervision order (*Re DH (A Minor) (Child Abuse)* [1994] 1 FLR 679). However, in the main, the use of private law remedies in public law cases seems to work. If Bill and the local authority were at odds on the outcome, it would definitely be necessary for him to join the proceedings in order to ensure his case was fully explored.

12.14.3　CARE VERSUS SUPERVISION

Reread s. 31(5), CA 1989 in *Cases and Materials* (12.8). Do you think this is a useful provision?

Whilst it may have seemed obvious from all your work so far that this should happen, the ability to make either the care order or supervision order needs to be made clear. The ability to do so stems from the fact that the criteria to be fulfilled to obtain the orders are exactly the same. However, the court, as arbiter, may disagree with the 'expert' opinion of social workers and the guardian ad litem when it comes to the nature of the state intervention and the welfare of the child. The debate over care orders or supervision orders is frequently found within the law reports.

Read the cases of *Re D* [1993] 2 FLR 423 (you have already considered this case at 12.12.3), *Re O (Care or Supervision Order)* [1996] 2 FLR 755, *Re B (Care or Supervision Order)* [1996] 2 FLR 693 in *Cases and Materials* (12.10.2).

On a separate sheet of paper write down some of the factors that appear to affect the decision as to which order is most appropriate.

Your list will have included some of these factors:

Re D

■　The father's history of violence and failure to acknowledge the same;

■　failure to undergo therapeutic treatment;

■　mother's inability to accept the level of risk posed and also inability to protect the child;

■ poor relationship with social services;

■ the ability to leave the child living with parents under a care order;

■ poor enforceability and safeguards under a supervision order.

Re O

■ The limited duration of the supervision order would mean more overseeing by the court;

■ the improvements that had occurred in relation to weight gain;

■ the co-operation with other agency workers (family centre);

■ the need to build a good relationship with the social workers.

Re B

■ The fact that the father had kept away from the children and the home;

■ the fact that if the father were to return EPOs would be applied for;

■ the effect on the mother if care orders were made;

■ the ability of the local authority to meet the children's needs under the supervision order if the order was subject to conditions.

Naturally, these cases only give you an illustration of the sorts of things that will be relevant to the balancing exercise that the courts will undertake. You should hopefully have noticed how strong the emphasis was on the children's welfare.

You may also find the article, *Supervision or Care Orders*, extracted in *Cases and Materials* (12.10.2) helpful on this issue.

By now you should be familiar with the welfare and welfare checklist concepts and they are not discussed further here.

12.15 The Consequences of the Orders

One of the fundamental distinctions between these two orders lies in the consequences, some of which you will have gleaned from your reading to date.

12.15.1 CARE ORDERS

Read ss. 33 and 34 in *Cases and Materials* (12.11.1) and on a separate sheet of paper draw up a list of the consequences of the making of a care order.

The consequences do not raise many theoretical difficulties, and in reality, they do not seem to raise many practical difficulties.

12.15.1.1   Section 33: suitable accommodation, parental responsibility

Starting with s. 33, you should have identified the following issues:

■ Once a care order is made, the child is to be placed in the care of the local authority. By this, the local authority has a duty to provide suitable accommodation for the child.

SAQ 245

What types of accommodation are potentially suitable?

There are several possibilities with regard to accommodation for a child in care. The child may be placed in foster care, which acts as a substitute family. If the local authority's care plan set out a rehabilitation scheme for the child and its family, then short-term fosterers would be used. If rehabilitation is unlikely, long-term fosterers would need to be found. All foster carers must be approved by the local authority before they can act as such (there are situations where a child can be placed without the requisite approvals, but this is where it is an emergency). Linked to long-term fostering, the child may be seen as suitable for adoption. Here the child may be placed with foster parents until an adoptive placement is identified. Children's homes are nowadays uncommon, and if used, tend to focus on older children, and often those who will shortly be reaching adulthood. Children's homes are also subject to approval and must comply with certain regulations. The local authority may decide to place a child with his/her wider family; even though there may be a blood tie, this would in effect be nothing more than a foster placement. Finally, the child may be returned to his/her parents. This is permissible but before the placement can take place, the local authority must comply with the requirements of the Placement with Parents Regulations 1991.

■ The local authority will gain parental responsibility according to s. 33(3) and may determine the extent to which parents can utilise their parental responsibility. The making of the care order will not extinguish that of the parents, but the local authority can restrict the use made of it by parents. To all intents and purposes, the local authority will be the parent. The ability to restrict the parents is dependent upon the placement. If the child is returned to its parents, the local authority will not be in a position to make all decisions for the child, but would expect to participate in major decisions. Likewise, good social work practice would indicate that where a child is in care, the local authority endeavours to encourage parental participation in major decision making.

When would this be unsuitable?

The continued involvement of parents would need to be assessed in the light of the child's welfare. In addition, if the plan for the child is adoption, it could be argued to be unfair to parents to continue to allow participation in decision making if ultimately all links will be ended (you will learn more about adoption in **Chapter 13**).

Not all decisions that form part of parental responsibility can be taken by the local authority.

What restrictions have you noticed?

In your reading of s. 33 you should have noted the restrictions in subsections (6) and (7) namely, the inability to change the child's religion, the inability to consent to the child's adoption or to appoint a guardian, the prohibition on changing the child's surname or removing the child from the UK for over a month. The last two are permitted if the agreement of all with parental responsibility is obtained or the court agrees it.

12.15.1.2 Section 34: reasonable contact

Must contact take place, or only when an order is made under the section?

Under s. 34 the presumption is for reasonable contact, in other words, that contact should take place and there is no automatic need for an order. It is only where the parents or individual seeking contact and the local authority disagree as to what is reasonable, or the local authority does not believe contact to be in the best interests of the child, that an order should be sought.

The issue of contact should be included within the care plan that is produced by the local authority for the final hearing and the court is specifically required to consider contact under s. 34(11). Failure to address this point may lead to the application being dismissed (at worst), and almost certainly being adjourned.

Can the local authority prohibit contact?

If the child is to be adopted, or the parents' behaviour to the child is such as to cause distress and harm, the local authority may wish to stop contact totally. This will need to be brought before the court, as the presumption of contact can only be rebutted by the making of an order. That order for 'no contact' will be under s. 34. However, in some cases the need to terminate contact may only arise as a matter of urgency. For example, if the child makes an allegation of abuse, claiming that the abuse happened during the contact. In this situation the local authority can terminate contact, without the need to go to court, for a maximum of seven days (per s. 34(6)).

To see how contact after a care order is viewed, read the case extracts from *Re B (Minors) (Care: Contact: Local Authority's Plans)* [1993] 1 FLR 543 and *Berkshire County Council v B* [1997] 1 FLR 171 in *Cases and Materials* (12.11.1.1).

12.15.1.3   Duration of the order

You will recall from your earlier reading of s. 31 that no court can make a care order in respect of a child who is 17-years-old.

You should also remember that this differs from s. 8 orders which cannot be made to last past the child's sixteenth birthday unless there are exceptional circumstances.

Read the extracts from s. 91, CA 1989 in *Cases and Materials* (12.11.1.2). How long can the care order last?

A care order will, unless brought to an end earlier, last until the child reaches majority at the age of 18.

It can be ended earlier by the court making a s. 8 residence order (which you may recall from s. 9, CA 1989 is the only s. 8 order that can be made with respect to a child in care).

The care order may also end on it being discharged (and on discharge the situation returns to how it was before the care order). Section 39, CA 1989, in *Cases and Materials* (**12.11.1.2**), deals with discharge and who can apply. Most discharge applications are commenced by local authorities. You should note the implication of subsections (4) and (5) of s. 39 since the same is not true of converting a supervision order into a care order.

12.15.2   SUPERVISION ORDERS

12.15.2.1   Consequences

As you did for care orders (see 12.15), draw up a list of the consequences of the order, having read s. 35 and sch. 3 Part I in *Cases and Materials* (**12.11.2.1**).

The main consequence of the supervision order is that the local authority will have to appoint a supervisor whose role is to advise, assist and befriend the child. As you can see from the Schedule, the child may also be subject to conditions in relation to residence, attendance at specified places or participation in specified activities. Medical and psychiatric assessments may also be carried out on the supervised child, although in respect of these conditions, the mature child can in effect veto them (para. 4(4)).

Treatment may also be specified, but only for the purposes of treating the child's mental health. It is interesting to note that this power overlaps with the powers available under the Mental Health Act 1983 to permit detention for treatment, and yet under the 1983 Act treatment can be given in the face of opposition whereas under the CA 1989, a mature child can veto treatment.

Does the local authority get parental responsibility under a supervision order, or the power to remove the child?

The answer is a simple no, unless of course the order permits the supervisor to require the child to live in a specified place (which may not be with the parents). In this situation parental responsibility for the child on a day-to-day basis will have to be delegated by the parents to the temporary carer or s. 3(5) will need to be utilised.

12.15.2.2   Enforcement

What powers does the supervisor have in the event of non-compliance?

Section 35 states that one of the functions of the supervisor is to consider whether or not to apply for the variation of the supervision order or for its discharge in the event that the order is not wholly complied with (s. 35(1)(c)(i)). However, the variation of the order is restricted to obtaining the right to impose conditions if those were not initially imposed. The success of this is questionable if the first attempt at supervision has failed.

Can the supervisor apply for the order to be varied to a care order?

Albeit that the supervision order can only be obtained after proving the same threshold criteria as for a care order, the 'trading up' of orders is not permissible. As you saw in the section on duration of care orders, the opposite is available. But this is justifiable only on the basis that the orders are being 'traded down' from care to supervision. If a care order is believed to be necessary, a supervision order having failed, a new application must be made, and the threshold criteria satisfied. The failure of the supervision order will of course be evidence of the need to make an order, but the making of the care order is not a certainty.

As you may recall from the case of *Re D* in **Cases and Materials** (**12.8.2** and **12.10.2**) (the father convicted of cruelty after a young child died in his care and order sought on child from subsequent relationship), the lack of enforcement powers for a supervision order may tip the balance in favour of a care order in some cases. It has been suggested that a supervision order will only work if co-operation already exists. If that is the case then to what principle should the court have regard?

You should immediately have thought of s. 1(5), the no order principle.

12.15.2.3   Duration

As the supervision order is less Draconian than the care order, it lasts for a shorter period of time.

How long do you think the order lasts?

You may remember this from your reading of cases earlier. The initial time limit on a supervision order is one year (sch. 3 Part II, para. 6(1)). It may, however, be extended upon the application of the supervisor for a period not in excess of two years (para. 6(3)), although any extension cannot take the supervision order beyond the child's eighteenth birthday or give a total period in excess of three years.

This necessity to renew the order, whilst it may be argued to be a time wasting exercise, at least requires the local authority to review the matter and to deliberate on the case. Again, this supports the idea of limiting the amount of time during which child care matters may be allowed to 'drift', and also supports the reduction of state intervention.

In addition to this time limit, the order may be brought to an end by an application to discharge by the same range of applicants as for care orders.

12.16   Appeals

Unlike the public law EPO, the making of, or failure to make, a care order or supervision order may be appealed. The court will have the power to make certain orders pending the appeal being heard, i.e.:

■   to permit the care order to take effect whilst the appeal is ongoing; or

■   to continue the existence of an ICO (if one was in operation at the time of the final hearing) pending the outcome of an appeal against the refusal to make a full care order/supervision order (s. 40, CA 1989).

12.17   Summary of Part Two

You have now finished the bulk of your studying on the public law intervention into families in respect of children and their care. You will look at post care matters, and options for the local authority outside the CA 1989 in **Chapters 13** and **14** when you consider adoption law and wardship. These areas also cover private law too. However, you should now be able to advise clients, whether they be individuals or local authority social workers in respect of the legal means to protect children. You should always commence your thought processes by considering voluntary action, or the legal steps which have the least Draconian intervention by the state. You should also be able to identify situations where a voluntary or 'softly-softly' approach is inappropriate.

To consolidate your work on this chapter, you should attempt the final stage of the case study below.

CASE STUDY

An emergency protection order is made in respect of all of the four children. A child protection conference is hastily convened, where what happened at school is explained. It is noted that Emma has not been back since the order was made.

The social worker who was allocated to the family at the initial case conference talks about the state of the house and the family dynamics.

The house is in a very poor state of repair, and Social Services have been assisting Mr and Mrs P in negotiating with the housing authority to get the major problems corrected, one of these being to get the indoor toilet fixed as only the outdoor toilet works. The house is unheated, and threadbare. The parents sleep on a mattress on the floor in the largest of the three bedrooms with the twins in a cot in the same room. Emma and Tom in the smallest room, have to share a single mattress which is urine-soaked, and has only one blanket, again soaked in urine. The social worker also reports that Emma and Tom are allegedly locked in the bedroom from about 7 p.m. each night. There was a cracked potty in the room, with faeces and urine in it. The room was smeared with faeces. No toys were found in the house at all.

As a result of the social work input, the children have been provided with a second-hand bed, and more bedding. Toys have also been provided, as has a calor gas stove and more fuel for the fire. A worker from the Children's Society has been going in daily to assist Mrs P with the younger children, and Tom had been found a place at nursery for two mornings a week.

From the report of the social worker and the Children's Society worker it is clear that Mrs P is left to cope on her own. Mr P is not bothered and always complains and derides his wife. From the contact with Mrs P and more investigation into her past it is believed that she will have great difficulty coping with the children (especially when the baby is born), as she does not seem to know what to do with them once past the crawling stage. Despite the intensive input, no progress has been made.

Stage Four   What are the long-term options? What are the consequences?

See *Cases and Materials* at the end of **Part Two** for an outline answer.

CHAPTER THIRTEEN

ADOPTION

13.1 Objectives

By the end of this chapter you should be able to:

- provide an explanation of adoption, what it is and what the effects are;

- describe the procedures for arranging adoptions;

- explain the legal requirements in adoption;

- highlight the distinctions between legal and non-legal requirements;

- relate the adoption legislation to the provisions of the Children Act 1989;

- advise hypothetical clients.

13.2 Introduction

The topic of adoption is one which will overlap both public and private law, although it will more frequently be more of an issue in public law since local authorities often regard adoption as the best means of promoting the long-term care of children. In private law, the majority of cases arise where step-parents wish to adopt their stepchildren. The law regarding both situations is fundamentally the same, there are a few small distinctions with procedures, which will be made apparent during this chapter. Your studying will take the form of considering the main issues involved in adoption law. You will also be introduced to some of the criticisms of the legislation, which may be undergoing change in the future.

13.3 What is Adoption?

13.3.1 A RECENT PHENOMENON

As a legal procedure, adoption was only introduced into our system in 1926 in the Adoption of Children Act 1926, albeit that many children prior to this were, in fact, in what would be perceived as adoptive relationships. The nature of adoption introduced in 1926 was not the same as today, the legal consequences being somewhat different. As child protection and the role of the local authority developed, 'adoption came to be seen as a method of providing homes for children (not merely legalising existing arrangements)' (Cretney and Masson, *Principles of Family Law*, 6th edn, Sweet & Maxwell, 1997).

Later, the legislation was changed, and eventually consolidated in the Adoption Act 1976, which still provides the basis of today's adoption law.

13.3.2   A DECLINING PHENOMENON?

Adoption became very popular and the 'heyday' for the process was in the late 1960s. In 1968 the number of adoption orders made reached nearly 25,000.

Look at the judicial statistics in *Cases and Materials* (13.1). What do the figures tell you ?

The total number of adoption orders made in 1995 was 5,317, less than one fifth of the 1968 figures. These figures represent a 16 per cent reduction from the number of adoption orders made in 1994, so it is evident that for some reason adoption is losing popularity.

Can you think of any reasons why this may be?

Once you have finished the chapter, you may wish to return to this SAQ and review, or add to, your answers.

Some reasons for the decline in adoptions are the change in society's attitude to single parenthood, and 'illegitimacy', the possible opportunities for women to work and raise children and possibly the availability of welfare benefits. It is now no longer unusual for single women to keep their children. This is true for women, and girls, of all ages. Neither is it expected that single mothers will put their babies up for adoption, or be pressurised into doing so. Those single women who did not wish to have their children adopted, but wished to hide the fact of their illegitimacy, were able to do so by adopting their own child, as a single person. The law recognised the child as legitimate. This can still happen today.

Additionally, today there exist other orders which may achieve similar aims to adoption. The residence order under s. 8, CA 1989 is a potential alternative to adoption for step-parents or other familial carers.

13.3.3   WHO IS ADOPTED?

With the trend away from adoption, there has also been a change in the type of children who are adopted.

If you had to give a stereotype of an adopted child, what would it be?

For the majority of people, the image of an adopted child is a baby, or very young infant, who will be adopted by a childless couple. However, that is not the reality. So called 'baby adoptions' are in the minority of all adoptions. In 1992 less than 10 per cent of adoptions were in respect of this group, with the majority of children being under 10 years at the time of the order.

Many more adoptions are now made in respect of children who come from divorced parents or from 'problem families'. Adoption is a potential long-term option for children in care, who are unlikely to be rehabilitated with their birth families. In many cases these children will have behavioural problems, or may be suffering from a varying degree of impairment. This changing face of adoption has led to the recent review of the law, and in addition to a change in emphasis on assessment of who wants to adopt and the qualities expected from adoptive parents.

13.4   What are the Effects of Adoption?

On a separate sheet of paper, write a list of the consequences that you can think of associated with adoption.

Once you have written this list, read the extracts from the Adoption Act (AA) 1976 in *Cases and Materials* **(13.2), namely ss. 12, 39, 42, 44 and 47. If necessary, go back and amend your list.**

Section 12 sets out the primary concept of adoption, i.e. the adoption order is one which gives parental responsibility to the adoptive parent(s) and extinguishes any parental responsibility held by the birth parents (or anyone else). The order in effect recreates the legal relationship between child and adoptive parents that would otherwise have existed between child and birth parents.

Will this relationship end when the child reaches majority?

Whilst in strict legal terms, parental responsibility does end on majority, the practicalities of life mean that the relationship which an adopted child has with its adoptive parents will not normally end at 18. Indeed, because the adoption order recreates a legal relationship, the rules on succession and intestacy will apply to the new adoptive family, and will last until death. Hence, an adoptive child becomes a child for the purposes of their adoptive parents' wills or death intestate (you should have gathered this from s. 42 which relates to the rules of construction for probate purposes). The ability to inherit on intestacy from the birth family is accordingly extinguished. In s. 42, AA 1976 the emphasis is on wills made other than by the parents; it is anticipated that an adoptive parent will amend any will to reflect the fact of the adoption.

The adoption order, as you can see from s. 39, AA 1976, operates to legitimise a child, and will treat the child as the legitimate child of the adoptive parents. Again, this reinforces the recreation in totality of the legal relationship with the adoptive parents.

Sections 44 and 47 illustrate two areas where links will be retained with the birth family, i.e. where there exists a peerage, dignity or title which is hereditary (not likely to affect many cases of adoption), and the ability to marry. An adopted child will remain within the prohibited degrees with all the specified birth family members in the Marriage Act 1949, sch. 1, and in addition will be prevented from marrying his/her adoptive parents. However, there is no prohibition on an adopted child marrying his/her adoptive sibling.

13.5   Who can be Adopted?

Whilst you have already seen that the nature of adoption has changed over the last decade or two, it is important to be aware of the legal restrictions on who can be adopted.

Reread s. 12(5) and (7). Also read the very short extracts from s. 13 in *Cases and Materials* (13.3). You will be looking at the rest of s. 13 shortly.

The limitations in law relate to the child's age and status. A child must be below 18-years-old (otherwise as you should know they are not a child), and cannot be adopted if he/she has been married. The reference to marriage presumably means a valid marriage or a voidable one. However, there are minimum ages required for a child before an adoption order can be made, set at either 19 weeks, or 12 months. These different ages relate to different types of placements which will be explained in **13.7**.

13.6   Who can Adopt?

The legal requirements concerning who can adopt are potentially weaker than the requirements placed on prospective adopters by local authorities who arrange adoptions. Any local authority which operates as an adoption agency may establish its own policy guidelines.

Read ss. 14 and 15, AA 1976, in *Cases and Materials* (13.4) and note down the legal requirements placed on adopters.

From these sections, you can see that a married couple, or a single person may apply to adopt a child.

What about a homosexual or lesbian couple: can they adopt jointly?

If a same sex couple wish to adopt a child, the only means to do so would be for one applicant to apply as a single person. If the adoption were to be granted, then the couple could utilise the CA 1989 to obtain a joint s. 8 residence order. In both cases the court may be unwilling to make the order due to the nature of the carers' relationship. Whilst the courts may not be as willing as they once were to accept the view that being raised by a same sex couple is detrimental or harmful to a child, there still remains some elements of concern.

ACTIVITY 206

To illustrate this, see the comments, in *Cases and Materials* (13.4), made by Lord Wilberforce and Lord Kilbrandon in 1977 in *Re D (An Infant) (Adoption: Parent's Consent)* [1977] 2 WLR 79 and the case summary and comment on *AMT (Known as AC) (Petitioners for authority to adopt SR)* [1997] Fam Law 225. Does it matter that the latter was a Scottish case? You will note that *Re D* was decided under the Adoption Act 1958 and concerned the child's relationship with a homosexual parent. The stance of the House of Lords is, however, interesting.

The restrictions placed on the applicants refer to age and residence. Applicants must have reached the age of 21 years before they can adopt. However, if the application is by a married couple, and one of them is the natural parent of the child, then you will see that under s. 14(1B) the natural parent need only be 18 years, as long as the spouse is 21.

In so far as residence is concerned, the applicant (or one of them) must be domiciled in the UK, Channel Islands or the Isle of Man.

These are the legal restrictions. Can you think of any others that may be imposed by an adoption agency?

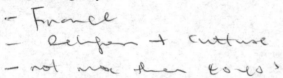

— France

— Religion + culture

— not more than £o,0o?

As mentioned above, any body acting as an adoption agency may impose its own requirements on potential applicants. Whilst local authorities fulfil the major role in acting as agencies (indeed under s. 1, AA 1976, every local authority has to establish services for adoption or secure them via an approved adoption agency), other bodies may be approved to act as such. In many cases these adoption societies are part of a religious body.

Frequently imposed criteria include:

■ a maximum age: often 35 or sometimes 40 if there are already adopted children in the family;

■ that couples are childless/infertile/not undergoing fertility treatment:

■ that potential adopters are non-smokers;

■ physical fitness, and that adopters are not obese;

■ preferred religion;

■ an unwillingness to use corporal punishment.

You may have thought of other possible conditions.

When an applicant wishes to adopt, there will be a variety of reports prepared on them, including such matters as health and lifestyle. You may therefore query why there need to be additional requirements such as the above. The primary reason is linked to the long-term welfare of the child. If a parent is unfit, unhealthy and overweight, it does not bode well for the future health of the child (or so the reasoning goes). It is also more likely that such a parent would be at greater risk of early death or disability or permanent ill-health.

SAQ 260

If an applicant is classed as being too old on local authority guidelines, can he/she challenge the decision?

NO Complaint Procedure

As the policy guidelines are not statutory, the only means of challenging the decision is by way of judicial review, arguing that the decision is unreasonable, or one that no reasonable authority would have reached on the facts. In addition, as the policy should be discretionary, it can be argued that applying it without recognition of the individual case and facts is a fettering of discretion. This argument was tried in the case of *R v Lancashire County Council, ex parte M* [1992] 1 FLR 109, but without success.

13.7 Who can Arrange Adoptions?

There are strict rules governing the placement of children for adoption, although, of course, ways round the provisions can be found.

ACTIVITY207

Read s. 11, AA 1976 in *Cases and Materials* (13.5). Identify the means by which a placement can be brought about.

Under the provisions you have just read, an adoption placement may only be made with:

■ an adoption agency;

■ a relative of a child (the definition of 'relative' is found in s. 72, AA 1976, also in *Cases and Materials* (13.5));

■ an order of the High Court.

Placement which has occurred in one of these ways will be termed a 'legal placement'.

Failure to comply with these requirements constitutes a criminal offence, and one which is punishable via proceedings in the magistrates' court. The offender, if found guilty, can be imprisoned for up to three months and/or fined up to £5,000 (s. 11(4)).

Where a local authority is arranging an adoptive placement, it will have to have regard to the suitability of the prospective adopters in light of the legal requirements under the AA 1976, and also its own policy guidelines. The assessment of the adopters is not purely done by social workers acting on behalf of the local authority, since all prospective adopters must also be approved by an adoption panel (or similar if the placement is by a non-local authority agency). The panel will comprise social workers, a member of the local authority social services committee, medical adviser, and two independent persons. The panel will not only consider the adopters, but also the suitability of this placement with these adopters and this individual child.

In addition to going through the panel, the agency will need to have regard to the wishes of the birth parents as to the religious upbringing of the child when arranging any placement (s. 7, AA 1976).

Reread the full text of s. 13(1) and (2) in *Cases and Materials* **(13.3). How does this affect the situation regarding placement?**

The section places a time restriction on the ability to make an adoption order. If the placement has been made by an agency, with a relative or the High Court, an order cannot be made until the child has lived with the applicants for at least 13 weeks (subsection (1)). However, you will know from subsection (2) that an adoption order can be made where the child has had his/her home with the applicants for a period of 12 months. This longer period applies where the placement has not been made in accordance with s. 11(1) – in other words where the placement has been carried out illegally. This 'illegal' placement situation may arise in many ways. It may simply be where a single mother leaves her child with neighbours whom she knows will be able to care adequately for the child, or it may be where a couple brings a child into the country from a foreign jurisdiction.

In *Cases and Materials* **(13.5) you will find the case of** *Re WM (Adoption: Non-patrial)* **[1997] 1 FLR 132 which illustrates this latter situation. The outcome of this matter was the making of the order.**

In many cases where the placement has occurred illegally it is unlikely that proceedings will be taken in the criminal courts, and in many cases the order of adoption will be made.

13.8   The Process of Adoption

There exist two possible routes for obtaining an adoption order in respect of a child, both of which are governed by the AA 1976. The first will be referred to as the 'standard route', the second as the 'freeing route'. Both have similarities, and the common aspects will be discussed in relation to the standard route only.

13.8.1   THE STANDARD ROUTE

Regardless of whether the adoption placement has been arranged by an agency or not, this pathway to seeking an adoption order can be used. Under this route, the applicants for the adoption order will make the application and the natural parents of the child will be the respondents. The child will already be living with the applicants, and this is normally with the parents' consent (although this is not always the case).

13.8.1.1   Reports

Once an application has been made, reports will need to be filed at court, from the local authority and a guardian ad litem or reporting officer. The local authority's report is often referred to as a schedule 2 report since the information that has to be specified will be found in sch. 2 to the AA 1976.

This report will need to be provided regardless of whether it is an agency placement or carried out under the other terms of s. 11.

If the placement is with relatives, say a step-parent, how does the local authority find out about the application?

You might understandably say that the local authority are told by the court once an application has been made. However, under the AA 1976, s. 22(1):

> An adoption order shall not be made in respect of a child who was not placed with the applicant by an adoption agency unless the applicant has, at least 3 months before the date of the order, given notice to the local authority . . . of his intention to apply for the adoption order.

The application need not have been made at this point, since the section merely refers to the intention to apply.

The purpose of giving notice is to enable the local authority to visit the applicants and to see how the child is being cared for in the home environment (s. 13(3)).

13.8.1.2   Secrecy

Adoption is traditionally a process bound up with secrecy. If you know anyone who has adopted a child, ask them how much they know of the birth parents. If they adopted some time ago, it is possible that they know nothing. To a degree this is changing, it has to if older children are being adopted who already know their birth family. However, this secrecy is maintained in the adoption process. Reports that are furnished to the court do not refer to any names or addresses, or any other means of identification of the parties. The adoptive parents can request that they are not named in the court proceedings and that they are allocated a case number by way of reference. The same level of secrecy is not always available to the birth parents.

13.8.1.3   The matters for the court

Once an application has been made, and the relevant reports filed, it is for the court to decide whether or not to make the order.

Which court will hear the application?

If you can remember the judicial statistics you looked at in *Cases and Materials* (**13.1**), you will know that all three courts with original jurisdiction can make adoption orders. The county court makes the majority of orders. Go back to the statistics and look at the differentials.

Why is it that the county court makes the majority of orders?

It is not possible to be conclusive as to the different usage made of the courts. The lack of general experience of adoption would militate against the use of the family proceedings courts. Arguably the expense of taking a case to the High Court, unless the matter is complex, means that this course of action has a low take-up rate. Hence, the county court with its legally qualified judges, and easy accessibility is the only remaining option. In dealing with an adoption case, there are certain matters that must be satisfied before an order can be made.

Put this jurisdiction onto your court hierarchy in 1.6.

Adopters and child

Write down the matters about which the court must be satisfied in relation to the adopters and child.

To answer this you need to return to the earlier parts of this chapter. The court must be happy that the adopters meet the criteria re age and domicile, and that they have had the child living with them for a period of at least 13 weeks (or 12 months if an illegal placement). The court must also be satisfied that the child is of the required age, i.e. 19 weeks, or 12 months minimum, not over 18 and never married. From the reports that have been furnished, the court must also be satisfied that a suitable bond is forming between the child and adopters and that the adopters are able to cope and provide adequate care.

Welfare
As with all other child-oriented legislation, the question of the child's welfare is also an issue.

Read s. 6, AA 1976, in *Cases and Materials* (13.6.1.1). Do you notice anything significant about this section?

Clearly this section requires the court to consider the welfare of the child before deciding whether or not to make the adoption order. The section will also apply to the local authority or agency when making the placement. However, you should have noticed that the emphasis placed on the child's welfare is not the same as that encountered in the CA 1989. In the CA 1989 the child's welfare is paramount; in the AA 1976 the child's welfare is the first consideration but the court must have regard to all the circumstances.

SAQ 264

Do you think this inconsistency is helpful? Does the 'first consideration' really equate to 'paramount'?

The AA 1976 was drafted at a time when other legislation referred to the child's interests as being the first consideration (i.e. the MCA 1973) and therefore not capable of overreaching all other factors. The lack of consistency has been criticised, not least because adoption applications are family proceedings. This means the court can make CA 1989 orders in an adoption application, and those CA 1989 orders would be decided on the basis that the child's welfare was paramount. In the review of adoption law, which resulted in a draft Bill being published in 1996, the intention is to alter this welfare provision. The Bill introduces a similar format to the CA 1989 with the child's welfare being paramount and the introduction of a welfare checklist.

ACTIVITY 213

You will find the relevant clauses and commentary from the government report and Bill in *Cases and Materials* (13.6.1.1). Note the similarities to the CA 1989, s. 1.

The decision on whether the making of the order is in the child's best interests will in effect be the most important factor, since unless and until this is decided, other questions cannot be answered.

SAQ 265

Is it going to be in a child's best interests to be adopted by a step-parent?

The statistics you have looked at highlight the fact that approximately half the orders made in 1995 were in favour of step-parents. This actually represents an increase from the previous year. The intention has been for many years to reduce the number of step-parent adoptions, but this does not appear to have worked. There are several reasons that can be put forward to explain the desire by step-parents to adopt:

■ it highlights the commitment to the new family by the step-parent;

■ it enables the child to be called by the surname of the new step-parent (if the father);

■ it prevents any interference from the birth parent;

■ it enables the step-parent to care for the child in the event of the death of the caring parent.

Whilst these may all be valid reasons, they do not really appear to be child focused. If the child is very young, he/she is unlikely to have had contact with the birth parent, or know who the birth parent is. However, most stepfamilies arise where the children already know both birth parents, and have some form of relationship with them. The making of an order will destroy any legal relationship with the birth parent, and this has been argued in itself to be detrimental to the child's welfare. Other criticisms are: the fact that second marriages are just as likely to end in divorce as first marriages; the change in name could confuse a child; interference may only be deemed as such by the carers and may in fact be legitimate intervention. It has also been suggested that birth fathers will agree to the making of adoption orders since it extinguishes the liability to pay child maintenance under the CSA 1991 and CSA 1995. However, it is difficult to validate this hypothesis purely on the statistics.

The review of adoption law has emphasized that step-parent adoption may not be in the child's best interests, and has proposed an alternative type of adoption order in these cases. You will find details in *Cases and Materials* (**13.6.1.1**).

Consent

ACTIVITY 214

Read s. 16(1), AA 1976 in *Cases and Materials* (13.6.1.1). What is the significance of this section? Consent procedure - Certainty or the Courts could dispense it. S 17 (1) A&CB 2001

Before the court can make any adoption order, it must be satisfied that all birth parents (with parental responsibility) have given unconditional consent to the making of the order. This is a matter which will be considered by the reporting officer or guardian ad litem in their report to the court. By 'unconditional consent', the parent must understand the full extent and impact of the adoption order, and not try to place restrictions on it, such as agreeing only on condition that contact will be continued post order. You will return to the issue of contact and adoption orders shortly, but you may wish to look at the extracts from *Re T (Adoption: Contact)* [1995] 2 FLR 251 in *Cases and Materials* (**13.6.1.1**) where there is a mention of 'unconditional agreement'.

ACTIVITY 215

See the brief extract from *Re T (Adoption: Contact)* [1995] 2 FLR 251 in *Cases and Materials* (**13.6.1.1**) on this point.

The unmarried father

— No rights unless he has P.R / or by way of maintenance then he must be consulted.

SAQ 66

Does the unmarried father have a say in the adoption process?

No —

If the unmarried father has obtained parental responsibility, under s. 4, CA 1989, then he will have to give his consent to the order being made, as the references to parent in the AA 1976 refer to a parent with parental responsibility. If he does not have parental responsibility, there is no guarantee that he will even know the matter is going ahead.

The guardian ad litem in carrying out the reporting process may contact the father to establish his views, as may the social worker involved from the local authority's side. Under the AA 1976 rules, if the unmarried father is paying maintenance by way of an agreement, or an order, in respect of the child, he must be made a party to the proceedings. An assessment under the CSA 1991 is arguably neither an order or an agreement but an administrative action which enforces liability, therefore many unmarried fathers will not be made party to the case automatically. If the father does find out about the proceedings and is otherwise unentitled to be a party, he can seek the court's leave to be joined, and in this situation the court has discretion to allow this to happen.

For judicial approaches on this issue, refer to the case of *Re B (A Minor) (Adoption)* [1991] Fam Law 136 and *Re L (A Minor) (Adoption: Procedure)* [1991] 1 FLR 171 in *Cases and Materials* (**13.6.1.1**).

If the alternative procedure of freeing for adoption is being used, the position of the unmarried father is slightly improved.

Read s. 18(7), Adoption Act 1976 in *Cases and Materials* (13.6.1.1) and write down why this is so.

Section 18 governs the freeing procedure, and under subsection (7) before the court can make an order, it needs to establish that the unmarried father will not be seeking a s. 4 parental responsibility order or a s. 8 residence order, or that if he did, he would not stand a good chance of succeeding. The only means to establish this is by making sure the local authority or guardian ad litem has had contact with the father. It is, however, questionable to what extent the adoption court should attempt to predict the future on the matter of s. 4 and s. 8, CA 1989. Whilst the court deciding the adoption matter will have family jurisdiction and will certainly have decided cases on these CA 1989 sections before, will it have sufficient information to hand to decide that the applications would be unmeritorious?

New mothers

You may have wondered, when reflecting upon the age of the child and the duration of residence with the prospective adopters, why there are two periods specified. The child must have lived with the applicants for a minimum of 13 weeks, but the child must be at least 19 weeks old. What happens in the first six weeks? This relates to s. 16(4) which declares that an agreement for the child to be adopted is ineffective if given by the mother less than six weeks after the child's birth. A placement can occur during this period (and often will do) but the agreement will be insufficient for the purposes of making the application, and the agreement can be revoked at any time.

Dispensing with consent

Not every placement or adoption application goes ahead smoothly, and often parents will refuse to agree to the making of an order which will remove all their rights as parents. Where a birth parent does not agree to the adoption order, even though a placement will have taken place, the court has the power to dispense with an agreement under s. 16(1)(b)(ii).

Read s. 16(1), AA 1976, and the grounds upon which a court may dispense with a parent's consent to adoption in s. 16(2), AA 1976, in *Cases and Materials* (13.3.1.1).

Which do you think are most commonly utilised?

Of the six alternatives, it is s. 16(2)(b), i.e. 'withholding his agreement unreasonably' that is most frequently used to dispense with consent.

What do you think the test of 'withholding his agreement unreasonably' should be?

The classic statement of principle for this issue was given in the case of *Re W (An Infant)* [1971] 2 All ER 49 by Lord Hailsham.

Read the extracts from *Re W (An Infant)* in *Cases and Materials* (13.6.1.1), noting that the case was decided under the Adoption Act 1958. The provisions in question are the same as the AA 1976.

What factors do you think will have a bearing on whether a parent is behaving reasonably?

Certainly the outcome for the child will be important since the court must have regard to the child's welfare (albeit this is only the first consideration). However, in today's climate of older child adoptions, the issue of contact is one which often affects the question of reasonableness. To illustrate this, read the case of *Re E (A Minor) (Adoption)* [1989] 1 FLR 126 in *Cases and Materials* (13.6.1.1) where the relationship between the child to be adopted (E) and a sibling (M) was in question. You should also look at the case of *Re P (Adoption: Freeing Order)* [1994] 2 FLR 1000 where a similar question arose.

Welfare and consent

From the above, you should have deduced that before a court can question the reasonableness or otherwise of the parents' decision on consenting to the making of the order, it must first have decided that the adoption order is in the child's best interests. It is in effect a two-stage approach.

13.8.2 FREEING

Freeing for adoption acts as an alternative to the standard route above (see **13.8.1**). It does so by creating an extra stage in the procedure. However, this does not mean that any of the legal considerations are ignored, just that they will be considered at a different point in time. The application to free a child for adoption is brought by the local authority or adoption agency, and will be against the birth parent(s). If the freeing order is made, and the child placed for adoption, any application for adoption will be made by the prospective adopters against the local authority or agency.

13.8.2.1 When can freeing be used?

Read s. 18(1) to (3), Adoption Act 1976 in *Cases and Materials* (13.6.2.1).

These provisions confirm that only an adoption agency can use freeing as a process. The situations where it can be used should have been identified as follows:

■ where the parents of the child agree to the making of a freeing order; or

■ where the parents do not agree to the making of a freeing order *but*

■ the agency is seeking the dispensing of consent to the freeing order *and*

■ the child is in the care of the agency.

Care is defined in s. 18(2A) as being where the child is in the care of a local authority. What this means should be familiar from **Chapter 12**, i.e. where the child is subject to a care order under s. 31, CA 1989.

A freeing order can be made even though the child has not yet been found suitable adoptive parents. However, if the local authority is asking for the parents' consent to be dispensed with, there must be a likelihood that placement will occur (s. 18(3)).

13.8.2.2 What does freeing achieve?

The making of a freeing order operates to declare that a child may be adopted, i.e. that there are no barriers (other than legal requirements) to prevent a placement going ahead, and an application being made. The freeing order will remove the birth parents' parental responsibility and give it to the agency (s. 18(5)).

If the order operates to declare a child free for adoption, what legal issues will the court have considered?

The legal requirements that the court must deal with are the same as under the standard route. At this stage in the procedure, the court will have considered that the making of an adoption order will be in the interests of the child, and that the birth parents have either consented freely and unconditionally, knowing the impact of the order, or that it is appropriate to dispense with the need for the parents' consent. These are the most problematic issues in the adoption process.

What will be the position regarding contact after freeing?

As you have seen from *Re P* in *Cases and Materials* (13.3.1.1), contact can operate to prevent the making of a freeing order. You should now contrast this decision with *Re A (A Minor) (Adoption: Contact)* [1993] 2 FLR 645 in *Cases and Materials* (13.6.2.2).

Which do you think is the better approach?

It is hard to evaluate the decisions since they appear to conflict. The distinguishing features are that in *Re P* the court believed that contact should continue after adoption and that the adoption order should only be made if this were to happen. However, in *Re A*, the court did not appear so committed to the idea of post adoption contact, and merely stated that the matter of contact could be reviewed at the adoption order application. Also in *Re A*, the issue had been raised some time after the making of the freeing order. Hayes and Williams in *Family Law: Principles, Policy and Practice*, London: Butterworths, 1995, have suggested that the approach of *Re A* was in reality contrary to the welfare of the child. Their criticism is extracted in *Cases and Materials* (13.6.2.2).

13.8.2.3   How long does freeing last?

The duration of the freeing order depends on whether a placement can be found easily for the child, whether the adoption application is pursued, and also depends on the birth parents. Under s. 18(6), the birth parents must be given the opportunity to declare whether they do not wish to be involved any further with regard to the child and decisions relating to the adoption. If a parent has not so declared (i.e. he/she does wish to remain involved), then s. 20 applies.

Read s. 20, Adoption Act 1976 in *Cases and Materials* (13.6.2.3). Write down the main effect of the section.

You will have realised that this section permits the birth parent to revoke the freeing order after 12 months have expired, if the child has not been adopted or has not been placed for adoption. This may seem an unlikely situation (if no placement was to be found, why take freeing proceedings?), but it does happen, e.g. in *Re A* (*Cases and Materials* (**13.3.2.2**)) the child had not been placed eight months after the order. The child may be hard to place due to its behaviour or medical condition, or its adoption placement may have broken down which occurs in a high percentage of cases. In some situations, the parent seeking to revoke the freeing order may not wish to care for the child, but instead to agree to a care order being made. This was the situation in *Re G (A Minor)* [1997] 2 WLR 747 (see *Cases and Materials* (**13.6.2.3**)).

If the parent has declared that he/she wants no involvement the agency can continue to try to place the child for adoption, or may, if a local authority, revert to long-term fostering.

13.8.2.4 Placement and after

When a placement is found for the 'freed' child, the agency will have to assess the prospective adopters as under the standard process. The adopters will need to comply with the legislative criteria and also those laid down by the agency. The placement must also be assessed as being in the interests of the child. Once placement has happened, the adopters are able to make an application against the agency.

Before the court can make the order, of what must it be satisfied?

At this second stage of the process, the court does not need to consider whether adoption per se is in this child's best interests as this was considered during the freeing application. The court must be satisfied that adoption of this child with these parents is in the child's interests, not quite the same test. The court will also have to go through the AA 1976 requirements of age, residence of the applicant(s) and the age and duration of placement of the child with them.

13.9 Protection during Placement

As you will realise from the material you have studied already, many placements with a view to adoption will take place without any legally enforceable rights for the adopters to keep the child in the event of the birth parents having a change of heart, or even the local authority with a care order changing its mind as to long-term placement. The AA 1976 provides means of protection for the adopters and child in these types of situations. Under s. 27, where an application for an order (either adoption or freeing) is made, the birth parent is prevented from removing the child or seeking its removal. Under s. 28, where an application is pending, or a notice of intention to apply has been given to the local authority, and the child has lived with the applicants for at least five years, the child cannot be removed. Finally, where the placement has been made by an agency, even if proceedings are pending, the agency can give notice to remove the child from the prospective adopters. If proceedings are pending then this removal can only take place with leave of the court.

Do these provisions help?

Although they do provide protection, it is only a protection of sorts. The protection depends very much on the making of an application. It is only where the child has lived with the applicant for at least five years that there is protection before the application is issued. You may feel these provisions to be acceptable, but do they promote the welfare of the child?

13.10   Post-adoption Issues

13.10.1   CONTACT

As you have learnt, contact and open adoptions seem to cause a lot of judicial comment. This is one area which is still in its infancy, and is hampered by the lack of compatibility of legislative considerations. If the draft adoption Bill is brought into the parliamentary legislative programme, some of these difficulties may be removed.

If a birth parent wishes to maintain contact after the adoption, but does not seek or obtain an order at the time the adoption is made, what can he/she do?

Once the order is made, the birth parent(s) will lose all status that they may have previously had. In this case, to obtain any CA 1989 order, they must first apply for leave under s. 10, CA 1989 as strangers to the child. It is suggested that leave will not be granted readily (*Re T (Adoption: Contact)* [1995] 2 FLR 251).

13.10.2   REVOCATION

Can an adoption order be revoked?

The principles behind adoption are clearly that it is an irrevocable process. The AA 1976 itself states that an adopted child may be made subject to a second adoption order, but there are no provisions to permit the order being overturned. This is not to say that the exceptional case will never arise where overturning the order is warranted. One such exceptional case arose in *Re K (Adoption)* [1997] 2 FLR 221 in connection with a Bosnian refugee, where the adoption order was revoked on the basis that it had been obtained without the true facts being known. However, even where the situation may have profound effects for the child, in many cases revocation will not occur.

Read, in *Cases and Materials* (13.7), the case of *Re K (Adoption)* [1997] 2 FLR 221 and *Re B (Adoption Order: Jurisdiction To Set Aside)* [1995] 2 FLR 1, to compare the judicial approaches.

13.11   Summary

You are now almost at the end of your study of family law. Adoption fits in to both public and private law spheres and is perceived to be a valuable means to achieve permanence in a child's life, especially in local authority care cases. You have seen how the law lays down a variety of regulations that must be complied with before an order can be made. Agencies, which carry out a large number of placements for adoption, often impose their own, often more rigorous conditions. An order can be sought using two different routes through the court system, depending on the applicability of the case itself. Whichever route is used, the fundamental legal provisions must be satisfied. The consequences of adoption are permanent transplantation from one family to another, and an order, once made, is rarely revoked.

To consolidate your knowledge of adoption and aid revision, try the following two activities (you will not find examples in *Cases and Materials*) and then complete the End of Chapter Assessment Question.

Draw flow diagrams, on separate sheets of paper, indicating the different routes to gaining an adoption order.

On a separate sheet of paper, identify the key players in the adoption process and list the legal and non-legal requirements applicable to them.

13.12   End of Chapter Assessment Question

Why are adoption applications from step-parents and relatives seen with some disquiet?
What problems can arise from this sort of application, and what alternatives exist?

See *Cases and Materials* (**13.9**) for an outline answer.

CHAPTER FOURTEEN

THE INHERENT JURISDICTION

14.1 Objectives

By the end of this chapter you should be able to:

■ explain the meaning of the inherent jurisdiction;

■ place the order of wardship within the inherent jurisdiction;

■ highlight the situations where wardship may be used in comparison to other orders;

■ explain who may be subject to the jurisdiction and the consequences.

14.2 Introduction

In this final study chapter you will be considering the inherent jurisdiction of the court to make orders in respect of children. As an area of law, the importance of the inherent jurisdiction has waned in recent years, in the main due to the impact of the CA 1989. There still exist situations where this jurisdiction is useful, and so you need to study them. This chapter will be comparatively short and you will not be expected to complete an End of Chapter Assessment Question.

14.3 What is the Inherent Jurisdiction?

The phrase 'inherent jurisdiction' is one with which you should be familiar: you have briefly looked at it in **Chapter 8**.

Do you understand what is meant by the inherent jurisdiction of the courts?

The jurisdiction is historically based and:

> [T]he inherent jurisdiction . . . has its roots in the feudal system and originates in the Crown's special duty as *parens patriae* to protect minors against injury of any kind . . . The main function of the court was originally to protect the property of minors whose parents were dead or unable to act; and in practice it was only the concern of the wealthy.' (Cretney and Masson, *Principles of Family Law*, 6th edn, Sweet & Maxwell, 1997)

Parens patriae is interpreted as meaning the 'parent of the nation'. Basically, under the inherent jurisdiction the court could do whatever it felt was necessary to protect the interests of the child (or adult if looking at, e.g. domestic violence). As such the concept of the inherent jurisdiction is very similar to the rules of equity, i.e. doing right in a situation even if statutory powers do not exist.

In so far as children are concerned, the use of wardship is the normal means by which the inherent jurisdiction is invoked. Wardship is part of the inherent jurisdiction, but is also an entity in itself since it has its own rules and consequences.

What orders would you expect to fall within the inherent jurisdiction of the court in addition to wardship?

One such order should be easily identifiable, i.e. the injunction which seeks to prohibit certain types of actions. However, you may not have identified the opposite type of order, i.e. a declaration which is permissive in nature.

If you can't grasp this concept, think of inherent jurisdiction as a set of rules and orders, with wardship being a subset within it. You may like to draw a Venn diagram to illustrate this point. If you do not know what a Venn diagram is, see the one in *Cases and Materials* (14.1).

14.4   Injunctive or Declarative Orders

Can you think of any situations where these types of orders may be used?

You could have mentioned any of the situations where an application for a specific issues order or prohibited steps order could be made, as these orders under the CA 1989 do much the same thing as those under the inherent jurisdiction. However, the case law would seem to indicate that in many of the cases where the inherent jurisdiction, instead of CA 1989 remedies, is used, there is a question relating to medical treatment of the child. Whilst the inherent jurisdiction declaratory relief could be used, it is also common for wardship to be used in this type of case.

Read the extracts from *Re R (A Minor) (Blood Transfusion)* [1993] 2 FLR 757 and *Re R (A Minor) (Wardship: Medical Treatment)* [1991] 4 All ER 177, in *Cases and Materials* (14.2), which illustrate when the inherent jurisdiction can be used, but also that the jurisdiction overlaps with s. 8, CA 1989.

Do you think that the court has made a s. 8 order in both of these cases?

As the court proceedings in inherent jurisdiction are still classed as family proceedings, the court will have the power under the CA 1989 to make a s. 8 order, subject only to the restrictions imposed by the CA 1989 itself. This is where difficulties arise for the local authority especially, since the CA 1989 has placed severe restrictions on the use that can be made of the inherent jurisdiction by the local authority which you will look at shortly.

Read the extracts from the case of *Re W* [1995] 2 FLR 466 in *Cases and Materials* (14.2) which illustrates that wardship may in some situations be deemed better for the child than CA 1989 orders.

14.5 Wardship

In practice this is the most frequently used area of the inherent jurisdiction in respect of children and, until the implementation of the CA 1989, over half of the applications to make a child a ward were made by a local authority. From this you can surmise that wardship (and the other orders within the inherent jurisdiction) will be available in private law.

14.5.1   WHO IS COVERED?

Write down whom you think can be made a ward, and who can apply to make a child a ward.

You should have recognised that you must be talking about a child, who will be an individual below 18 who has never been married. A child must have an independent existence from its mother before it can be made subject to an order. In *Re F (in utero)* [1988] Fam 122 an application was made by a local authority to make an unborn child a ward. The application failed due to the child not being in existence, in the sense of not yet being separate from its mother and independent. The child does not need to be habitually resident in the jurisdiction, nor does the child have to be in the jurisdiction when made a ward of court. It is unlikely that a child will be made a ward whilst abroad, unless of course the child has been abducted.

The applicant who is seeking to make the child a ward does not need to have any relationship or connection to them. However, if an application is lodged where there is no link, or a very tenuous one, the court may not be minded to make the order unless it is clear that making the child a ward is in the child's interests. Cretney and Masson illustrate this ability to apply, although not related, by the following list of cases:

■ *Re D (A Minor) (Wardship: Sterilisation)* [1976] Fam 185 (educational psychologist);

■ *Re B (A Minor) (Wardship: Medical Treatment)* [1981] 1 WLR 1421 (doctor);

■ *A v Berkshire County Council* [1989] 1 FLR 273 (guardian ad litem).

As you can see, the nature of the applicants' profession may suggest why they were seeking to make the child a ward.

14.5.2   WHERE TO APPLY

The jurisdiction to grant wardship orders lies primarily with the High Court Family Division, although many aspects of wardship may be dealt with in the county court (s. 38, Matrimonial and Family Proceedings Act 1984). The procedure will involve one or more directions hearings prior to the final hearing, and it is these directions appointments that will take place in the lower court before a district judge (on a general basis). The final hearing is normally dealt with by a High Court judge although it is possible that a county court judge (acting as a High Court judge) may deal with the matter.

14.5.3 WHEN DOES WARDSHIP BECOME EFFECTIVE?

Imagine you are the aunt/uncle of a young child. The parent, your sister, is a drug addict. Because of her addiction you believe she should not care for the child. You do not really want to involve the social services, so you apply to make the child a ward. When would you expect that wardship to become effective?

Most legal orders only become effective once they have been made at the final hearing. If action needs to be taken prior to the final hearing, interim orders may be made. Wardship does not quite work like that. The child will become a ward of court, and subject to all the consequences of wardship as soon as the application has been lodged at court, regardless of whether it is served on the other parties and regardless of a hearing. This state of affairs does not last indefinitely – this temporary protection will only remain for 21 days after the application has been filed at court (RSC Ord. 90) – hence within this time frame the applicant must ensure that a hearing takes place at least to decide if the wardship should continue.

What happens if an issue needs deciding immediately?

Not all cases of wardship involve emergency situations, but if something needs to be done as a matter of necessity or urgency, then an ex-parte hearing can take place. Such a hearing would not act to satisfy the requirements of the Rules of the Supreme Court — that a hearing take place within 21 days to prevent the wardship lapsing.

The fact that wardship is 'immediate' in its effect is one of its great advantages. In private situations this immediacy can be used if, for example, the child has been abducted and it is believed the child will be removed from the jurisdiction.

Would any CA 1989 order be as effective?

Whilst a s. 44 emergency protection order could be sought it will invariably involve a few hours' delay. This in itself may not be such a detriment to warrant the more expensive High Court application, but the fact that the wardship will last at least 21 days (unless there is a hearing in that time) is certainly more advantageous.

When non-emergency cases are dealt with, the use of CA 1989 orders may increase. As you have seen in *Re W*, however, the wardship jurisdiction may be preferable.

Look at the case of *Re K (Adoption and Wardship)* [1997] 2 FLR 221 (*Cases and Materials* (14.3.1)) which you will recall from Chapter 13. Following the setting aside of the adoption order, why was wardship continued?

In this situation, it appears that the need to protect the child and ensure the reintroduction to her Bosnian family was the priority. By retaining wardship, the court could be in control.

The procedures for concluding wardship applications are not subject to the timetabling requirements of the CA 1989, and in practice it would seem that many wardship cases will take much longer to reach final hearing (Masson and Morton report in (1989) 52 MLR 762 that approximately 25 per cent of cases took over one year) than s. 8 residence orders and particularly s. 31 care orders. This would certainly be the situation in *Re K*, dealing as it did in private law and the possible long-term reintroduction to the Bosnian family.

14.5.4 CONSEQUENCES OF WARDSHIP

The nature of wardship may be another reason for its being preferred in some situations to the CA 1989 remedies. When a child is made a ward of court, the court will in effect 'step into the shoes' of the parent, and no act can be taken with respect to the child without the court's permission or authority. Any exercise of parental responsibility by anyone else, unless in accordance with the directions of the court, will be unlawful. The only sanction presumably would lie in contempt proceedings.

If the court takes over the parental role, does this mean the court will provide day-to-day care etc.?

Practically, the court cannot fulfil a parental role in full, but must delegate some of the parental duties and responsibilities to others. This would include the day-to-day care of the child. The issue of providing care for the child may be one which would necessitate an ex-parte order on the filing of the application if the protection of the child was at issue. In many cases the person to whom care will be delegated will be the applicant.

ACTIVITY 229

Read the extract from *Re S (Wardship: Education)* [1988] 1 FLR 128 in *Cases and Materials* (14.3.2), which illustrates the 'totality' of wardship but also shows that not all aspects of parental responsibility may be delegated totally to the carers.

14.6 The Local Authority and the Inherent Jurisdiction

14.6.1 RESTRICTIONS

ACTIVITY 230

Read s. 100, CA 1989 in *Cases and Materials* (14.4.1).

Write down the ways in which the use of the inherent jurisdiction has been limited for the local authority.

You will have found the restrictions on local authorities in subsections (2) and (3). The latter simply prevents any application under the inherent jurisdiction by a local authority unless the local authority has obtained the leave of the court. Leave may be granted in the situations covered by subsection (4) which is discussed below.

The court is also prevented from using the inherent jurisdiction to involve the local authority in child care. Thus under subsection (2):

■ the court cannot use the inherent jurisdiction to put a child into the care of a local authority;

■ the court cannot use the inherent jurisdiction to put a child under the supervision of the local authority;

■ the court cannot use the inherent jurisdiction to put the child into accommodation provided by or on behalf of the local authority;

- the court cannot use the inherent jurisdiction to make a child subject to a care order a ward of court;

- the court cannot use the inherent jurisdiction to confer parental responsibility or any aspect of parental responsibility on the local authority.

Even though this is directed at the court, it provides a severe limitation on local authorities too. For an additional interpretation of the restrictions in s. 100(2), see the extracts from the article entitled *The Children Act 1989: Local Authorities, Wardship and the Revival of the Inherent Jurisdiction* by Parry in **Cases and Materials (14.4.1)**.

14.6.2   WHY s. 100?

The restrictions that have been created by s. 100, being so comprehensive, must have some justification.

Can you think of any?

You were told earlier that almost half of the applications in wardship pre-CA 1989 were made by local authorities. This extensive use was one reason for seeking to reduce the powers of the courts and the local authority in respect of inherent jurisdiction. Local authorities had come to utilise wardship to combat the perceived problems with the Children and Young Persons Act 1969 which provided their powers of intervention for child protection. The grounds available under the 1969 Act were thought to be inflexible and backward looking. Wardship with its ability to consider future perceived harm (without existence of past harm), its speed and the variety of options once made, was a more attractive proposition. With the implementation of the CA 1989, and the new powers to take a child into protective care, the faults of the old law were removed. The intention was that the CA 1989 powers should be perfectly sufficient for the local authority to act to protect a child, without the need to resort to the inherent jurisdiction.

To illustrate further the reasons for the implementation of s. 100, read the extracts from the Joseph Jackson Memorial Lecture, given by Lord Mackay, and published in the *New Law Journal*, in *Cases and Materials* (14.4.2).

14.6.3 WHEN CAN THE INHERENT JURISDITION BE USED?

As you have seen, there exists a means by which the local authority can use the inherent jurisdiction, having obtained leave to do so.

If you have not already done so, read s. 100(4) and (5) in *Cases and Materials* (14.4.1), and note down the situations when the court will grant leave for the local authority to use the inherent jurisdiction.

The local authority must satisfy two criteria before leave will be granted for the application. The granting of leave, you must remember, does not mean that the order will be granted, it is just the first hurdle to overcome. The first condition is that the making of an order under the inherent jurisdiction will achieve something that the local authority could not do using the orders available to it under the CA 1989. In other words, the inherent jurisdiction is being used to plug gaps that exist in the legal regime. Secondly, the making of the order will prevent the child suffering significant harm which would otherwise be suffered.

Can you think of any examples when the inherent jurisdiction will, or could, be used?

From your earlier reading on public law you will have come across a couple of situations where the inherent jurisdiction would be the only means of protecting a child.

Do you recall who can be made subject to a care order or supervision order? Under the CA 1989 a court cannot make either of these orders if the child has reached his/her seventeenth birthday. If a child of 17 is believed to be at risk of suffering significant harm, how can the local authority protect him/her? The only conceivable way would be to use the inherent jurisdiction, since the local authority cannot be expected to use s. 44 EPOs repeatedly.

You may also recall the case of *Nottinghamshire County Council* v *P*, which considered the inability of the court to force a local authority to apply for a care order, and also considered the powers of the court to make s. 8 prohibited steps orders to remove a parent from the matrimonial home. It was decided that a prohibited steps order could not be used in this way since it was not an action relating to the exercise of parental responsibility. Whilst this gap has now been plugged by the FLA 1996, in similar situations of actions not being part of parental responsibility, the inherent jurisdiction may be the only option.

Other cases where the inherent jurisdiction will commonly be used are medical treatment matters, i.e. where children require medical attention and are either refusing to consent or their parents are refusing. You will recall that this is so from the case of *Re R (A Minor) (Wardship: Medical Treatment)* [1991] 4 All ER 177 in **Cases and Materials (14.2)**.

14.7 Summary

As you have seen, the inherent jurisdiction can be used in both public and private law cases, although following the CA 1989 the use made by local authorities has declined. The inherent jurisdiction is used in respect of children normally by declaring the child a ward of court. In so doing, the child's parents or others with parental responsibility are usurped from their role and the court becomes the decision maker for the child. Wardship is used primarily where a range of decisions needs to be made, it is a more rounded order since wardship covers *all* decisions relating to the child. In contrast the inherent jurisdiction will be used where a specific question needs to be decided or referred to the court. As a residuary power, and as a means to plug any apparent gaps in the statutory code, the inherent jurisdiction is crucial.

CHAPTER FIFTEEN

THE END

Well, you've made it, unless, of course, you are the sort of person who reads the last chapter immediately after the first chapter to see if you will like the book. This should have been an enjoyable, but also an academically testing course of study. Inevitably there will be areas of family law that have not been addressed, or have only been skimmed over. The intention was to introduce the major areas to you, and also to give you a flavour of some of the less legalistic issues that have shaped and moulded the legal codes. The social context within which family law is placed is central to assessing the ability of family law to regulate the way in which we live today with our spouses, partners and children. You will no doubt have found arguments and ideas with which you do not agree – fine, but always make sure you can justify any arguments against a proposition. This is even more crucial if you are trying to argue against the implementation or effectiveness of family law (or any law for that matter).

Now you have finished, try not to forget what you have learned. Keep up to date, read the newspapers and legal journals if you can, to ensure that you will be able to talk authoritatively on family law and family living.

If you hated the course – well – that's life!

INDEX

Abortion 7
Access orders 209
Adoption 270, 277–98
　arrangement of 283–4
　child protection during placement
　　295–6
　effects of 279–80
　nature of 277–9
　post-adoption issues 296–7
　process of 285–95
　types of adopters 280–3
　types of children 279, 280
Adultery, divorce and 37, 41, 45
Age
　divorce settlement and 79
　void marriages and 25
AIDS/HIV, voidable marriage and 31–2
Annulment of marriage 22–36
　bars to 32–3
　consequences of 33–5
　void marriages 22–7, 34
　voidable marriages 22–3, 28–32, 35
Appeal
　against care/supervision orders 275
　against divorce settlement 88–90
　against emergency protection order
　　247
Arrest 123, 138–9
Assets, divorce settlements and 74–7

Banns 15–16
Behaviour
　conduct of parties in divorce settlement
　　80
　unreasonable behaviour fact in divorce
　　cases 42, 45
Bigamy 25, 27, 34
Birth rates 7

Care orders 203
　appeals against 275
　consequences of 269–73
　criteria for 252–61

Care orders – *continued*
　final hearing 266–9
　process 261–6
Ceremonies of marriage 16–18
Child assessment orders 238–41
Child Support Agency 143, 144, 146,
　149, 157
Children
　abuse of 219–23
　　definitions of 219–21
　　extent of 221–3
　　investigation of 228–34
　　physical abuse 176, 177, 179–80,
　　　220, 221
　　sexual abuse 147, 179, 180, 220
　adoption of 270, 277–98
　　arrangement of 283–4
　　child protection during placement
　　　295–6
　　effects of 279–80
　　nature of 277–9
　　post-adoption issues 296–7
　　process of 285–95
　　types of adopters 280–3
　　types of children 279, 280
　care and protection of 190–1
　　Child Protection Case Conferences
　　　235–7
　　local authorities and 223–8
　　long-term orders 252–75
　　short-term orders 237–48
　day care of 225–6
　definition of childhood 168–71
　discipline of 196–7
　divorce and 57, 59, 72, 143–66, 203
　domestic violence and 131
　education of 175, 191–2
　inherent jurisdiction and 299–308
　law relating to 167–87
　　private law 188–217
　　public law 218–76
　medical treatment of 192–5
　naming of 195–6

Children – *continued*
  parental responsibility for   188–203
    automatic   197–8
    definition of   188–9
    delegation of   199, 201
    interpretations of   190–7
    joint/individual   202–3
    loss of   203
    matters included in   189–90
    parental responsibility agreements
        199–200
    parental responsibility orders   200–1
    residence orders and   201, 205
    unmarried fathers and   198–201, 203
  rights of   171–4, 209–10, 227
  state intervention and   174–8
  support and maintenance of   143–66
    Child Support Act   143–51
    departure from formula   158–9
    formula for   151–7
    non-applicability of Child Support
        Act   159–65
    relationships and   142–3
  void marriage and   34
  wardship and   203, 300, 301–6
Church of England, marriage and
    14–16, 18
Civil marriage   14, 16–17
'Clean break' provisions in divorce   67,
    69, 83–4, 154
Cohabitation   4, 5, 6, 38
  domestic violence and   131, 136–7
  maintenance and   69, 98
  property ownership rights and   102,
      109–10
  welfare benefits and   98
Common licence, marriage under   15
Common-law marriage   11–13
Conduct *see* behaviour
Consent
  divorce and   43
  marriage and   19, 29–31, 33
Consummation, voidable marriage and
    28–9
Contact orders   204, 209–13
County court
  adoption and   286
  annulment and   35
  divorce and   47
  domestic violence and   120
  wardship and   302
Court of Appeal, divorce and   88
Court Welfare Officer   233
Courts
  inherent jurisdiction of   299–305
  see also county court; Court of Appeal;
      family proceedings court; High
      Court; High Court Family
      Division

Criminal law options on domestic
    violence   121–2
Cultural differences   2
Curtis Committee   177
Custody orders   184, 205

Day care of children   225–6
Declarative orders   300–1
Desertion, divorce and   42–3, 45
Detrimental reliance   111–12
Disability, divorce settlement and   79
Discipline of children   196–7
Divorce   5, 8
  bars to   45–6
  children and   57, 59, 72, 203
    child support and maintenance
        143–66
  'clean break' provisions   67, 69, 83–4,
      154
  delay of   86–7
  domestic violence and   135–6
  facts in   40–5
  financial arrangements and   58–9,
      66–70, 73–91
  grounds for   39–44, 53
  historical perspective on   37–8
  law on
    Family Law Act   49–65
    Matrimonial Causes Act   37–48
  mediation and   52, 60–3
  modern presumptions of   38–9
  numbers of   7, 37
  prevention of   85–6
  problems with   46, 47, 49–50
  process of   46, 52–60
  property and   66–7, 70–2, 73–91, 154
Domestic violence   100, 118–41
  civil remedies against   122–30
    Family Law Act and   130–9
  criminal law options on   121–2
  definitions of   119
  historical development of law on   118,
      119–20
  stalking and   139
Duress, marriage and   30

Economic activity, gender and   7, 8
Education of children   175, 191–2
Education supervision orders   192
Emergency protection orders   241–8, 304
  consequences of   244–7
  criteria for   241–4
  procedure   247–8
Estoppel, proprietary   116
European Convention on Human Rights
    174
Ex parte orders   126, 129, 137, 139, 247–8
Exclusion orders   128–9
  enforcement of   129

Extended families   2

Family   1–10
  definitions of   1–5
    social and legal   3–5
  enforcement of law on   8–10
  prevalent family groupings   5–8
  prohibited degrees of marriage within
      23–5
Family proceedings court (magistrates
    court)   9
  domestic violence and   120, 126–30
  emergency protection orders and   248
Fathers
  unmarried   4, 146
    adoption process and   290–1
    parental responsibility and
        198–201, 203
Financial arrangements
  on divorce   58–9, 66–70, 73–91
    commencement of orders   84–5
    decision making process   73–84
    maintenance orders   68–70
    new partners and   76–7
    prevention/delay in divorce and
        85–7
    variation and appeal of orders
        87–90
  without divorce   92–117
    maintenance   92–8
Foster care   270
Fraud
  divorce settlement and   89
  property transfer and   105–6
Freeing for adoption   293–5

Gender
  domestic violence and   120
  economic activity and   7, 8
  maintenance and   67, 69
  void marriages and   26–7
Gifts   104–6
Guardian ad litem   248, 262

Hague Convention on Child Abduction
    208
High Court, domestic violence and
    120
High Court Family Division
  divorce and   47
  wardship and   302
Hindu religion, marriage and   18
HIV/AIDS, voidable marriage and   31–2
Homosexual/lesbian relationships   4, 27
  adoption of children and   281
  domestic violence within   131
  grounds for divorce and   41
  privacy and   119
  property and   106

Households, changes in   6–7

Incomes
  child maintenance formula and   151–7
  divorce settlements and   74–7
  of women   7–8, 75
Information sessions, divorce and   54–5
Inherent jurisdiction   299–308
  injunctive/declarative orders   300–1
  local authorities and   305–8
  nature of   299–300
  wardship   203, 300, 301–5, 306
Inheritance, divorce and   76
Injunctive orders   300–1
Instalment orders   69–70
Interim care orders   264–5
Intolerability in divorce cases   41, 45
Irretrievable breakdown of marriage   39,
      40, 43–4, 53
  statement of   55–6
Islam, marriage and   18

Jewish religion, marriage and   18
Judicial separation   35

Legal aid   9
  divorce and   63
  mediation and   61–2, 63
Lesbian relationships see homosexual/
    lesbian relationships
Living standards, divorce settlement
    and   79
Local authorities
  children and   174, 177, 180, 185,
      214–15, 218, 223–8
  accommodation   208–9, 226–8, 270
  adoption   280, 282–3, 284
  Child Protection Case Conferences
      235–7
  inherent jurisdiction   305–8
  investigation of abuse   228–34
  long-term orders   252–75
  short-term orders   237–48
Lump sum orders   69–70, 82, 162

Magistrates court see family proceedings
    court
Maintenance
  of children   143–66
    Child Support Act   143–51
    departure from formula   158–9
    formula for   151–7
    non-applicability of Child Support
        Act   159–65
    relationships and   142–3
  divorce and
    commencement of orders   84–5
    concept of   66–7
    decision making process   73–84
    financial orders   68–70

Maintenance – *continued*
prevention/delay in divorce and 85–7
variation and appeal of orders 87–90
without divorce 92–8
Marriage 7, 11–21
annulment of 22–36
ceremonies 16–18
consent to 19, 29–31, 33
development of law on 11–13
formalities of 13–18
consequences of non-compliance with 19–20, 25
irretrievable breakdown of 39, 40, 43–4, 53, 55–6
judicial separation 35
pre-marriage requirements 14–16
promotion of stability of 45
property and financial arrangements without divorce 92–117
evaluation of shares in equity 115–16
maintenance 92–8
occupation rights and matrimonial home 98–102
ownership rights 102, 106–16
proprietary estoppel 116
resulting trusts 103–15
registration of 19
venues for 16, 17–18
violence within *see* domestic violence
void marriages 22–7, 34
voidable marriages 22–3, 28–32, 35
see also children; divorce
Mediation, divorce and 52, 60–3
Medical treatment of children 192–5
Mental disability, divorce settlement and 79
Mental illness, voidable marriage and 31, 33
Mesher orders 72
Mistake, marriage and 30–1
Molestation 123, 131
Mortgages, property arrangements without divorce and 101, 116

Naming of children 195–6
National Society for the Prevention of Cruelty to Children 176, 238, 243–4
Need
calculation of 78–9
test of 78
Non-disclosure, divorce settlement and 89–90
Non-molestation orders 123–4, 130–3, 137
application for 126, 131–2
duration of 126, 133

Nuclear family 2

Occupation orders 133–7
Occupation rights 98–102
Ouster orders 124–5
application for 126
duration of 126
Ownership rights 102, 106–16

Parents
absent 145
adoptive 280–3
adoption process and 285–95
consent to marriage by 25
denial of parentage 146
parental responsibility 188–203
automatic 197–8
definition of 188–9
delegation of 199, 201
interpretations of 190–7
joint/individual 202–3
loss of 203
matters included in 189–90
parental responsibility agreements 199–200
parental responsibility orders 200–1
residence orders and 201, 205
unmarried fathers and 198–201, 203
poor care of children by 259–60
single parents 8, 75, 143, 146, 278
support and maintenance of children 143–66
unmarried fathers 4, 146, 198–201, 203, 290–1
Pensions
child support and maintenance and 155
divorce and 60, 70, 81–3
Periodical payments orders 68–9, 70, 162
variation of 88
Perjury 34
Personal protection orders 127–8
enforcement of 129
Physical disability, divorce settlement and 79
Place of safety orders 177–8, 245
Police protection of children 230–1
Polygamous marriages 27
Pregnancy, voidable marriage and 32, 33
Prohibited steps orders 205, 214–15, 245, 301
Property
arrangements without divorce 92–117
children as 175
divorce and 66–7, 73–91
child support and maintenance and 154, 162, 164
commencement of orders 84–5

Property – *continued*
    decision making process 73–84
    new partners and 76–7
    prevention/delay in divorce and
        85–7
    property orders 70–2, 82
    variation and appeal of orders
        87–90
  evaluation of shares in equity 115–16
  occupation rights and matrimonial
      home 98–102
  ownership rights 102, 106–15
  proprietary estoppel 115
  purchase in name of another 103–4
  resulting trusts 103–15
  voluntary transfers of 103, 104–6
Proprietary estoppel 116

Quakers, marriage and 18

Rape within marriage 120
Reconciliation 45, 56–7
Refusal of contact 212–13
Registration of marriage 19
Religion
  divorce and 46
  marriage and 14–15, 18
Remarriage, maintenance and 69
Residence orders 184, 195, 201, 204,
    205–9
Roman Catholic church, marriage and
    18
Royal Society for the Prevention of
    Cruelty to Animals 176

Secularisation trends 8
Secured periodical payments orders 68
Separation
  grounds for divorce and 43, 45
  judicial 35
  property and financial arrangements
    without divorce 92–117
  evaluation of shares in equity
    115–16
  maintenance 92–8
  occupation rights and matrimonial
    home 98–102
  ownership rights 102, 106–16
  proprietary estoppel 116
  resulting trusts 103–15
Sexually-transmitted diseases, voidable
    marriage and 31–2, 33
Short Committee 178
Sikh religion, marriage and 18
Single parents 278
  employment and 75
  support and maintenance of children
    and 146
  welfare benefits for 8, 143

Single person households 6–7
Social security *see* welfare benefits
Solicitors
  divorce and 52, 55, 62–3, 73
  mediation and 63
Solicitors Family Law Association Code
    of Practice 73
Specific issues orders 204, 214–15, 301
Split residence orders 206–7
Stalking 139
Step families
  adoption within 277, 288–9
  child support and maintenance and
    143, 159
  marriage within 24, 25
Supervision orders
  appeals against 275
  consequences of 269, 273–5
  criteria for 252–61
  final hearing 266–9
  process 261–6

Tenancies 102
  domestic violence and 132
Transsexuality, marriage and 26
Trusts, property and financial
    arrangements without divorce
    103–15

Undertakings, acceptance of 124, 137–8
United Nations Convention on the Rights
    of the Child 1989 173–4
United Nations Declaration of the Rights
    of the Child 1959 173

Venereal disease, voidable marriage and
    31–2, 33
Violence *see* domestic violence
Void marriages 22–7, 34
  age of parties 25
  already lawfully married 25
  disregard of formalities 25
  gender and 26–7
  parties' rights in 34
  polygamous marriages 27
  prohibited degrees of marriage 23–5
Voidable marriages 22–3, 28–32, 35
  consent and 29–31, 33
  consummation and 28–9
  existing pregnancy and 32, 33
  mental illness and 31, 33
  parties' rights in 35
  venereal disease and 31–2, 33
Voluntary transfers of property 103,
    104–6

Wardship 203, 300, 301–6
Welfare benefits 175
  maintenance without divorce and 98

Welfare benefits – *continued*
     single parents and   8, 143
     support and maintenance of children
          and   148–9

Women
     economic activity by   7, 8
     incomes of   7–8, 75
     property and   104–5
     violence against *see* domestic violence